SEEING NEW HORIZONS

A Blind Aviator's Journey After Tragedy

Dr. Barry Hulon Hyde

PAGE PUBLISHING, INC.
Conneaut Lake, PA

First originally published by Page Publishing 2020

ISBN 978-1-68456-757-7 (pbk)
ISBN 978-1-68456-759-1 (hc)
ISBN 978-1-68456-758-4 (digital)

Printed in the United States of America

The obstacles people face can be motivating or hold them back from achieving their goals. The accomplishments that I have made gave me courage, motivated me, and may have inspired others. This story will share the life changing experiences and turning points that lead me to where I am today.

Childhood

I entered this world on February 3, 1972, at Cabarrus Memorial Hospital in Concord, North Carolina. My parents, Barry Edward Hyde and Brenda Claudine Absher, were married June 22, 1968. My brother, Todd Edward Hyde, was born two years and two days earlier than I was. I was the second of two sons.

My first name came from Dad, a rodeo cowboy who made a living in construction, and Hulon, from the father of one of Brenda's friends in Arkansas. They met him when the senior Barry was competing in a rodeo there and thought he was a great person. "So we named Hulon after him," Brenda said. "We had never heard the name before, and my husband liked it."

While growing up, my family and I traveled frequently to Southern Rodeo Association competitions, where my dad participated in saddle bronc, bareback and bull-riding events. My dad loved horses, and it was his dream to be a professional cowboy. At age sixteen, my dad started rodeoing, or riding horses. The years of 1970 and 1972, he received the award of All Around Cowboy of the Year for the Southern Rodeo Association. In order to be the All Around Cowboy, you had to participate in two or more events. The events to choose from were bareback riding, saddle bronc, bull riding, calf roping, and steer wrestling.

Dad competing at a rodeo

We lived at 218 Blackwelder Street beside my mother's parents until 1976. The first broken bone I suffered occurred in 1975 at the age of three on the front porch of the Abshers, and it was the left elbow. I fell on my grandparents' front porch after it had been raining. The raw iron posts were slick, and I slipped from one after climbing up it. Surgery fixed the break with a pin and stitches. The doctors provided demerol and later found out that I was allergic to the medicine. I was in a comatose state for a week before reaching consciousness.

On the evening of January 9, 1976, my father was participating in a rodeo in Raleigh at the state fair. Dad was on a horse riding bareback, and his eight seconds led to significant brain injury as well as a broken nose, collarbone, and broken jaw. He was riding a horse bareback, and his spur caught the D ring on the saddle and stuck. The horse was dragging him around the arena with the back feet kicking him in the head. Ten other cowboys jumped into the arena and bulldogged the horse, trying to free Dad. My dad's injuries were so significant doctors pronounced him dead three different times because his heart stopped beating. The first time was on the arena floor, the second in the ambulance, and the third on the operating table. I feel this was a blessing to have my dad revived so many times. This trauma is one part of life that is preparing my family and me for the future.

During 1976, my family and I moved two blocks west beside my dad's parents. We lived at 2705 Vale Avenue until 1985. This house is where my grandpa's twin brother and my grandmother's sister had lived before they died.

The injury to my face in 1976 occurred at this house when I was chasing my brother Todd. I went to jump over one twin bed; however, I did not jump high enough, and I fell into the other bed's rail with my cheekbone. I remember blood was just spurting out of it and Mom and Dad took me to the emergency room for stitches.

A trip to Midland, Texas, was to visit my uncle Charles, and my aunt Annaliese took place with my dad, my grandpa, and my grandma Hyde. My dad and I drove with my grandparents while my dad was recovering from the injuries he had suffered at the rodeo competition. My German aunt Anneliese, who was married to my dad's brother, Charles Hyde, removed the stitches in my face. We visited our family for several weeks four months after Dad's accident.

Kindergarten began in 1977, and my mother drove the school bus and worked in the cafeteria at Landis Elementary School. During attending kindergarten, I met one of my best friends, who is still a very close friend today, Deric Harrington. On August 16, 1977 Todd, cousins Kelly and Chad, and I were on the school bus that afternoon when Jason Moon's mom at his bus stop on West A Street had told Mom that Elvis had died. We were located beside Fairway

Drive in Kannapolis down the street from the West A Church of God, about three-fourths of a mile away from home.

At this time during my childhood years, we attended fly-ins at my dad's first cousin, Bet James, at their grass strip in Kannapolis. Several times a year Bet and her husband, Ferrell, would have a bunch of their fellow aviator friends attend and some would camp out and stay all night. The fly-ins always occurred on the James's grass airstrip on Saturdays and Sundays. These aviation-filled weekends always involved a bunch of Piper J-3 Cubs. Ferrell James II gave me my first airplane ride in a Piper J-3 Cub during one of his dad's fly-ins. In addition, Ferrell Jr. is the pilot who took me up in his dad's 1930 Waco. I feel the fly-ins and the flights I received broadened my interest in aviation. These flights increased my interest to learn about aviation and increased my desire to become a pilot.

Ferrell James Jr. was nicknamed Son. This man was a cousin since his grandmother and my grandmother were Dobbin sisters. I would work for his father and mother doing yard work and working in the flower beds. As I grew older, the work experience grew for me depending on what I was doing. I would be in Ferrell II's company frequently. I remember one time in particular, he brought me home after doing some work for his parents in his El Camino. This was when the street my family and I lived on was still dirt or gravel. He gave me a very awesome ride going down the road fishtailing.

In 1979, I suffered another broken bone. I ran through the yard chasing my Aunt Leisa and her girlfriend Relena as they drove up the road. I did a half flip, came down on my left shoulder impacting a rock on the ground breaking the collarbone. I had to wear a shoulder brace for several months. My brother and I grew up playing sports instead of going to rodeos. Todd was two years ahead of me; therefore, we would be on the same team one year and the next year Todd moved up to the next team. When Todd and I made it to high school, my brother was the pitcher and I was the catcher. We both received letters as well as made All-County and All-Conference as baseball players. Our dad and Uncle Randy were All-County and All-Conference in basketball when they were in high school. Todd and I graduated from my dad's high school. Dad's name was on the wall in the gym as the first year of South Rowan High School in basketball in 1962. Uncle Randy's name was on the wall as well. I wanted to have my name up on the wall beside their name. The year 1990 was the last year of the three-year high school. I had to settle for runner-up in basketball. Unfortunately, I was not able to have my name beside my father's.

I began playing T-ball and soccer at age five. Todd and I played soccer and baseball with friends such as Scott Lippard, Josh Ferguson, Brandon Beaver, Trent Littlejohn, and Deric Harrington. These people are still my friends today. I began playing basketball in China Grove on Saturday mornings with the people previously mentioned as well as some more people like Chad Sides, Chris Beaver, and others. I went from T-ball to Little League in Landis, North Carolina. I played for the Larry Macy Braves, the Landis Lions and Stamper Electric. Some more people that played were our cousins Kelly and Chad Hyde, Scott Yoder, and David Clayton.

In the mid to late 1970s, Mom took Todd and me to Blowing Rock in the mountains of North Carolina. We met Fred Kirby and watched the cowboys and Indians as they acted around Tweetsie Railroad. This trip was when I had my left arm in a sling after breaking it at my grandparents.

Began Working for the James's

At age twelve, I went to work for the James's mowing their yard and remodeling houses during the summer. I learned to be a mason at South Rowan High School. A friend and cousin's employee, John Ridenhour, taught me how to hang and fill sheetrock and how to paint. I also learned how to do some carpentry and many other things. The skills I learned awarded me Masonry Student of the Year as a senior in high school. Hyde's Maintenance began, and I became self-employed. I worked for my cousins, the James, who were father and son, and they were both pilots for Piedmont and then US

Airways and owned rental property. The work I did after high school involved maintenance and painting on the James's rental property. Ferrell James employed me, and I helped him remodel twenty houses while overseeing the maintenance on forty houses and 120 apartments. They had a hangar full of airplanes and parts and a runway beside Kannapolis Lake in North Carolina. I would go to work and see the airplanes in the hangar, and I wanted to sit in one and pretend I could fly the airplane. Many times my cousin Ferrell Jr. would take me flying in a Piper J-3 Cub or his dad's 1930 Waco biplane. In addition, Ferrell Jr. took me fishing and flying quite frequently. I feel working for a pilot and being around airplanes influenced and propelled me toward becoming a pilot.

While living on Vale Avenue in Kannapolis, the Hyde grandparents lived next door to us. My mom's parents, or Virgie Almarie Elledge and Claude Absher, lived two-tenths of a mile east. My brother and I would ride our bikes everywhere, and we spent a lot of time at Grandma and Grandpa Abshers. They had a garden that we helped with by tilling it and picking potatoes, green beans, greens, tomatoes and corn. We also canned vegetables and picked blackberries on the bank of the branch. We kept up their yard as well.

One of the first concerts I attended was at Carowinds in the early eighties. This concert featured several bands, but the one that was memorable was 38 Special. The friends that attended with me were Deric Harrington and Scott Lippard.

During 1984, a childhood friend, Chad Wingler, and I were playing in Sunday school while spring cleaning was going on. As Chad and I were on the stage behind the curtains, we looked at the dining area, and people were mopping the floor. My grandpa was one of the people. After we looked out there everything was fine, a few seconds went by when we heard someone gasping for air. We looked out the curtains one more time and saw my grandpa lying on the floor. It was almost as if he was having a seizure as he sucked for air. The church members called 911, and later that afternoon, the doctors pronounced him dead. This was my first big loss of someone who was close to me. The loss of my grandpa taught me how important he was to the family.

Each Christmas, my grandpa was the first person to visit early in the mornings. I always looked forward to showing my gifts to him. In addition, during his time in my life, I remember each weekend he and Grandma would play card games called Rook. They always had a house full to play cards each weekend.

In 1985 and in my seventh grade year, my family and I moved to Enochville, which has a Kannapolis address. The family and I moved five miles west of where we previously lived. Today, my mother still lives in this house. The house is a red brick and a ranch-style house with a fenced-in backyard. Family and friends helped with the move. One couple that helped with the move was Bobby, Sherry, Josh, and Heath Ferguson. Another couple was John and Beverly Barringer. Kenny and Dolores Carpenter helped as well. The family members that helped were Ferrell and Bet James.

I met one of my best friends in seventh grade at Corriher-Lipe Middle School during band class, Mike Cook. He had been a very good friend to me before the accident and after this dramatic event in my life. We have done lots of partying together. He comes to pick me up and takes me to his family events as well as other times. Mike and I have been friends for thirty-five years.

One more friend that I made at Corriher Lipe was Carrie Reavis. She and I were good friends through junior high school. After my accident, she and I have reconnected and now are closer than ever.

Another concert I remember was at the pavilion on the Grand Strand at Myrtle Beach during the summer in the mid-eighties, and the band featured was Survivor. I remembered this concert because I entered underage. I attended this concert with Deric Harrington, and we were on vacation with his mom. People packed the Magic Attic, and it was loud. Deric and I went together to Myrtle Beach every summer, and one year we went four times over the summer. I would go with him, his mother, his sister, Marsha Dedmond, and sometimes his aunt.

Middle school began at Corriher-Lipe, and I attended basketball camp in seventh grade at Catawba College in Salisbury, North Carolina. Chris Beaver attended this camp as well. The next year, I went to summer basketball camp at Winthrop College in South Carolina.

The next heart-wrenching loss I experienced was the loss of my grandpa Absher in 1987. He was in declining health, and I was helping my grandma take care of him. I had been staying the night with them, and one night when I stayed with a friend, Grandpa fell and broke a hip. The fall was tragic, and he never came home from the hospital. This death was a great loss to the family.

After ninth grade, I attended another basketball camp at Appalachian College in the mountains of North Carolina. While attending South Rowan High School the following year, I attended another basketball camp at Davidson College in Davidson, North Carolina.

My tenth grade year was in 1988. I was in a driver's education with two friends. One girl was Carla Meeks and the other girlfriend was Lorna Doyle. Lorna is a great friend. We are good friends, and we still talk today.

During the ninth grade school year at Corriher-Lipe, I worked with John Ridenhour remodeling a house on Moriah Street in Landis, North Carolina. Ferrell James ended up with five on a street that I helped in making it ready to rent once again.

My mom and dad gave me permission to drive a 1973 Volkswagen Bug that they had bought for my brother. My brother received a "driving while impaired" ticket and lost his license on a Friday evening with a friend and his passenger, Scott Yoder. They dropped me off at my uncle and aunt's, Kit and Leisa Caldwell. Afterwards, I had to learn to drive the straight-drive vehicle so I could take us places like school. Driving was good practice, and my mother and father taught me how to drive this stick shift vehicle.

While attending South Rowan High School, I made some great friends. Lorna Doyle, Wendy Crawford, Sammy Donaldson, and

Kim Bonkowski were great friends. We all partied and had lots of fun, especially after graduation in Myrtle Beach.

In 1989, the summer after eleventh grade, I attended basketball camp in Mars Hill, North Carolina. This basketball camp is where I won the slam dunk contest. I performed a backward 180-degree dunk with the ball in both hands. I received a shirt, certificate, and a plaque with the basketball camp name and year on it.

Later in 1989, I won the high school slam dunk contest that I attended. This contest took place with JV and varsity teams only from South Rowan High School. The contest came down between Jeff Wilkerson and me. He did a one handed dunk, and I did another backwards 180-degree dunk. I was rewarded a shirt and a certificate.

While attending South Rowan High School in 1990, I worked with John Ridenhour remodeling four town houses in Landis. Ridenhour worked on closing up windows, inside and outside, fixed the doors so they would all close properly, hung sheetrock and filled some sheetrock as well and I assisted him in doing these tasks. I remember digging out the basement and moving that dirt out back to fill in where utility buildings built by Ridenhour and me were placed. I also had to dig another foot down for the drainage pipe and then cover it with gravel, so that it could drain under the concrete floor. In addition, my dad and I removed a couple of trees that we cut up and used for firewood. All four units needed maintenance when someone moved out. The yard needed mowing, the appliances needed cleaning, and the unit needed painting, and the carpets needed steam cleaning. I painted all four of these units off and on over the upcoming years.

During baseball season in 1990, I received another letter—All-County and All-Conference for the second year in a row. I finished the season by hitting seven homeruns. Two of those homeruns came in Kannapolis during an Easter tournament. One hit was a homerun with the bases loaded over the right field fence. The second homerun I hit went directly over center field in another game, and I received three RBIs after hitting this one. I received a plaque for the Most Valuable Player of the tournament.

During my senior year, I also received the recognition of Masonry Student of the Year. I received the recognition and certificate but was not awarded the tool bag I was supposed to receive because I did not attend the awards ceremony since I had baseball practice. This award took me three years to receive it however; the masonry teacher did not feel I deserved it simply because I was not there to receive it in person.

Mom, Dad, and I flew to Las Vegas in June of 1990 so Dad could be a groomsman for Mom's cousin, David Absher. Dad was a groomsman along with Shawn, Kevin and David's brother Ed Absher. Shawn was the best man, and the wedding took place June 22, 1990. We visited David and his new wife, Peggy, his daughter, Robin, and David's sons Sean and Kevin. David and Peggy had a pool party at their house, and dancers came to party as well. David's topless dancer had a very nice set of fake breasts, and she looked to be a white female. She was wearing a thong that had straps over her shoulders, and most of the skin above her hips was bare. This woman put on a good show and earned her money. Peggy's dancer was an Italian person who came in wearing leather attire. He danced good for Peggy and the crowd and earned his money.

The trip to Las Vegas in June of 1990 was a great trip. I met Rebekah and Curb, and Rebekah is Garvey Elledge's daughter. Garvey was Grandma Absher's brother who lived in Arizona. The hottest day I had ever encountered happened with the temperature reaching 117 degrees for me on this trip.

Masonry Job

After graduation and the Myrtle Beach trip, I went to work for McGee brothers. These brothers owned a masonry business, and I went to work as a laborer mixing mud and moving bricks so men could lay brick on homes in Charlotte, North Carolina. I worked so hard for several days I suffered heat exhaustion, which is close to a heat stroke. This hard construction work taught me that I did not want to work this hard, and I learned to do something different, like wanting to fly airplanes.

Private Pilot Training

My mom says I was around airplanes all the time, and I had my life all planned out. I was hoping to retire at about age forty-five or fifty years old.

I graduated high school on June 1, 1990. My friends and I went to Myrtle Beach, South Carolina, for ten days to celebrate graduation. After returning home, then, I began working full-time for James Enterprise. In the fall, I started college at Rowan-Cabarrus Community College, and that is where I met my first serious girl-friend. I began taking flying lessons at the Statesville Municipal Airport. In early 1991, I helped the James's remodel a farmhouse in Georgia. Afterward, I went back to working on my degree from RCCC, flew on the weekends to build flight time, and worked on preparation for the ground written test. This gave me the lifelong goal that I wanted to establish—that is, to become a commercial pilot while working in real estate and rental projects on the side.

I took off from school during the fall of 1991 through the fall of 1992. In addition to flight training, I helped the James's remodel their home place in Royston, Georgia, during the spring of 1992. As we were remodeling the old home, we stayed in their mobile home down the road from the house. This place had a chicken coop along the driveway that we burned down. The house had the chimneys replaced, new plumbing, new heat and air unit, a new roof, new back porch and front porch, along with some new wood in places. In addition, there was new screening on the walk around porch; painted inside and out, upstairs and downstairs; and stained and pol-ished floors. It also had two bathrooms installed with new toilets and shower stalls and washer and dryer hookups. This process took about two and a half months.

During late 1991 and through mid-1992, I began working on becoming a private pilot at Catawba Valley Aviation located at the Statesville Municipal Airport. I had two flight instructors. My first was Neil Plyler, and the second instructor was David Meadows. It took me about nineteen hours to be ready for soloing. I flew the airplane solo at the Statesville Municipal Airport on December 21, 1991. The airplane was a Cessna 152, a single-engine, 108-brake horsepower, two-seater airplane. I felt very confident in my ability to complete three takeoffs and three landings to a full stop during the solo. The sensations were exhilarating and extraordinarily awesome being in control of the airplane.

I continued to fly, working on the private pilot's license and preparing for the written test. During 1991, I took a ground school with my brother, John Barringer, and Ken Carpenter for the written test at Rowan-Cabarrus Community College. I flunked this test and had to go about studying for the test in a different way. Therefore, I began studying on my own, and I retook the test at a fixed based operator (FBO) at Sugar Valley Aviation in North Carolina. On this test, I scored a 100 percent. I was very pleased, and when I took the check-ride with Margaret Morrison, the FAA examiner at Statesville, she stated that she had never given a check ride to someone that scored a 100 percent on the private written test. I felt very blessed when they hung the results on the wall in the Statesville Municipal Airport. I received my private pilot's license on June 26, 1992. After my check-ride, I did not cross paths again with Margaret until 2012 at FAA Headquarters in DC. I am very proud of this accomplishment. I continued to fly in accordance with meeting the requirements for the cross-country time to begin the instrument rating before leaving for flight school, flying Cessnas out of Statesville or flying Jimmy Kipka's C-172. From this period, I did my fifty hours of cross-country requirements and built some nighttime as well. I worked and built up flight hours, trying to get in enough time to earn several certificates. The instrument rating, commercial license, flight instructor license, and a multi-engine rating were completed.

Barry with airplane pre-accident

Associate Degree in Business Administration and Accounting Certificate

I attended Rowan Cabarrus Community College with a high school friend, Jason Ritchie, and we graduated together. Jason and I are still close friends, and we visit with each other at Concordia Lutheran Church. I really enjoy the company of his family.

In addition, Elizabeth Hudson and I attended college together. That is where we met, and we dated for three and a half years. College graduation occurred in 1995, I graduated with an associate degree in business administration along with an accounting certificate. Elizabeth taught ballet, tap, and jazz at the Salisbury School of Ballet. I helped the business with two dance recitals on backstage at Catawba College. She never went flying with me, and she never cooked me a meal while we were a couple.

The vacations Elizabeth and I shared occurred in Aurora, Illinois, where she was originally from, and her sister and brother-in-law still live there. I remember being there one Christmas when the temperature was sixty degrees below zero. I smoked cigarettes at the time, and it was so cold I could not stand outside long enough to smoke an entire cigarette. In addition, I remember spitting on the ground, and it became frozen before it hit the ground. Several times, when we were there, we rode the subway into Chicago. Elizabeth was a shopper, and we shopped at Lord and Taylors, Marshal Fields, Saks Fifth Avenue, and Hecht's in downtown on Michigan Avenue.

Elizabeth, her dad, and I drove to Long Island, New York, for her cousin's wedding, and it was an awesome trip. We saw Fifth Avenue, where Macy's was located, and where the David Letterman Show was recorded. We drove by the Statue of Liberty and saw the buildings like the World Trade Centers, and driving through all the tunnels was an experience. Another learning experience I witnessed was how dirty the city of Manhattan was. For example, where we parked in a parking deck in Manhattan, we went to ride on the elevator, and a bum covered with newspapers as he was lying on the concrete was asleep. There was trash all around the wastebasket, and the smell was awful.

In 1993, Elizabeth and I flew by using Mom's buddy pass with the airlines to fly to Las Vegas. We went to some shows, and one in particular was held by the Tropicana Hotel.

One concert Elizabeth and I attended was the Aerosmith Concert at the Blockbuster Pavilion. This concert was very good, and we had great seats under the canopy, twenty rows from the stage. This concert packed the pavilion.

While working for the James family, dating Elizabeth, and attending school, I invested the rest of my time into flying. Ferrell Jr. flew with me a good bit, and we went on some trips together. We flew to Greenville, North Carolina, to visit Chris Beaver, Scott Lippard, and some people. We flew to the beach for the weekend and met up with a couple of friends, as their employers had a meeting there as well. During this time I met Mark Trammell, a friend of Ferrell Jr., that I also flew with frequently. Ferrell Jr. and I spent time working together, fishing, flying, and chasing pretty women, though not necessarily in that order. We put his canoe in Kannapolis Lake rather frequently and caught lots of bass and a large amount of catfish on a regular basis.

Barry & Cousin Ferrell with fish

Ferrell Jr. and I flew Jimmy Kipka's Cessna 172 anytime we wanted. One flight I remember taking place was when we were flying down the Yadkin River. Two guys were fishing on a canoe. We buzzed by them very quickly, and I am sure this flyby scared them. Another flyby I remember vividly is when Buddy Chastain was married to Ferrell's sister, Rebekah. He was mowing a grass field on a tractor and going away from us, and he did not know we were flying that afternoon. He was standing on the tractor as he was mowing, and he did not know we were coming to buzz him. When we flew over him, he almost jumped off the tractor because we scared him so much.

Todd's Wedding

On November 9, 1994, my brother married Terri Leigh Eddleman. Dad was Todd's best man, and I was a groomsman. The wedding was at St. David's Lutheran Church in Kannapolis, where we were all members. The wedding party took place at the Moose Lodge in Kannapolis as well. Todd had our cousin-in-law Steve Ansley sing in the wedding, and he, Scott Seamen, Brian Heileg, and Brent Ross sang at the party. Todd and Terri had a big turnout in attendance, and it was a fun celebration.

Concerts

I attended several concerts at the Independence Arena and the Charlotte Coliseum. The concerts I remembered from the coliseum were Guns N' Roses with Skid Row opening for them. I was impressed with this concert, the crowd, the loudness, and the performance. In 1997, Todd, Terri, Gene and Lynn Gowayns, and I attended Cheap Trick, who opened for ZZTop in the coliseum. They played some good songs. However, ZZTop never moved around on the stage. Also during another concert, KISS performed. They were dressed in their makeup and wore the big shoes, and they could not move. They rocked the coliseum, and I was glad I attended.

During the mid-nineties at the Ritz, located beside the Independence Arena, I saw Jackyl, Vince Neil, and Gilby Clarke. These entertainers were impressive, loud, and packed the arena. Jackyl's lead singer carried an oil container around with him and drank out of it. Ferrell James II went with me to see Gilby Clarke, who played a favorite song, "Cure Me or Kill Me," and he played the guitar very well. Ferrell also saw Vince Neil with me, and he performed well also. He sang and carried a microphone around on the stage. He was also at the pavilion in his band, Mötley Crüe, without their original drummer.

In Fort Mill, South Carolina, where the Charlotte Hornets training facility was located, I saw the Black Crowes perform, and I was there in 1994 with Ferrell James II, Jason Wright, and Eric Little. The facility was packed, and there were two people dressed as crows dancing on the stage and the speakers. Some of my favorite songs were played, like "Twice as Hard," and I was happy with their performance.

I also saw Mötley Crüe with their drummer Tommy Lee, but they were missing their lead singer, Vince Neil. This show was in the company of Christopher Marlowe.

Blockbuster Pavilion had many concerts I attended. Charlie Daniels and Hank Williams Jr. also performed. Charlie Daniels was impressive. Hank did not perform very long, and I believed he was intoxicated. Another good show was Elton John. He performed many favorites, packed in many people, and played the piano like nobody I had ever seen. Another concert was Metallica. The pavilion had the most people I had ever seen in it, and it was pouring down. It rained throughout the entire show. Mike, Jackie Cook, Chris Marlowe, and I all went to see this band, and I remember Marlowe and I got muddy and had to ride in Mike's car like that. The Steve Miller band performed two years in a row and packed people in the pavilion. ELO—Electric Light Orchestra—and America were fine shows, and so were BTO, Bachman, Turner, and Overdrive.

Money Spent

The work I performed for James Enterprise helped me purchase a dirt bike, three Toyota Celicas, and a Ford van I used for work. The pay I earned also paid for a brand-new Toyota Celica in 1994. I also used what I earned to pay for all flight time I pursued. My earnings also paid for my education. I bought a mobile home in 1994 and renovated it before renting it out. James Enterprise helped me in finding this piece of rental property, and I spent my evenings in mid-1994 for a month and a half renovating the 1965 model mobile home. I borrowed $11,000 and invested around $3,000 on things like used appliances, carpet, linoleum, paint, shower stall, sinks, blinds, curtains, plumbing, and electrical and miscellaneous items. The mobile home rented for $375 per month, and the banknote was $225.69 per month. The extra $150 paid the taxes and insurance for the year. The rental property began its lease for one year and four months and then sold to James Enterprise. I now had enough money to pay for my instrument rating, the commercial license, the flight instructor certificate, and the multi-engine rating. I sold my work van, my motorcycle, and everything I did not need to help me pay for flight school. I went to American Flyers, a flight school in Addison, Texas.

Cousin

In addition, Ferrell James II spent time with me taking me flying. He also had a Bultaco motorcycle, and he could ride that motorcycle doing a wheelie all the way up the runway. Later he owned a Honda 600 XL, and he could ride that motorcycle on one wheel as far as the road would let him. In 1995, he tried to pop a wheelie on a Yamaha 125 on gravel. The motorcycle rolled over on him, tearing the (ACL) anterior cruciate ligaments in the knee.

Flight School

The trip to American Flyers in Addison, Texas, took place in October of 1995. The evening before leaving, I stayed the night at Deric Harrington and Brandon Beaver's in South Charlotte off Arrowood exit at Coffee Creek Apartments. The car was packed for the trip, and I left Charlotte early that morning and drove for thirteen hours. I stayed the night in Monroe, Louisiana, and drove the rest of the way that Sunday morning.

The money I saved after selling most of my work material and vehicle helped pay for my flight school training. I spent four months at the Addison Airport in flight school and received the certificates I trained to receive.

The airport had only one runway and an approach off both ends. The south end of the runway had several tall buildings close by, and the north end was clearer. The most flown airplane was N9502D, a Cessna 172 RG. This airplane satisfied the requirements for the high performance endorsement.

The first certificate I received was my instrument rating in November 1995 by training in N9502D, a Cessna 172 RG, and an ATC Frasca Simulator. It was very enjoyable flying in a simulated environment by wearing foggles or a hood. Performing procedure turns, shooting approaches, and witnessing the approaches was very fun, live or simulated. One of the most fun approaches I remember was when my flight instructor Colin Bailey and I performed the ILS approach into Fort Worth Meacham Field. I remember flying the approach in the clouds, and we popped out several hundred feet above the ground. It was awesome to experience that successful flight.

The second license I sought was the commercial license in December of 1995. Mom and Dad visited one weekend, and they flew into Dallas / Fort Worth Airport. Mom fixed me some meals and put them in the freezer. Over Christmas, I flew home on US Airways and spent a week for the holidays. Ferrell Jr. and I flew N8222L, Jim Kipka's Cessna 172. I executed the commercial maneuvers up to the practical test standards with Ferrell onboard watching. After returning to Addison, Texas, the scheduled check-ride was with a different examiner I had for the instrument rating. This oral was a piece of cake, and the flight went good, all but the crosswind landings. He wanted me to practice crosswind take-offs and landings more and then come back for a reexamination.

My parents enjoying themselves

The long commercial cross-country was 350 miles round trip, with landing points more than fifty nautical miles apart. That day I flew from Addison Airport to Midland Airpark in Midland Texas. However, I had a magneto misfiring or a little water in the fuel or something going on, so I elected to land at Abilene, Texas, to have the airplane checked out. No problems were found, and my trip continued. I have family in Midland, and my cousin Christian Hyde came to visit me when I called upon reaching the airport. I flew a Cessna 172 RG, N9502D. Christian came out to the airplane and checked out the airplane, and we visited for a short while. The FBO fueled the airplane, I filed a flight plan, and then I flew to San Angelo, Texas. My cousin Tommy Hyde worked for the FBO, and we visited briefly as well. That evening, I did make it safely back to Addison after dark.

Kevin Sutton, Tommy Hyde's son-in-law, is married to Ginger, Tommy's youngest daughter. He worked on his commercial license at American Flyers. He would visit Homestead Village, where I stayed, and we shared our experiences with each other. We would also talk about certain issues and questions for the written exam.

During January 1996, I received the flight instructor airplane license. One of the training flights for this license became memorable in several aspects. The first memorable aspect was when we flew over the South Fork ranch that was for the 1980s TV show *Dallas*. The entire backside of the ranch had plastic covering it. I could not figure out if this plastic was there for maintenance reasons or if the show removed the plastic. One more aspect of memorable training took place when I learned to land the airplane from the right seat. This training was in a Cessna 172 RG. The airport used for my first landing from the right seat was at the Fort Worth Alliance Airport. In addition, at this time, the press covered the removal of some homes, trailers, woods, etc. for the protests of building the Texas Motor Speedway that we flew over during training.

In addition, in January, I received the multi-engine rating at the Redbird Airport located in south Dallas. That rating came by flying 7.2 hours in a Beechcraft Travel Air with the owner and instructor Clyde Frederickson. He was a very good instructor and gave me good pointers on engine-out procedures. His big saying was "Dead foot, dead engine." The scheduling of this check-ride was on a Sunday morning. My dad flew in the previous evening, and I picked him up at the DFW airport. He and I were up that Sunday morning, and I had my car packed, as we were going home after the check-ride whether I passed or failed. Fortunately, I passed, and I paid this examiner $200 for the check-ride. I received this check-ride for only $895, which included the examiner fee. Dad and I drove back home to North Carolina, but we did not arrive until 7:00 a.m. Monday morning. The Dallas Cowboys lost the Super Bowl on this Sunday.

Flight school ended up costing about $30,000, and because I did not have quite enough to cover the flight costs and living expenses, my mom and dad took out a second mortgage on their home to help me with the remainder of the cost.

After flight school, I returned to Kannapolis and went back to work on rental property. In addition, I worked for G&G Turf and Irrigation located in Cornelius, North Carolina. This business was an all-around sprinkler business, and we installed new sprinkler systems around Lake Norman and in the Ballantyne neighborhood in South Charlotte. I worked with Mark Trammell and Jody Banet. Sometimes we would install new sprinkler systems, and sometimes we would have to fix a broken sprinkler head. This company employed two Mexicans, and these men were sending their money back to Mexico.

Sprinkler Work

While working for G&G Turf and Irrigation, I spent a lot of time at Deric Harrington and Brandon Beaver's condominium at Admiral's Quarters on Lake Norman. We would party at a dance club called Twisters and go to several bars, one named Irish Que. These friends later moved to Alta Harbor, an apartment complex on Lake Norman.

Employment at a Flight School

In October of 1996, I went to work at a flight school, Lancaster Aviation at the Concord Regional Airport, located in Concord, North Carolina. I flew with many people, helped eight individuals become pilots, and helped two other pilots add to their pilot's license. Working seven days a week and twenty months of work added up to over 1,200 flight hours of instruction given and 1,600 hours total time in airplanes. I was doing what I loved and wanted to do. The time I was not working, I was fishing with my cousin Ferrell James Jr.

The flight school had the owner Lanny Lancaster, Larry Morris, and me as full-time instructors. On the weekends, we would have two other available instructors to instruct, Dan and Jerry Goodson. At the time of the crash, Lancaster and Larry had already parted ways. Larry Morris ran Tarheel Airtech out of an office upstairs above our office. Jeff Olson, Christine Lundon, Chuck Morris, Scott Linville, Dan Black, Lancaster, and I instructed for the flight school at the time.

The thirteen airplanes included in the flight school were for rental and instruction; those airplanes were used in sightseeing or for rides, even for photography. The airplane list was from four Cessna 150s, a Cessna 172, two Diamond Katanas, one Piper Cherokee 180, three Pa-28R-200, Piper Cherokee Arrows, one Aeronca Champ used for tail-dragger training, and one Piper Twin Comanche. I helped in the previous mentioned tasks and gained valuable experience.

At the flight school I worked at, I helped pilots go through student training—some up through soloing the airplane and some up to attaining eight private pilot's licenses, one for a commercial license, and one for a flight instructor license. In addition, the flight school offered biennial flight reviews, instrument competency checks, and checkouts for insurance purposes in the airplanes for rental of aircraft. The private pilots were Tony Hammond, Thaddeus Sergeant, Steve Gordon, Jason Graves, Ken Carpenter, John Meeks, Mick Cobb, and Jimmy Fenning. In addition, I helped Kevin Fiala train for his flight instructor license. An employee of the flight school was Larry Morris, and he was like the chief pilot. He would fly with our students during the three hours of prep for the check ride to make sure the students or pilots were ready for their check ride. The FAA examiner used in giving these practical tests was Pat Smertzler. Her home was in Hickory, North Carolina, and she drove down to the Concord Regional Airport to exercise the check rides.

Students or pilots would rent an airplane with or without an instructor. The instruction given costs $25 per hour at the time, and I was only paid $10 an hour when I began in 1996 and only $12 per hour in 1998. The Cessna 150s would rent for $45 an hour, the 172 and Piper Cherokee 180 would rent for $65 per hour, the Diamond Katanas for $85 per hour, and the twin Comanche for $135 per hour, and all rentals were rented wet, fuel included.

The flight school's busiest time was on the weekends. I did most of the flying with students and pilots on the weekend versus the rest of the week. During my twenty-month work span, I did fly occasionally eight hours at a time on Saturdays, like during the fly-ins where we hauled passengers all day. Speaking of fly-ins, I sat in the pilots' meeting with the organizers, pilots involved, and the gorgeous Patty Wagstaff as they put a game plan together for the fly-in. She performed two air shows at the Concord Regional Airport in 1997 and in 1998. She performed the air show in her Extra 300 airplane, and it was one hell of a performance.

The students' and pilots' training, insurance requirements to rent one of the flight school's airplanes, the biennial flight review, and maneuvers played part in the instructor's expectations of the pilot. Certain maneuvers performed by the pilot or student pilot, like power on and off stalls, medium and steep turns, maintaining altitudes and headings, emergency procedures, forward and side slips, simulated engine-out procedures, normal and crosswind takeoffs and landings, short field and soft field takeoffs and landings were all practiced as well.

In December of 1996, I remember flying with a student who was a father of a Western Carolina University student. We flew in a Cessna 172 N7771U to the Jackson County Airport, which overlooked Western Carolina University in the North Carolina Mountains. The airport overlooked the Western Carolina University campus and the town of Cullowhee. I remember that the FBO was empty and part of the displaced threshold had caved off the side of the mountain.

There were several flights in particular that I remember occurring. Shortly after working for the flight school, I would let the students fly us to Florence, South Carolina. The students that I let fly us down there needed their three solo controlled field takeoffs and landings. Most of the time, I would exit the airplane at the end of the runway and watch closely the takeoffs and landings performed by the students.

The weekend of March 31, 1997, the Absher side of the family met in Wilkesboro to celebrate my grandma Absher's 80th birthday. I flew N46047, a Cessna 172, from the flight school in concord to the Wilkesboro Airport. Mom, Dad, and Margie, Mom's sister, picked me up, and we went to surprise Grandma Absher. We spent a couple of hours with her, and we all sang "Happy Birthday" to her. Dad and I flew back together, and I flew him over Dale Earnhardt's farm as well as other places like over Statesville and Mooresville. We flew over Ferrell James's grass strip, and we went back to Concord Regional Airport where we landed.

One flight I remember took place with Jimmy Fenning in his Piper Cherokee 180. At the time, he was working as Mark Martin's crew chief on Jack Roush's race team. We flew up to an airport east of Greensboro to practice traffic pattern operations as well as takeoffs and landings.

One more time I flew that I can recall was when John Barringer, Ken Carpenter, and I flew to Camden, South Carolina, to buy a Piper Tri-Pacer for Ken Carpenter. We flew down in John Barringer's Piper Super Cruiser to purchase the airplane and fly it back to Barringer's grass strip in Kannapolis. Ken Carpenter and I would do some flight training out of Barringer's strip, but we did a lot at Rowan County Airport or at the Concord Regional Airport. Pat Smertzler gave him his check ride for his private pilot license.

One of the first flights that I went on personally while employed at the flight school was when I went to meet some people in Myrtle Beach, South Carolina. This flight took place in N46047, a Cessna 172, in instrument conditions. It was a Saturday morning around 10:00 a.m., and I called the flight service station to file the instrument flight plan. At the time, Myrtle Beach was reporting a ceiling of 1,500 feet, visibility was five miles, and they were reporting light rain and fog. I had a passion to make this flight, so I did a preflight on the airplane, took off, and contacted air traffic control on approach to Charlotte airport and I was on my way to the beach. I flew in the clouds all the way until popping out on the approach into Myrtle Beach. I could see the ground below and the hotels along the coast, but I was still in the clouds looking out the front windshield. Therefore, I requested a go-around, the air traffic controllers vectored me around and aligned me back up on the initial approach fix, and I continued inbound until I felt comfortable with the approach to follow through with a landing.

In May of 1997, Tommy Hyde came out to the airport, and I took him flying in a Cessna 172. We flew around Kannapolis, Landis, China Grove, Rockwell, Albemarle, Mooresville, and Statesville. This flight may have been our first flight together with me at the controls.

During 1997, I saw Jack Roush fly into the Concord Regional Airport in his P-51 Mustang. He took the man that played coach on TV, and they flew for a while. Someone was there making pictures and videoing the flight.

Crisis in the Tobacco Field

I wrote this article at UNCC in one of the first English classes that I took after recovering from the accident. In the summer of 1997, as a young flight instructor at the Concord Regional Airport, I faced a crisis with Jason Graves, one of the students I was instructing. At the time, this was the most dramatic crisis I had experienced in my eighteen-month career as a flight instructor.

Jason had arrived at the point in his training that required him to fly a solo cross-country, a flight that is longer than fifty nautical miles one way from point A to point B. On the last leg of his trip, Jason began to fear that the airplane was out of fuel and decided to land the airplane in a tobacco field. After putting the plane down in a field behind a woman's home, Jason telephoned me. He was upset but otherwise okay; he was mostly worried about how we would fly the plane out of this field.

I flew a Cessna 172 to Siler City Airport to meet Jason and the woman whose house was close by the field used as a landing area. As we made our way back to the plane, we began to deal with the crisis of just how we would get that plane back out of that field. I considered my options, which were to (1) attempt to fly the airplane or (2) have someone drive to the site, remove the wings, and put the airplane on a trailer and drive it home.

"Wow!" I exclaimed when I saw the plane. "How did you get this airplane here in one piece?" I was very impressed. It took a lot of bravery to land on this soft surface with a full crop of tobacco.

Since this sand hill's dirt was so soft, we would have to do a special type of takeoff, what the FAA calls a soft-field takeoff. Fortunately, these takeoffs were a part of our training. Before executing this takeoff, however, I had to be sure we had enough fuel to get us to the Siler City Airport. We examined the time sheet and concluded we had just under an hour of fuel left in the tanks. That should do it.

Next, we had to chart our way out of the field. In the middle of the field was a small direct road leading to a water stand, which was approximately ten feet high. That road would be our runway.

It was time to get this plane in the air. I executed a short field and soft field takeoff. In order to do so, one must take advantage of a phenomenon known as ground effect. This phenomenon occurs when a plane flies at a height not more than the length of its wingspan. At this height, lift produced by an air cushion allows the plane to remain airborne at a lower speed than normally required to fly.

As soon as I got the plane off the ground, I experienced this ground effect. I immediately steered to the right to avoid the water stand. The left wing just barely cleared the water stand, and the right wing almost hit the tobacco plants as we turned to miss it. However, we made it back to Siler City with just enough fuel in our tank to continue on to the Stanley County Airport for fuel.

I returned to the airplane I had flown in and followed Jason's plane to the Stanley County Airport, where he obtained fuel. We made it safely back to Concord; we were grateful the crisis was over.

In retrospect, I would make this same decision again. The alternative to resolving this crisis would have cost too much and would have taken more time. Even though the decision was risky, we successfully made it.

Renters

While working at the Concord Regional Airport for Lancaster Aviation, Robert D. Raeford, a commentator on the *John Boy and Billy Big Show* on the radio, would come and rent the Aeronca Champ. I would go out to the airplane with him and hand prop the airplane for him. This airplane is the only one he would rent, and it was a tail-dragger.

Air Show

During the spring of 1997, the Concord Regional Airport had an air show that took place. The flight school where I worked gave passenger rides in a Cessna 172 and two Piper Arrow 200s. Airplanes were on static display, and Patty Wagstaff was the aerobatic performer in an Extra 300. It was neat to sit in the pilot's meeting with her on that Saturday and Sunday at that event.

Personal Flights

The summer of 1997, I rode with John Meeks and one of his friends in N46047, a 172, that the flight school sold Meeks. We did some flight training on our round trip flight to Raleigh, North Carolina, to see a concert. The concert was of Jimmy Buffet located at Walnut Creek amphitheatre. We arrived in the early evening and it was a night flight home, which we arrived early the next morning. We saw Jimmy Buffet's two Beech Hawker jets on the tarmac at the airport. The concert was very entertaining, and he played many favorites. In one tune, he rode above the stage in a car with a girl driving. He was impressive and well-liked.

In addition, an awesome flight with Scott Pope in a Beech King Air 200, N300N, took place while I worked at the flight school. Scott asked me to ride along, and he would see to it that NASCAR would pay me for the trip. That morning, I met Scott at the airport. We departed around 4:00 a.m., and we flew up to Cape Cod, Massachusetts, to pick up Bill France Jr., his wife, and their child. What made this trip so memorable to me was as we flew on a northbound heading past Manhattan, New York, we were able to see the Statue of Liberty, the World Trade Centers, and all the buildings making up downtown Manhattan. The World Trade Centers along with the Statue of Liberty in the bay stuck out and are very vivid in my memory. It was neat flying at 24,000 feet in a pressurized airplane and then shooting the instrument approach into Cape Cod Airport with Scott. He allowed me to fly some, but I primarily talked on the radio.

Another flight I remember for one of my students that took place was the check ride that Jason Graves flew on with the examiner Pat Smertzler. The check ride took place in a Cessna 150, N6219K, a two-place, single engine, 100-brake horsepower airplane. It was during the summer, and it was hot and bumpy that day. The examiner and Jason went out and flew for about an hour doing maneuvers and air work when Jason got motion sickness and tried to vomit out the window during the flight. He did so, and most of it came back inside of the airplane. Jason received his license even after becoming sick.

In late 1997, the boss of the flight school wanted to buy a newer 172 to use in the flight school. Therefore, since my mother was a flight attendant, she was able to let us use buddy passes to fly with, and she had so many a year to use. She gave one to me to use to fly to Orlando, Florida, to purchase a Cessna 172 that the boss had wanted to purchase. I flew down as a passenger on US Airways, checked the airplane out visually, checked the maintenance logbooks out, paid the owner, and flew N77934 back to Concord. I stopped in South Carolina for fuel and arrived back to the Concord Regional Airport around 8:00 p.m. that evening.

Several months after returning home with the newer Cessna 172, Ferrell James II, my brother, a friend, and I went flying one evening after dark. My cousin sat in the left seat and flew the airplane. I sat in the right beside Ferrell, my brother sat directly behind me, and our friend Alvis Hill sat in the other seat. We flew to Tanglewood to see the Christmas lights, which were west of Winston Salem, North Carolina. In addition, we came back from there over Lake Norman, and as we were heading back to the east, we spotted the *Catawba Queen*. The *Catawba Queen* is a large boat that has parties on it, and this night they were busy partying.

Barry & brother Todd

I received the multi-engine instructor license on February 2, 1998. Rich Burns, an examiner out of the flight standards district office in Charlotte, gave me the check ride. We flew a Piper Twin Comanche for the check ride, and it was a nice day for it. I executed the flight and met the practical test standards, and Burns awarded me my temporary addition to my license.

The flight with Loren Edwards in Ricky Rudd's Beech King Air 350, N313MP, took place on several occasions. The latter time was in the evening, and I thought it was awesome to feel the landing sensation that Loren let me feel during the flight and landing at the Winston Salem Airport. We drove his truck back at dusk that evening.

Some flight instructing I did was for Randy Humphries in his Piper Saratoga. We flew the airplane to Nashville, Tennessee, and we watched him race his midget cars. We made this trip on several occasions. Each time we would not return to our home airport until after midnight on those nights.

A fun flight I instructed on took place with Dr. Kevin Craft. He and I, along with one of his friends, flew to Georgia to the Fulton County Airport. We took a cab to our motel, got ready for the evening, had some dinner, and then went to Tattletales downtown Atlanta. This bar was a very nude bar, and there was only standing room inside the bar. Everyone was having a great time watching the girls do private dances for the guys. Then we went to a dance club.

Another Air Show

The second air show I worked was at the Concord Regional Airport. The flight school carried passengers around the traffic pattern for ten dollars per person. I flew almost eight hours on that Saturday and almost as much that Sunday. In addition, I sat in the pilot's meeting with Patty Wagstaff once again. She and a passenger arrived in a Beech Baron 95 with her pilot. She performed in the air show in an Extra 300 and put on one hell of an air show!

Airline Job

My mother was friends with the chief pilot—they both worked for US Airways Express. This airline was the commuter for US Airways. Mom had been talking with the chief pilot, and they had set up an interview for the second week of June 1998 for me. My dream of becoming an airline pilot was about to come true.

Details Leading to Airplane Crash

June 1, 1998, which started out as a routine day, changed my life forever. I boarded N7794Y, a Piper Twin-Engine Comanche, and the pilot had the left engine already running. I was a passenger and a safety pilot on this flight. The flight departed Concord Regional Airport at 3:55 p.m. en route to Livingston, West Virginia. The airplane went off Roanoke's radar at 4:32 p.m.

June 1, 1998

June 1, 1998, began similar to any other day. That morning I went by the bank to deposit my check the boss from the flight school had given to me the previous evening. Next, I went to the drive through at Hardees and then went straight to the airport. When I arrived, I asked Misty Smith, a girl behind the counter, to make sure to tell the linemen to top off N7794Y. The day was a beautiful day, and the flight school was very busy. I flew with four pilots before boarding the running Comanche.

Flight Details before the Crash

During the afternoon around 2:30 p.m., Brian, Lanny Lancaster's attorney, came into the office and asked if I would go with him to practice takeoffs and landings in the Cessna 172. While performing takeoffs and landings, Robert Anderson arrived early and began the preflight on the Comanche. Brian and I flew until around 3:45 p.m. that afternoon. We taxied onto the ramp, pushed the airplane back on the flight line, and tied it down. I filled out his logbook, signed it, and then took out a bill out of my pocket and billed him for the flight time. I tore the front off the bill and gave it to him, and I put the second copy in my pocket. However, I did not write his name on the receipt.

I came out of the airplane and went straight to the Comanche, and Robert Anderson already had the left engine running. I boarded, and I asked him if we were full of fuel. He said, "Yes, we are full of fuel." When I asked about the oil, he replied, "Oh shoot, I forgot to check the oil." I replied, "Taxi us up to the terminal, and I will go in and charge two quarts of oil. That way we will not have to buy oil when we arrive there, and they may not have the kind we need."

He fired the right engine up, we taxied up, and he shut the right engine down. I went in and asked Misty for two quarts of oil. She gave me two quarts of oil, and she wrote the bill up to charge Lancaster for the oil. I went out and boarded the airplane. Robert fired the right engine up, and we went to runway 2, did a before-takeoff checklist, and then took off.

ATC Tapes

We departed the Concord Regional Airport around five minutes before four o'clock, and as Robert was climbing out, I asked him if I could buzz my cousin's airstrip in Kannapolis. I did from the west, and I flew around, came back, and buzzed it from the east. My cousin Ferrell Jr. was standing out on his front porch watching. I handed control of the airplane back to Robert, and I started writing down the flight plan material. I contacted Greensboro Approach and continued flying on. As I was filing the flight plan with Raleigh Flight Service Station, Greensboro told us to contact Roanoke Approach, and they gave us the frequency. I contacted Roanoke Approach and said, "Roanoke Approach, 77Niner4Yankee."

Roanoke replied, "N ended in Yankee, try again."

I said, "Yes, sir, good afternoon, 77Niner4Yankee."

Roanoke stated, "77Niner4Yankee, Roanoke Approach."

I said, "Yes, sir, we are off the two-hundred-ten-degree radial from you guys, forty-five miles out. We are about level at ten thousand. Request flight following up to Greenbrier. We are a twin Comanche."

Roanoke stated, "Niner4Yankee, ident please."

I keyed the mic. Roanoke said, "Niner4Yankee, radar contact forty-five miles southwest of Roanoke. Roanoke's altimeter, 29.75. Say aircraft type."

I replied, "PA-30, Niner4Yankee."

The controller said, "Roger, I will have a code shortly." The controller then stated, "Twin Comanche, Niner4Yankee, squawk 0461.

I replied, "0461 for Niner4Yankee."

Sixty seconds went by and there was no chatter on the mic. Then, I asked, "What about radar contact for Niner4Yankee?"

The controller responded, "Sir, I gave you radar contact forty-five miles southwest."

"Okay, Roanoke. Niner4Yankee, we are descending through nine thousand. We are losing the right engine, we need priority!"

"Okay, where do you want to go?"

"We would like to come and land at Roanoke."

"If you do not want closer, I will bring you in to Roanoke."

"Roanoke is fine, sir."

"Roger. Fly heading 030 vectors toward the Roanoke Airport and advise me if you need any more assistance."

I remarked, "030, we will advise, Niner4Yankee."

"And maintain your altitude as long as feasible."

"Right now, we are at 8,300." Five seconds went by, and then, I could hear the mic click on and back off. Twenty-two seconds went by, and the controller said, "Twin Comanche, make the heading 040, and uh, if you do experience, uh, anything else that makes you want to get on the ground faster, I have three airports closer than Roanoke."

I said "Okay, 040 for Niner4Yankee, and we will let you know." After twenty-two more seconds went by, the controller said, "Twin Comanche Niner4Yankee, how many souls on board and fuel?"

"We have two souls on board, and we are full of fuel."

"How many gallons would that be?"

"I am estimating eighty-five gallons."

"Roger."

The controller responded to me after forty-five seconds, and he said, "Twin Comanche, Niner4Yankee, radar contact is lost. I will pick you up as you get closer in."

I said, "Roger, Niner4Yankee." No one said anything for thirty-seven seconds, then a Cherokee 16Whiskey climbed through 2,300-contacted departure. The controller replied, "8416Whiskey Roanoke Departure, radar contact, climb to your requested altitude."

The pilot replied, "16Whiskey."

After twenty-eight seconds passed, the controller told 16Whiskey to proceed on course. The pilot replied, "On course for 16Whiskey." After thirty seconds passed, the controller said, "Twin Comanche Niner4Yankee, say altitude."

I replied, "Niner4Yankee, uh, is at 5,700 feet."

The controller said, "Okay, sir. Um, are you unable to maintain altitude? Are you coming down fast?"

I keyed the mic, and after a second Robert Anderson said, "Niner4Yankee. Uh, we are losing directional stability, and uh, there is a little trouble holding altitude."

"Okay, sir, you are getting down into an area where our minimum vectoring altitude, uh, if we were to see you, is six thousand feet. Correction, uh, five thousand feet, so you are well below my coverage at this time. When you are able, proceed directly to the, uh, Winthrop VOR, 114Niner, and that will bring you direct to the field."

Three seconds went by, and Robert responded, "Roger, Niner4Yankee, 114.9."

The controller said to the pilot, "Catawba 3490, Roanoke Departure, radar contact, climb and maintain one zero thousand."

The pilot responded, "Climb and maintain one zero thousand for Catawba 3490."

"Catawba 3490, turn right heading three one zero, join Victor 258 and resume own navigation."

The pilot replied, "31zero to join and resume own navigation, Catawba 3490." The pilot checked in after thirty-five seconds of silence, "Trans Auto 141 at 2,500."

The controller replied, "That is Trans Auto 141 at departure. Radar contact, climb and maintain one zero thousand."

"One zero thousand."

After 22 seconds, the controller instructed the pilot of Trans Auto 141, "Turn right on course direct Pontiac."

The pilot responded, "Direct Pontiac."

After forty seconds went by, the controller told 3490 to contact Washington Center 127 point Niner Two.

The pilot responded, "Twenty-seven niner two, Catawba 3490."

I exclaimed, "Roanoke, Niner4Yankee needs assistance to the closest airport!"

The controller said, "Niner4Yankee I have lost radar contact with you about ten miles or so ago. Um, so, sir, I really do not know where you are closest to. The last time I saw you, you would be closest to the Blacksburg Airport, and that would be on an approximate heading of 350 degrees."

I said, "Okay three five zero for Niner4Yankee. We are at four thousand continuing to descend here."

"Okay, sir, that is my only guess, uh, on the heading three five zero and, uh, maintain as, uh, as, uh, high as, uh, altitude as you can.

"Uhh, we are doing the best we can do."

"Okay, full power, and uhh, be sure to step on that good engine.

"We are doing it, man, and it looks like, uh, we are descending about a thousand feet a minute."

"Uhh, sir, I heard the, uh, the stall warning going off in there. If, uhh, if you are in the stall, you might need to pick up speed to maintain altitude.

I exclaimed, "We are turning, looking for a field!"

Another pilot said, "48X-ray with you, seven thousand."

The controller said, "Four eight X-ray, Roanoke Approach, expect the visual approach to the Roanoke Airport, uh, the altimeter 2niner seven four."

The pilot said, "Two-niner seven four, four eight x-ray."

After fourteen seconds, I said, garbled, "Niner four Yankee is going in!"

The controller asked, "Niner4Yankee, are you still with me?"

The pilot of 48x-ray said, "He said he was going in."

The controller asked who heard that report, and the pilot of 48x-ray claimed he did. The plane crashed into a stand of pine trees between two houses close to a softball field that we were trying to land on. The blessings began by someone being home in one of the houses and a woman thought the sound of the airplane crashing was the garage door opening. A minute went by, and she did not hear her husband, so she went outside to greet him and saw the garage door was still down. She then heard something and saw the airplane close to the house, and she did not know what to do. She dropped to her knees and prayed, and it dawned on her to run inside and call 911. The paramedics and firefighters were holding their meeting at the fire department right up the road from the crash scene. Paramedics converged on the crashed plane. The medic saved my life. I was that near death.

Airplane wreckage at crash site

Trooper writing report of crash

Notes Made from the Scene of the Accident

Virginia State Highway Police Trooper Doug Holly, 1-800-542-5959
Five minutes on scene
Lifeguard 10 airlift
Forty-five SW of ROA, ROA Tower, engine problems, lost altitude, lost radio contact

Anderson—Con.—he was piloting, was on left, commercial pilot
Hulon—not Con. (on right)

FAA left at 1:00 p.m. today
Plane had fuel
Switches not on for fuel

Anderson—no one to contact
Hulon—turned over to FAA

4:32 p.m. 911 call
Sheriff's first, state trooper next
Inboard (outboard) SWTS
Floyd—SW of Roanoke

FAA Investigator—John H. Phelps, NEW phone number from faa.
gov December 2009: 405-954-7519. Old phone number at time of
crash: 804-222-7494, ext. 231

Brian Rayner, NTSB, 202-314-6367

New Path for Flight Studies

I remained in the hospital for three months. I remember nothing but my dreams about the doctors and nurses along with many beeps and buzzes of the medical devices keeping me alive. It was horrific. When I started coming to, I could not see anything, which made it scarier. What I was seeing was not clear. My brain was not accustomed to me not being able to see.

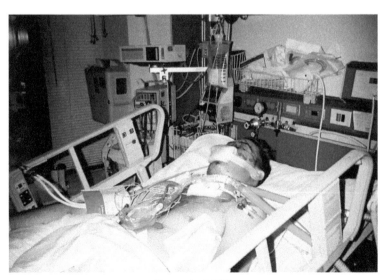

Barry in ICU

Lawsuit

My mom knew an attorney, Rusty Almond, and she worked with this man. Rusty Almond and Pappadackus assisted in investigating the plane crash. These attorneys were close friends to Tony Meneo, an attorney out of Raleigh, North Carolina.

Memorandum at Concord Regional Airport

On June 23, 1998, a memorandum that went out to the Airport Service Workers (ASWs) stated, "Lancaster's Aviation, Inc., please note, 1. Please do not fill wing tanks on N8209C, Aeronca Champion without pilot's permission. 2. Do not fill wing tanks on N3031K, Piper Arrow above tabs without pilot's permission. Thanks." Misty Smith wrote on this memo these are the only two airplanes not allowed fuel nightly.

Charlotte Rehabilitation

The day of July 5, 1998, I was in the Charlotte Rehabilitation sitting with the family on a Sunday afternoon. My mom, dad, and my brother were talking to me and asking questions. The doctors wired my mouth shut, and the tape they recorded me on sounds as if I was mumbling and making no sense.

I said, "A piece of red rawhide."

Mom said, "A piece of meat?"

I said I was like a piece of rawhide.

"The plane crash did that to you."

"I know. I have seen more red places on them." She then told me to wipe my mouth. It didn't help. It did not help at all. Todd asked me if I remembered where the brakes and all that stuff were on my wheelchair and everything. He said, "You are doing well, and you are going to have to start using the phone. You are going to have to start walking more with a walker and keeping your weight off your right leg. You just keep doing all of those things, they are going to let you out of here, and we are going home."

I said, "That is what that one old boy said that made me stay two days in a row."

Todd said, "I know you know Paul and that is who it was."

"Son, do you know where you are at? You are going to have to have a place to sleep. Do you know who gave you a haircut yesterday? Do you remember that? Do you remember that?"

I said no.

Dad: "You do not remember getting a haircut yesterday?"
Me: "Probably not."
Dad: "I bet you do."
Me: "I thought Todd gave me one haircut."
Dad: "He did."
Me: "How did he give me any?"
Dad: "Todd gave you a haircut yesterday and a shave. Did you know that?"
I said yes, and Todd said, "And a shower."
Dad: "Do you remember telling him that you were ready to get out of the barber's chair?"
I said, "Yes, what is his name?"

Dad laughed and said, "You were telling the truth. I am ready to get out of here."

Dad said I was ready to go, and I said that was what I was ready for as well. Dad said, "It will come. That day will come around here."

I said, "Call it. I was thinking it was coming."

Dad replied, "Well, it is coming, but it is down the road a little ways. It is coming every day. You are going to get better every day. It is going to take a lot of hard work on your part though."

I said yes.

"You can do it."

Then my brother said, "We are pulling for you. Randy Hyde is coming down here to see you this weekend. Brandon came by and saw you. Do you remember Brandon coming by and seeing you?"

I said yes and that Brandon paged me about three or four times a week.

Dad said he would probably be coming by and seeing me often, since he worked over here and came by to check on me.

I said to my mother, "Mom, I love you."

She replied, "I love you too, darling."

"I am sorry."

"Sorry for what?"

"Just, everything."

"I know you are, but it is not your fault."

Todd said, "It is not your fault though."

Mom said, "It is not your fault."

I said, "Yes, I know, but a lot of it is my fault."

Mom and Todd asked why, and Dad said, "Why do you say that?"

I said, "Because I am in a position where they get me."

Dad said, "You could not help the position you are in."

Mom added, "Because you are in this position."

"Yes, I know, but I should be in a different position."

Dad said, "Well, you are lucky to be here. You could be in the ground and buried."

I said, "Let us go somewhere else."

My brother said, "Where do you want to go? It is warm out here. You wanted to get warm?"

I said, "I want something to eat."

Todd said, "You want something to eat?"

I said yes, and Mom asked me if I wanted her to go inside and get me a milkshake. "I have some of that chocolate shake stuff, and I might find you some ice to put in it," Mom said. "Do you want another drink of tea? This is tea Mom made at home. This is not their tea. Do you want a drink?"

I said no, and Mom said, "You do not want anymore?"

I replied, "This is not your tea."

Todd said, "This is Grandma Absher's tea."

"I do not want any right now."

Todd asked me if I remembered going in and buying two quarts of oil, and I said I did. He asked me, "Do you remember going straight out there, just getting right in, and leaving?"

Dad also asked, "What time was it? Do you remember?"

Todd added, "Do you remember what time it was?"

I replied, "What day is it supposed to be now?"

Todd answered, "Today is July 5, and it is 1998. How old are you?"

I said, "How old am I? I guess I would be twenty-eight, if I had another year to go."

"No, you would be twenty-seven instead of twenty-eight."

"I guess, I would be twenty-seven."

Dad asked, "What year were you born, Hulon?"

"Shoot, I do not know, 1926, 1946?"

Mom said, "No, 1946 is close to when your mom and dad were born. You were born in 1972."

I said okay, and Dad asked how old Todd is. "How old is your big brother?"

I said, "Todd was born at the old stuff over at Grandma's place, 1942."

Todd asked, "How old am I, Hulon?"

"I do not know, I forgot."

Dad asked me if I remember where I lived and what the address was. I answered Aunt Mae's house.

Dad said, "Aunt Mae's?"

Mom said, "Honey, you live in Enochville."

Todd stated, "We moved from Aunt Mae's, you remember that? We moved over there beside Terri's, Leslie's, Shanda's, and all of them. What is that address?"

"I do not remember, I do not remember."

Mom said, "2814 Countryside Drive."

"That is Aunt Mae's house."

Todd said, "That was 2705."

"That was Grandma Hyde's."

"Grandma Hyde was right beside us, and that was 2703. Do you remember me, you, and Ferrell going down the Yadkin?"

I said yes. Todd asked if I remembered him falling, and I said, "I think so. I remember us both falling."

He said, "Do you remember us both falling? Yes, see you did. You were laughing at me, and you got out and then you busted your butt. Do you remember telling me that you fired me?"

I said yes. "It looks like I might not be able to go to class tomorrow."

Todd said, "No, you do not have to worry about it."

I said, "My right foot and leg hurt badly."

Mom said, "Do you want to elevate it?"

"Oh, it hurts!"

"Does that feel better?"

"No, it hurts."

"Does it hurt worse? Do you want to put it down?"

"Yes, put it down. Right there. Man, it feels good back here."

Dad asked, "Does that breeze feel good?"

Mom asked, "Can you smell the air? That person sitting in there told me you wanted a steak and a hamburger, like a Whopper," and I said I did.

Mom said "When?"

"Last night, I wanted something so bad, and they would not even feed me because they knew I couldn't eat it. Now if that was not that unfair, then I do not know what was, and it pissed me off. I would not do that to anybody."

Brother said, "There are many things you need to remember," and I said sorry.

Mom said, "Remember you were just a passenger in that airplane."

Todd said, "You remember you were just a passenger?" and I said yes.

Mom stated, "You were not flying the airplane."

Todd stated, "You were not instructing or anything, were you?" and I said yea.

Dad asked me if I remember the man's name that I was flying with, and I said no. Todd asked me if I had ever met him, and I said, "I could not even remember going over there to a Charlotte place or little Charlotte, which is down. US Air, we used to call it something Charlotte." I was very confused and couldn't answer questions that made any sense.

Todd said, "Piedmont."

"No, I do not remember."

Mom said, "CC Air?"

"Anyway, I do not know, man. They had to be so mean. What do you want, what do you want? What did you open the door for? Who told you that you could do that? I can remember those people being like that, and I went on beside the airplane. You think I would be a nice person to him or help him out a little bit?"

Todd said no and I said nope. I stated, "I mean just as mean as they were the night before to me."

Todd asked me if I liked flying with him. I answered no, I did not like flying with any of them.

Todd said, "As long as you were flying, you were happy, right?"

"I wish I was flying."

"I know. You know why you cannot anymore, right?"

I answered yeah.

"You were in a plane crash."

"Yeah, I have learned a lot from the start."

"Was he flying the airplane, or were you flying the plane?"

"He was flying it, man, and all I was doing was riding along."

"Riding along?"

"Have you people changed my flip-flops?"

Todd asked, "Hulon, was he a smart-mouth to you?"

"That one person was."

"That one person was?"

"Yeah."

Todd asked if he cussed a lot, and I said yeah.

Todd asked, "Do you remember going in and getting two quarts of oil?" and I said yeah. He asked what I did after that, and I said I did not know. I stated that the plane was so young I did not remember.

Mom stated that the engine needed oil in it. I said, "If that is what it needed, then that is what I gave it."

Todd said, "Yep, do you remember losing an engine?"

"No, I do not remember anything, and I am telling you."

"Well, every once in a while, it comes back. You are talking about it every once in a while. You are going back through it, seven thousand, six thousand, five thousand. It is like you are going down. You are replaying it in your mind."

I said, "Identifying the engine."

"Huh?"

I said again, "Identifying the engine."

"Identifying which one went out?"

"Yes."

"Which one went out?"

"You have to identify it and see."

"The right one or the left one?"

"Yeah. I will explain it to you when I am not so tired."

Brother asked me if I was getting sleepy. I answered yes, and he asked me if I wanted to go back in and lay down for a little bit.

"Yeah, I am out of energy. I thought maybe Mom would get up and fix me some breakfast."

"Well, it is getting about suppertime, and it is about 3:38 p.m. in the afternoon. You have been up for a while. They said you stayed up all night."

"I have."

He then asked about what I had been doing. He said, "Everything?"

"Goofing off to flying airplanes, everything. It is just like right now. If I would have known that we had an engine out, you better believe I would not be sitting here waiting on them."

Mom asked, "Do you know where I am sitting from you?"

I answered, "Yes, straight across from me."

"Where is Todd sitting from you?"

"Left of me. He is about eleven o'clock or ten o'clock."

"Where is Terri sitting from you?"

"Terri? I do not know."

Terri spoke up and said, "I am right here."

I said, "Terri is probably ten o'clock. Just guessing, I do not know."

Todd asked, "Do you see any light today?"

"No, both eyes are shut."

Mom said, "No, your right eye is open, baby."

"Nah, it is closed."

Mom said it was open, and my brother said it was open.

Mom said, "It is open wide. Your left one is closed."

Brother asked me, "do you feel any weaker or stronger today? Your arms ought to be sore. Are you sore in your arms?"

I said I felt weaker.

He said, "Because you are getting stronger. Do you remember going and lifting weights, and you would feel sore the next day?"

I said yes, and Todd said, "That is how it is going to be. You are going to be lifting that walker, holding that leg up. You are going to get sore."

"I know."

Todd continued, "But it is not doing anything but making you stronger, and you like being strong. You always lifted a little bit, at least once or twice a week, did you not?"

"I tried."

Todd laughed and said, "You tried, and we all cannot be perfect. How many days a week did you work, Hulon?"

"How come they do not call and see how many men they have out there and see if they are cooking anything?"

"How many days a week did you work?"

"Two or three, I do not know."

"Bull, you worked every day, all day." Mom and Todd said seven days a week. I said, "Probably."

Mom asked if the doctor had been in to see me today. I said, "No, two or three came to see me yesterday. He said he is proud and was like, 'Barry, do you even know you are here?' He said let me see how you sound."

Todd said, "They came in there to check your breathing and everything. When you had the crash, Hulon, you collapsed both lungs."

"Yeah, one said, 'Let us change your breathing machine. I said, 'Okay, what do you want me to do?' He said, 'Simulate doing this,' and I said okay and that worked out good. Today it was nice, and it really worked out good. I was pulling and receiving it."

Terri asked, "Does that hurt your leg, Hulon, to do that?"

I said yeah, and she said, "Well, don't do that."

Brother said, "No, does it feel better there?"

I said, "I am trying to make it feel better."

"Just get it in a comfortable position, and that is why they say you cannot put any weight on that leg."

Dad asked, "Do you remember Lauren coming to see you yesterday?"

I said yeah, and Dad said, "Do you remember touching her?"

"Barely."

"Barely?"

Mom said, "Do you remember her giving you a kiss?"

I said yeah, and dad laughed and said she went to church with them that morning. I said yeah.

Mom said, "everyone was asking about you at church."

Todd said, "Yea, everybody is worried about you."

Mom added, "They are praying for you," and Dad said, "You have many people praying for you, Hulon."

I said, "Well, that is a good thing, man."

Todd said, "I know."

Dad said, "There are many people who really want to know."

Mom said, "Put this one over that one."

I said I wanted something to eat, and Dad said, "Are you ready to eat?"

"Nothing big."

Todd said, "Not yet, but we will go in and get you something though."

I said, "Well, I will get something to drink."

Mom asked what I wanted, and I said I did not care.

Dad asked, "A milkshake?"

I said, "A hot and a hat, hot and hat.", struggling to communicate with my mouth wired shut.

Mom said, "A hot and hat?"

"A hot and a hat sandwich."

Terri asked, "A hot and ham?"

I said, "Hot and ham. If I could bend over, give me a sandwich, cut it off, give me a sip, and give me a bite. Get me an old people's treat." Frustrated from not being able to eat solid food, since I was only getting fed through a belly tube, I wanted something soft like old people with no teeth eat.

My brother said, "Old people's treat?"

I said yeah, "We ate treats the other night. I want a thing of sausage."

Dad said, "A sausage biscuit?"

I said yeah, and Dad said all right. "Do you want Grandma to fix some of those good homemade biscuits?"

I said, "Yep," and Dad said all right.

Brother said, "Grandma can cook," and I said, "Yeah. They could also fix bacon."

Mom asked, "Why are you taking your sock off?"

"I have something in it."

She asked me if I could get it out, and I answered, "Yes, I think so."

Mom explained, "Hulon, you have got to feel the back of your sock."

Dad said about me needing some toe care, and Mom continued, "You are putting it on backwards."

Dad said, "Cut his toenails. That would probably help him feel a little better."

Mom said, "Sit it up here. You have it on backwards."

Brother said, "You are doing well. You just keep trying to get it on and everything."

Dad said, "You have to get your damn days and nights together, son, so you will not be awake at night so much and you can sleep."

I said, "Yeah, I know."

Dad continued, "Get your days and nights together. You are going to need it when they start working you out during the day."

Mom said, "When you come home, Mom and Dad cannot stay up with you all night. We have to get up, and so you have to sleep in the nighttime."

"I know, and I am ready right now."

Todd asked, "Are you ready to go lay down on the bed?"

"Hell yeah, I am ready to go lay down now."

Mom said, "Next Sunday, they said we might be able to take you home for a while. You want us to bring you back? Would you like that, or do you want to stay over here?"

I answered, "I like eating with y'all. I like being around y'all, and I like being with y'all."

Todd said, "I know. We love you eating with us too, brother."

Dad said, "We want you there with us."

Todd stated, "We love you coming around every day," and I said, "I think I miss doing so."

Todd continued, "There are many things that you miss doing and want to do now, although I am not there. That is terrible."

I said, "That is just like Lauren. I can picture her sitting up on that thing Grandma had and turning the damn turn."

He replied yes, and I said, "I can see her turning the turny, getting things done."

"Turning the steering wheel."

Dad laughed, and Todd asked me if I remember the push bag that she had. I said yeah, and Mom said, "Well, at least you were able to see her baby, and you can remember what she looks like in your mind." I said yeah, and Mom added, "You may not be able to see her again. You will just have to remember what she looked like. You remember Momma, Todd, Terri, and Daddy?"

I said, "What Todd call them, they could buy one right now."

Mom asked, "Buy one what?"

"Something to eat."

My brother said, "We will go in and get you something to eat."

I said, "Yeah, here we go."

Mother said, "Here we go," and my brother said, "let us go."

Terri laughed and Todd said, "Wait a minute." They took me inside.

I said, "Both engines were running."

He said, "Both engines were running?"

"Yeah, the most important people sitting behind the two main engines are the most important." All three of them sat there and looked at each other. I said, "I am going to tell you what the most important thing is always to fly, and I was supposed to do something. There is no way I would sit behind that engine."

Todd said, "No, that is a bad place if you ever crash."

I said, "Yeah, I always sat two or three spaces back, you know. I said that was fun and that I had a blast. It showed the whole tape of him the other night. I stated that was a 1946 model airplane, and that plane that big Ferrell has got, that is a 1946 model, I cannot imagine."

Todd said, "That is an old plane, isn't it? What year is that Piper Comanche down there?"

I said, "Oh gosh," and Todd continued, "It is a nineteen sixty something—what is it?"

"The Twin Comanche?"

"Yes."

"Probably a 1949, a 1950."

"What year is it, a 1962, '62 or '65?"

"Yeah."

Mom asked, "What?" and Todd said, "The twin."

I said, "That is it, and it might be a fifty or sixty-year model."

Todd said, "It is a sixty model, hold on. I got you."

"I know."

A couple of my good friends, Mike Cook and Chris Beaver, also came in to visit me while my family was there.

Mike asked how the leg is doing and I told him that leg was in bad shape. "It has been real sore, man and has hurt worse today than it has the whole time."

I told them about what the doctors said, "Well, you should do this and you should do that, man." I said, "I have tried everything I know to do. They finally turned me loose today. I think I can go back to flying."

Someone asked me, "You could flex it like that right now, can you not?"

I exclaimed, "I could flex the heck out of it, but what good would it do when you can only move it three inches, you know?"

They said, "The way it hurts?" and I said yeah.

My brother said, "You cannot put any weight on it, can you? What did he tell you, zero weight?"

I asked Todd, "Could you change this stuff on here? How I put that on there? Well, I don't know how that was on there, and a lot of it is still there."

Todd asked why I was taking that off. I answered that I was not, I just wanted to put it up here. Mom asked if someone changed the thermostat. I said turn it off. I asked, "Do you have a decent lighter on you? Without a lighter, we could not see it right here.

Todd said, "We could see it."

Mike said, "Oh yeah, I see it."

I said, "You see all that damage?"

Chris Beaver said yeah, and I said, "It goes all the way through here. The other one is not like that one."

Todd said, "I didn't cut the heat up."

I said, "It is so sore,"

My brother said, "What shirt?"

I said, "That is not funny, man."

Mike said, "It looks like the taping is good though."

I shared with Mike about all the stuff that they made me do yesterday. I asked Todd, "What did they make me do yesterday or the day before?"

He said, "Here on you?" I said yeah, and he said, "You have been learning how to get out of that wheelchair and into a bed, out of it, and to the parallel bars using a walker."

Todd asked, "We just want to know if you are sore or if you are not sore."

I said, "I am sore. They think am I sore or not? But I am. They have me tomorrow, all day."

Todd said, "Today is your day off."

Chris said, "The only day off is today."

I said, "You know what, they can probably do without me tomorrow. I will probably sleep in all day."

Todd said, "You had better sleep in today. They are going to work the hell out of you tomorrow."

Mike said, "You had better go to bed early."

Chris added, "Call in sick."

Dad spoke up and said there is not any calling in sick at this place. Mike laughed, and Todd said, "They would come and get you."

I said, "Well, I would have to."

Mike said, "Hey, it is all good getting you stronger now."

Chris said, "It is no worse than basketball practice."

I said, "Yeah, it is bad." Mike laughed, and I said, "especially when we are out there doing pulls around a damn thing, like 360 pulls, on the same one."

Mike replied, "Oh man."

"If you have a two-hundred-and-fifty-pound person out there and they tell you, 'Hey, do not put your right leg on anything—'"

Todd said, "Well, you do not weigh two hundred and fifty pounds no more, brother."

I said, "I hurt badly."

He replied, "I know." I complained that my neck hurts. Mike asked if my arms are sore. Chris asked how my arms felt.

I explained, "My arms, they feel all right I guess. In a couple of days, they will be sore."

Mike said, "They will work that soreness out."

Todd said, "That is what you need. You know from lifting weights, you get sore and that will get you stronger."

Dad asked Mike how his little ones were doing. Mike answered, "Oh man, we wore them out yesterday."

Dad laughed, and Mike shared about the family reunion at his mom and dad's the day before. He said, "They swam all day."

Dad asked, "They were wide open all day?"

He replied, "Yes, nonstop."

Todd asked Mike, "How is your job going?"

Mike said, "Man, I love it with a passion over there, I really do."

Chris said to me, "If you are tired, then take a nap."

I said, "Everything is starting to come together now."

Mike said he had the routine down now, and he said I was just meeting people now.

Rehabilitation

For the next two years, I underwent surgeries and learned the required skills for the blind to function and keep their independence. My parents sent me to the Rehabilitation Center for the Blind in Raleigh, where they taught me new skills and continued my rehabilitation. I had days of therapies—physical, mobility, cognitive, occupational, and speech.

Erased from my memory was the last six months of 1998. After the crash, a helicopter airlifted me to Roanoke Regional Hospital where they pronounced me dead on arrival (DOA). At the crash site, I sustained many injuries. I had collapsed both lungs, and my right leg was broken in four places, the knee, both bones in the shin, and ankle. I had a significant brain and head injury. The head trauma affected my lower jaw, which was broken in four places. My upper jaw was broken from my face, I had four teeth destroyed, and my nose was crushed when my head hit the dash. I also had my left eye knocked out, the right eye blinded, my tear ducts destroyed, and three cracks in my cranium. I lived in a coma for twenty days during my twelve weeks in the hospital. That twentieth day I woke up and told my father, "Happy Father's Day!"

The first thirty days were in Roanoke. I had family and friends visit me. A special visit my grandmother talked about was the one where she held my hand. She consoled me and asked me, if I could hear her, to squeeze her hand, and I responded. This squeezing of my grandmother's hand was a sign to all my family and gave them hope I was going to live.

Spitfire Aviation, an air carrier based at Concord, flew me back to Concord. The next two months I spent at the Charlotte Rehabilitation Center. Paralysis on the left side of my body took place, and I was bedridden. The rehabilitation process helped me learn to eat and speak again. I learned to walk once again and learned to think although the trauma caused short-term memory loss.

The day I arrived home from the rehabilitation center, a white dove came to live in the backyard at my parents' house. It stayed for a few months and then disappeared.

Several months after coming home from the hospital, my condition and behavior made me suicidal. I was waking up and literally coming to my senses. I believe I was realizing that I was going to be blind! It had taken me a long time to accept that I would be blind forever. I honestly thought my family was putting me to bed in the basement, and we did not even have a basement.

The hospital released me to my family after Mom signed papers stating she would take care of me. I needed twenty-four-hour care, and my mom helped me get through the dramatic situation. The loss of my three senses—smell, taste, and sight—and my limited mobility required total care. This included eating, bathing, dressing, and living in general.

These are instructions from Tony Mineo, the attorney—his guidance for the client.

"My Day"

1. The purpose of "My Day"—we have talked to you about "My Day" when you were in the office. We would like you to start making notes and we would prefer that you do your final writing of "My Day" in private and then mail it to this office. It is strictly confidential.

2. How these injuries have affected your life—why we call it "My Day" is that we want you to take a normal day, from the time you get up until the time you go to bed, and explain in detail how this occurrence has changed your life. For example, the way you put on your clothes, the way you get in and out of bed, the way you take a bath, etc. By your life, we mean your working life, your playtime, your hobbies, your life as a husband or as a wife, etc. This includes your disposition, your personality, your nervousness, etc. We need to know how it has affected the marital relations between you and your spouse.

3. Your pain and suffering—we want a description of your pain, both at the scene of the occurrence and at all times thereafter. We want to know whether it is a shooting pain, throbbing pain, etc. We want your words and not anyone else's. We are interested in your pain during any hospital treatment and your pain and discomfort since the injury. It may be helpful to keep a diary on these matters and on your "My Day" material regarding how it has affected your life.

4. Start at your head to remember your complaints and injuries. A good rule to follow in order to remember all of your problems is to start at your head and, in detail, go down through all parts of your body moving from your head, neck, shoulders, back, etc., and explain in detail any problems that you have with each part of the body. Give details with regard to your medication and what it is for if you

know. For example, medication in the hospital for pain or afterwards for nervousness, etc.

5. Do not use the words "I can't"—please do not use the words "I cannot", because cannot means physical impossibility. For example, you cannot use your left hand, because you do not have one. However, other than this definition of "can't," we think you should stay away from it. Do not say, "I can't do it", "I can't do it", "and I never do it". We would prefer you would use words such as "I am not able to do it as well" or some other words meaning the same thing. You should always work towards the idea that "I am trying and I will continue to try and do more things." Everyone will admire you more if you try. About your activities, such as your housework, your yard work, your work at the office or factory, you should detail what things you are able to do and what things you are not able to do as well as before. If your injury seriously hampers your activities, then you should also show how many things you are not able to do now.

6. "My Day" witnesses—we would like you to contact your friends and neighbors, persons, on a separate sheet of paper for each witness, give us his name, address, and telephone number. Have him or her describe or you describe in detail on a separate sheet of paper what each witness knows about how this injury has changed your life. For example, your neighbor could tell about how you are not able to work as much around the house, or your friends could tell how you don't bowl now, or you don't do some other type of hobby. It is better if these witnesses are not your relatives. It is all right if they are your friends, because they would be more likely to have observed you. Again, please pain word pictures and give details and descriptions of specific instances. It is impossible when being too detailed.

7. Loss of wages or loss of potential income—one of the major things in your case may be the loss of income or

potential income. We will need copies of your W-2 forms, and your income tax returns for at least the last five years. If this injury has prevented you from being advanced in your employment or has prevented you from obtaining employment, please give us the names, addresses and telephone numbers of witnesses who may prove this for you. We would also like to know in detail what services prevented you from performing around the house, such as supervision of the children, and all the other services performed by either a husband or a wife.

8. Keep a copy of your answers—please keep a copy of the answers that you give us in working up your material on "My Day" because this will be helpful to you for the trial, depositions (your sworn statement), and for the answering of interrogatories (answers to questions). If you cannot type, make yourself a copy by using a ballpoint pen and carbon paper.

9. Questions or help in answering "My Day"—if you need any help in writing your "My Day" please call this office for an appointment.

10. Start making notes—the best way to write "My Day" is to start right now making notes. Then after a few weeks, prepare the copy for us and the copy for yourself. As time goes on, prepare additional information and send it to the office.

11. Use your imagination—you know your own life better than we do. Use your imagination and go into all aspects of your life. Explain to us, in detail possible, how this occurrence has affected your life. Paint a word picture, so that we can sell our most important product—YOU.

Summary of Medical Service/ Bills for Barry Hulon Hyde

Charlotte Medical Clinic, Inc.
1001 Blythe Boulevard, Suite 500
Charlotte, NC 28203
POC: Pam—704-355-5188
Account No. 127152
Dates of Service: 7/10/98, 7/13/98, 8/24/98
$ Amounts: 160.00, 109.00

Carolina Neurosurgery & Spine Associates
1010 Edgehill Road North
Charlotte, NC 28207
1-800-344-6716
Account No. 79620
Dates of Service: 7/15/98
$ Amounts: 5,158.00

Head Neck Medicine Surgery
102 Highland Avenue, Suite 104
Roanoke, VA 24013
540-343-4423
Account No.: 17564
Dates of Service: 6/1/98—6/7/98
$ Amounts: 9,066.25

Charlotte Radiology
P.O. Box 30488
Charlotte, NC 28230-0488
704-362-1945
Account No.: 016064320
Dates of Service: 7/1/98—8/25/98
$ Amount: 1,544.00
Dates of Service: 7/1/98—7/28/98
$ Amount: 707.00

Southeast Anesthesiology Consultants
P.O. Box 33632
Charlotte, NC 28233-3632
704-377-5772
Account No.: 949071
Dates of Service: 7/15/98
$ Amount: 3,482.00
Dates of Service: 8/5/98
$ Amount: 376.00

I.D. Consultants, P.A.
814 East Boulevard
Charlotte, NC 28203
704-331-4715
Account No.: 16927
Dates of Service: 8/25/98—4/1/99
$ Amount: 804.00
Dates of Service: 7/17/98—10/19/98
$ Amount: 561.00

Pathology Association of Roanoke
(On behalf of Roanoke Memorial Hospital)
P.O. Box 11763
Roanoke, VA 24022-1763
540-772-2280
Account No.: 220*1521913
Dates of Service: 6/5/98
$ Amount: 282.75

Charlotte Plastic Surgery Center
P.O. Box 220977
Charlotte, NC 28222
704-348-2460
Account No.: 63747
Dates of Service: 7/29/98
$ Amount: 26,437.00

Carilion Roanoke Memorial Hospital
P.O. Box 12865
Roanoke, VA 24029-2865
540-224-1500
Account No.: ARM 1521913
Dates of Service: 6/1/98—6/29/98
$ Amount: 16,439.17

Neurosurgery, Inc.
1030 S. Jefferson Street, Suite 106
Roanoke, VA 24016
540-982-1149
Account No.: 54-1769283
Dates of Service: 6/1/98, 6/7/98, 6/10/98
$ Amount: 3,862.75

Anesthesia Associates of Roanoke, Inc.
P.O. Box 13306
Roanoke, VA 24032
540-345-0289
Account No.: 158605
Dates of Service: 7/9/98
$ Amounts: 2,491.00, 1,222.00, 1,034.00

Vistar Eye Center, Inc.
P.O. Box 1789
Roanoke, VA 24008
540-344-4000
Account No.: 413081
Dates of Service: 6/1/98—6/9/98
$ Amount: 2,605.00

Carilion Faculty Physicians
P.O. Box 11643
Roanoke, VA 24022
1-800-540-1487

Account No.: 484149
Dates of Service: 8/7/98
$ Amount: 9,190.00

Carilion PT Transportation Service
P.O. Box 12533
Roanoke, VA 24026
540-343-1487
Account No.: L999910382
Dates of Service: 6/1/98
$ Amount: 4,343.00

Carolina Medical Center
1000 Blythe Boulevard
Charlotte, NC 28203
704-355-2000
Account No.: 949071
Dates of Service: 7/15/98 - 7/23/98
$ Amount: 48,079.44
Dates of Service: 7/23/98—8/11/98
$ Amount: 25,433.67

Charlotte Mecklenburg Health Service RH
P.O. Box 34728
Rehab Phys.
Charlotte, NC 28234-4728
704-393-4808
Account No.: 99092
Dates of Service: 6/29/98—7/15/98
$ Amount: 793.00
Dates of Service: 7/23/98—8/2/98
$ Amount: 273.00
Dates of Service: 7/16/98—8/5/98
$ Amount: 1,740.00

Charlotte Institute of Rehabilitation
1100 Blythe Boulevard
Charlotte, NC 28203
704-355-4300
Account No.: 99092
Dates of Service: 6/29/98—7/16/98
$ Amount: 19,523.21

Charlotte Eye, Ear, Nose & Throat Associates, Inc.
1600 East Third Street
Charlotte, NC 28204-3282
704-358-4111
Account No.: 288068
Dates of Service: 7/3/98—7/10/98
$ Amount: 823.02

Radiology Association of Roanoke
P.O. Box 12668
Roanoke, VA 24027-2668
540-772-2280
Account No.: 114*031521913
Dates of Service: 6/1/98—7/29/98
$ Amount: 492.60

Pathways Home Care
487 Lake Concord Road, NE
Concord, NC 28025
704-723-6182
Dates of Service: 2/1/99 Speech Therapy
$ Amount: 1,492.60
Sanchez, D.D.S., P.A. & Keshairi Sanchez
1815 South Ridge Avenue
Kannapolis, NC 28083
$ Amount: 2,003.00

Northeast Medical Center
920 Church Street North
Concord, NC 28025
704-783-3000
Dates of Service: 11/5/98—11/17/98
$ Amount: 280.00

Northeast Eye Center
33 Lake Concord Road, N.E.
Concord, NC 28025
Dates of Service: 8/17/98—Present (not sure of end date)
$ Amount: 500.00

Assetcare Assetcare
P.O. Box 11745
Roanoke, VA 24022-1745
540-776-3277
$ Amount: 282.75

Charlotte Pathologist
C/o Carolina Medical Center
1000 Blythe Boulevard
Charlotte, NC 28203
Dates of Service: 7/9/99
$ Amount: 148.00

Bayada Nursing
9009 J.M. Keynes Drive, Suite 12
Charlotte, NC 28269
704-971-4600
Account No.: 7755
Dates of Service: 05/01—Present (not sure of end date)
$ Amount: 14,432.00

Total Care of the Carolinas
320-H Copperfield Boulevard

Concord, NC 28025
704-793-4220
Dates of Service: 02/00—04/01
$ Amount: 16,800.00

Chesapeake Rehabilitation Equipment
1002 South Kings Drive
Charlotte, NC 28207
704-376-5555
Account No.: 12628/File No. 4416
Dates of Service: 09/98 Wheelchair Rental
$ Amount: 759.40

Dr. Sam Chewning
Miller Orthopedic Clinic
1001 Blythe Boulevard, Suite 200
Charlotte, NC 28203
704-373-0544
Dates of Service: 9/9/98 Surgery
$ Amount: ???

Martin's Drug Company
1113 North Main Street
Kannapolis, NC 28081
704-932-9111
Prescriptions
$ Amount: 500.00

Edwin E. Johnston & Associates, Inc.
2010 New Sharon Church Road
Hillsborough, NC 27278
919-732-8864
Artificial Eye
$ Amount: 1,800.00

Dr. Martin Scobey
Carolina Medical Center
1000 Blythe Boulevard
Charlotte, NC 28203
704-355-2000
Dates of Service: 9/2/98 GI Procedures and Bronchoscopy
$ Amount: ???

Lifeguard of America, Inc.
P.O. Box 13612
Roanoke, VA 24035
540-342-7637
Dates of Service: 6/1/98 Helicopter Transport
$ Amount: 8,004.00

Grand total of all charges listed above: $234,033.61

Nurses and Home Healthcare Aid

It was necessary for me to have weekly checks performed by a special nurse, Davida Widenhouse. She kept a visit on me frequently, and she made sure things were in place that I needed. Davida and her daughter Mackenzie are still close friends today. Her brother-in-law took us flying when we go to Daytona. One home healthcare lady that took care of me and both grandmas, Rhonda Hill, really witnessed change in our lives.

Fishing Trip

Ferrell James II and I went fishing one night at High Rock Lake. We went in his boat and fished with live goldfish or large minnows. He and I only caught four fish, and I caught the largest catfish I had ever caught. It weighed twenty-four pounds. Those four fish fed about thirty people. My dad and Larry Morris were two people I remembered sharing this fish with us. Ferrell cooked them in our backyard.

Surgery

The last reconstructive surgeries were on July 15, 1999. My face had many plates and a number of screws removed. I feel that I can now set off a metal detector. I have four screws, three in my knee, and one in my head. I also have a titanium rod between the tibia and fibula, which is between the knee and ankle on the right leg. The three screws in my knee held the rod in place. I have two teeth bridged in, a new nose constructed from bone out of the right hip, and a prosthetic eye.

Rehabilitation Center for the Blind in Raleigh

One month after the last reconstructive surgery, I attended the Rehabilitation Center for the Blind in Raleigh. This school teaches newly blind individuals. I learned Braille; mobility with a pointer cane as well as my support cane; JAWS, which is a speech computer program; living skills; and social skills.

The different obstacles that occurred while attending the Rehabilitation Center, were many. I learned mobility; how to type again; JAWS, the screen reader; how to fold money and make belts; and how to warm food by the use of the microwave. It took a long time for the teachers to learn that I could not smell or taste along with no sight.

While walking with a support cane and a pointer cane, some-one walked into me, and it was by another blind person. Someone else walked into me in the hallway, and I thought the impact broke my nose. Another time someone walked into me was by a junior student, who was running down the sidewalk.

During the time at the Rehabilitation Center for the Blind, I took several Amtrak Railroad trips from Kannapolis to Raleigh. I stopped in Greensboro to visit with my uncle Randy. We made a trip to a Chinese lounge and spa for a massage.

Chris Beaver, a great friend whom I played basketball with, helped me on trips back and forth to Raleigh. He lived close by as I stayed in Raleigh, and he would pick me up on Fridays and I would ride home with him. He would drive back on Sunday evenings.

My cousin, Donna Albright Denar and her family would pick me up at the center and they would take me back to their house to visit. Her dad, Bub, drove me to their house as well. It was nice having family along with friends that were so close by the center.

A lady at the center that I remember helping me the most was Barbara McGinnis. She was responsible for teaching me to use a screen reader, which was Job Application with Speech (JAWS). I think she helped me make it typing 8 words a minute. I still had a long way to go. Barbara, had a lot of faith in me, and she kept challenging me. She and I are still great friends today. I called her for many years as I was working on completing my degrees.

Concerts—Post Recovery

Two concerts I had attended since losing my sight were Tom Petty and the Heartbreakers. He performed at the pavilion in Charlotte and the Walnut Creek Amphitheatre in Raleigh. I was happy with the performance and both times, I had seats in the disability section, which was close to the stage, and had on my earplugs. The band played many tunes, and they were very loud. I attended the one in Raleigh when attending the school for the blind. My uncle Randy Hyde and cousin David Albright, Donna's brother, attended the performance in Charlotte at the pavilion. We rode the golf cart from the parking lot all the way to our seats because my leg would not let me walk that far.

Dad

The next turning point in my life was losing my father. On December 30, 1999, my dad died from a massive heart attack. I was home from Raleigh during the Christmas break. My dad and I lived through life-changing experiences, and now it was time for him to leave this world. Our loss brought our family closer together. My mom and I supported each other through this difficult time in our lives. During this time, the white dove came back to the house for a few days. My dad's mother, three brothers, and one sister survive my dad. My brother and his wife, their children Lauren and Austin, my mother, and I survive him also.

During the Christmas holidays during 1999, dad, my *hero*, had a massive heart attack, and a few days later, he died. The family shared the first Christmas with Austin and enjoying everyone's company. The day of Dad's heart attack was spent cutting wood with Ferrell, Ferrell II, Robert O'Neal, Tim, and me sitting in the truck listening to them run the chainsaws and loading it. All of us ate hotdogs at the tailgate of his truck where I was sitting. Dad seemed fine, and we all had a good day together. That evening, we had dinner at Grandma Abshers. Mom was staying with Grandma since she just had a hip replaced. On Dad's way home, he took me by Ferrell II's house. Ferrell II took me home, and I was asleep when Dad had his heart attack at 2:30 a.m. Instead of waking me up, he called Mom at Grandma's. She rushed home and woke me up, and I listened to the medics work on Dad. Dad had several surgeries; however, the main artery Dr. Christy was repairing in the back of the heart kept splitting. The doctors pronounced him dead at 6:55 a.m. with Mom, Todd, and me beside his bed. Mom asked Dr. Christy afterward to examine Todd and me to make sure our hearts were normal, and they checked out fine.

Passion

I finished attending the school for the blind in Raleigh in January of 2000. Losing my dad and still trying to figure out what caused the plane crash motivated me, but it was difficult at the time. I wanted to continue my love and passion for aviation. I started studying for my advanced ground instructor (AGI) license. I continued to study, and I passed the written test on June 6, 2000. Rich Burns, a safety inspector administered the test for the Federal Aviation Administration (FAA). This license allowed me to teach sports, recreational, private, commercial, and airline transport pilots (ATP), as well as flight instructors on the ground.

Studying for AGI Written

As I was attempting to reestablish some goals in my life during 2000, I wanted to continue my love in aviation; therefore, I began studying for the AGI license. Doug Goodnight, Larry Morris, mom, and Jason Wright helped me study by calling out questions and the choices to me that were out of the Gleim test booklet. We spent many hours' one on one reading and answering questions. Burns, spoke with people in Washington and Oklahoma to try to figure out the best way to test me. Burns orally tested me at Concord Regional Airport in a testing center. On June 6, 2000, I scored an 80 percent. At that time, I became the first and only blind AGI in the world for the FAA.

Meeting Lincoln

On June 12, of 2000, I received a very special gift in my life! Two years and eleven days after a life-changing accident, I received my guide dog from Southeastern Guide Dog Inc. School. My guide dog was named Lincoln, and he was my inspiration to live and carry on!

At Southeastern Guide Dog Inc. School, fifteen recipients were in training together. All the recipients matched with their dog that we went home with. They were in the kennel for eight weeks and then handed off to the puppy raisers for twelve months. The guide dog school receives them back for three to five months of training before they are assigned to their blind users.

When I started training with Lincoln in Palmetto, Florida, we attended twenty-six days of learning how to cope and use a guide dog. Some of the things we did were obstacle walking, bridge crossing, railroad crossings, and night walking. Training also included city travel in the downtown area of Tampa. We spent three days in training, doing things like traffic light crossing, climbing stairs, escalator travel, going through revolving doors, and mall travel.

One day at training, Lincoln walked me too close to the curb, and I fell and skinned my elbow and knees! At the time, I was learning as much as Lincoln was. Here I was still learning with a leg that had been broken in four places, which had a titanium rod in it, and I was giving up walking with a support cane and a pointer cane. I was trying to learn to walk in this situation; however, this was very complicated.

At home in Kannapolis, Lincoln and I walked throughout the entire neighborhood together. This was where my mother lived, and the entire backyard was fenced in. In addition, he could run and play with his Kong toy! We walked down my brother's dirt driveway to his house quite frequently. He loved my mother, as you would not believe. He had so much personality and was so happy to be with me. He was so lovable, and I never thought I would have this kind of relationship with a dog.

Adjusting with Lincoln near University of North Carolina at Charlotte

Mr. Lincoln and I were living in the city now, and we adjusted awesomely! The summer of 2001, we walked 1,800 steps one way to class on Monday, Wednesday, and Friday. Some days it was frustrating as hell trying to walk to class. I had certain landmarks I used rather frequently. Two out of five days, I had trouble. There was a garbage truck picking up a dumpster, and Lincoln stopped. The garbage truck started backing up toward us, and I did not know if he saw Lincoln and me. That was scary. In addition, one day a big truck parked on the side of the sidewalk with a piece of equipment on its trailer with brake trouble. Lincoln and I had to go out onto the street with the traffic, and that was frightening as well. There was no way I could do this—that is, walking back and forth without my blessed guide dog! Therefore, you had better believe this dog was a very special and God sent to allow me to do this with him. We were hardly ever apart; however, we were occasionally though. We went everywhere together. You name it and we had done it, except ride a train. Lincoln was born six months and two days after my plane crash, so I believe that his existence here was to help take care of me, and he did a fine job! I had him so spoiled that his eighty-five pounds occasionally slept in the bed with me! This wonderful guide dog had even been flying in an airplane with me many times! I must say, Lincoln was special!

Training with Lincoln

In June of 2000, I attended the Southeastern Guide Dog School in Florida. On June 9, my mother and her sister Margie drove us to Marco Island, Florida, to Ferrell and Bet James's condominium. Then, on June 11, they drove me to Palmetto, Florida, on Sunday. The introduction was Sunday, and we did not receive our guide dogs until Monday after lunch. However, that night, I dreamed the dog I received had the name Lincoln. He gave me his first kiss that day, and I was happy with his presence. A kiss tells it all; we made a perfect connection with each other. That was neat having fifteen dogs in the same room; this was where the training started!

The first step of this training was for me to give up the use of my support cane and pointer cane. The instruction that I received was to give my support to my guide dog.

We would have to be awake by 7:00 a.m. every day. We would take the dogs to eat breakfast and then to busy and clean up with a bag. Of course, I learned always to keep extra bags in my pocket.

After breakfast, we would do thirty minutes of discipline. We would line up and work together and individually with our dog. Outside of the busy area was where the obstacle course was set up. Cones, bicycles, towels hanging from limbs over the sidewalk were obstacles in our way during training. We would load onto the buses to go to other places for training, such as the mall, the training center in Palmetto, as well as downtown Tampa. This was where we did road crossing with streetlights, curb crossing, elevator travel, escalator climbing, revolving doors, and some mall travel. The buses carried eight or nine of us including our guide dogs. At the training center in the suburban area of Palmetto was where a car with one of the drivers would block the sidewalk, and we would have to decide what to do. During this training, trust was continuously progressing.

It took me about a week to trust my dog. We would always end up back at the school by 4:00 p.m. We would feed the dogs dinner and eat ourselves. Every Sunday, we went to play with the dogs and reward them once a week by playing with their toys and running with another dog.

The trainers always made us attach a leash to the dogs at the foot of the bed. I got in trouble because I let Lincoln in the bed with me. I would rather share the room with Lincoln rather than who they had assigned me.

The guide dog school, which was a nonprofit organization, provided a leash, a collar, a dog tag, a harness, and a license. Lincoln's tattoo is the identification number in his ear.

The guide dog school not only provided for Lincoln, they supplied accommodations for me also. They taught us how to take care of our dogs. This would include his shots, medicine, baths, treats, and diet. Lincoln had grown from eighty-six pounds to a healthy one hundred pounds since I received him. At the time, I did not know I was overfeeding him, and I did not know that he was overweight. The one thing I have found out was no amount of training will teach you how to love your dog!

There are things people are learning about how to treat guide dogs. For instance, people should know that they are supposed to act as if the dog is not there. This dog is my eyes, and people should understand that is why I use him. He wears a sign to make people aware that he is a working dog. This means no rubbing, no talking to, and no feeding while he is in his harness.

Instrument Ground Instructor Written

I began studying for another aviation license. The instrument ground instructor license that I took on October 19, 2000, which was the next test, I passed for the FAA. This instrument license allows me to teach pilots interested in adding an instrument rating onto their license. Rich Burns, an FAA inspector and examiner, was the one who gave me this test and the previous test on the AGI. The FAA awarded a certificate to Inspector Burns for me being the first blind man in the world for the FAA to receive these ground certificates.

Rich Burns, the inspector who orally gave me the tests, said a few words. "Barry's an incredible young man. I am impressed as hell at what he's accomplished," said Burns, who confirmed I was the first and only blind person to be awarded the licenses. "His heart is so into it, and his accomplishment makes you think if you've got problems, think what Barry has gone through." Burns is still to this day a very close friend.

Braille Certificate

This point in my life, I began my home study course from Hadley School for the Blind. I am right-handed, but I read Braille with my left index finger. Reading and writing Braille was hard, and I was trying to learn how to play the guitar. The guitar string was putting a callus on my fingertip, so I gave up the guitar for Braille. I accomplished another goal by learning Braille and receiving another certificatte.

Hyde's Properties

The year 2000 was a very good year for me. In the last few months of this year, I began Hyde's properties, and my mother helped me buy my next rental property. My mother also bought JAWS, the computer program for the blind, and a computer for me. JAWS was the acronym for the screen reader I used for the computer. The name is Job Application with Speech. This screen reader is what has allowed me to continue my studies and help me in writing the papers for school.

Frightening Spell

On December 12 of 2000, I had an episode where I passed out three times within ten minutes. Therefore, I stopped taking all my depression and antiseizure medication. The medicine caused this spell; therefore, I was unaware that this reaction was from the brain injury.

Kendra Harrington

In January 2001, I met a girlfriend, Kendra, and her mom, Sharon Harrington. One important memory I shared with Kendra took place at my mom's house in Kannapolis, North Carolina, and we were listening to the race, which was taking place at the Daytona International Speedway. We witnessed the traumatic crash of Dale Earnhardt. This man was my dad's favorite driver as well as most of my family's and my favorite driver.

Kendra and I shared many commonalities. She had lost her sight to diabetes at age nineteen. Her kidneys had stopped working, and the doctors put her on the transplant list. She had received two kidneys from a twenty-month-old baby, and the life of those kidneys was ten years. Once they had stopped working, then she had to go on dialysis.

Kendra gave me the inspiration to carry on and accept my blindness. I feel God placed her in my life to strengthen and encourage me to carry on. She had attended UNCC as I began, and she graduated with a master's degree in human resources during my second year of working on my bachelor's degree in history. Kendra's mother and she were a great addition to my life. Her mom, Sharon, is still a great friend today, and I cherish her.

Barry & Kendra

Achievements

I began drinking coffee for a short while and quit smoking cigarettes on February 28, 2001.

Bachelors of Arts Degree

During late April of 2001, Mom, Todd, Terri, and Terry Carpenter, Mom's husband, moved me to Mallard Green apartments in Charlotte, North Carolina. Lincoln and I lived there for the next three and a half years. Mom was my living aid, therefore; Bayada Nursing paid her to clean the apartment, cook for me, do my shopping, and paid my monthly bills.

One important aspect of my life came after I returned home with Lincoln. Ironically, the day I arrived, the white dove had returned. Mom and my brother saw the white dove and told me about it. I felt this was my dad looking down at us, and saying, "That is a good-looking dog you have there. I am glad you are home, and I am checking on you." The dove sat on brother's barn behind my mother's house. They have not seen the dove since.

Kendra and my uncle Rudy Hyde proofread the writings of the papers for class. They also helped me find sources and relevant information for tests and the writing.

Lincoln and I went to Mom's most weekends and holidays. However, sometimes I stayed at the apartment, and Kendra came over and stayed the weekend. Other times, Sharon and Kendra brought *Chili's* over for dinner for us.

Rehabilitation

Another part of my rehabilitation process was beginning school at the University of North Carolina at Charlotte during the first summer session in May of 2001. This education process helped me build my memory back to where it was before the brain injury from the crash. I moved to Charlotte to live on my own, and I lived within walking distance of the school. Lincoln and I walked 1,800 steps one way to class every day that we had class. Several semesters Lincoln and I walked 2,300 steps when I had class in the music building. I went to school during the summer semester of 2001. I slowly found out how hard attending school was going to be. The university only accepted and transferred in twenty-five credit hours from my associate's degree out of the total 120 hours needed. The first obstacle that Lincoln and I encountered was guiding me to class. The books I had to read were books on tapes or emailed to me with active links. I recorded lectures with tape players and transcribe notes. The technique I use to study was time-consuming. My tape players were used frequently to study, and I listen repetitiously to my notes.

Lawsuit Details

On Thursday, October 24, 2001, the airplane insurance check valued at $100,000 came by FedEx from Tony Meneo. He wanted me to sign it and send it back to him. This insurance money was for the loss of my eyesight. The division of the money was into four parts: the attorney received $40,000, or 40 percent; Medicare received $33,333.33; a private investigator received $10,000; and I received the rest totaling $17,000. This money went to Mom. She used it to catch up on bills, and to live on.

On October 23, 2001, I received a letter from the office of the university attorney of the University of North Carolina at Charlotte regarding subpoena record request, dealing with Barry Hulon Hyde versus Robert E. Anderson. It stated as follows:

> Dr. Mr. Hyde, pursuant to 34CFR Section 99.31 A9I. This letter notifies you that we received a subpoena, copy attached from attorney Robert D. Potter Jr., requesting the Register

to produce by November 16, 2001, and all University academic records pertaining to you. We will comply with the subpoena unless otherwise ordered by the courts. If you wish to prevent such compliance, contact your attorney immediately. Sincerely, Sylvia Hadder, Paralegal, University of North Carolina at Charlotte.

NORTH CAROLINA COURT OF APPEALS

On May 10, 2001, BARRY HULON HYDE, Plaintiff-Appellant, v. ROBERT E. ANDERSON, Individually, LANCASTER AVIATION, INC., a North Carolina Corporation, LEONARD LANCASTER, Individually; the CITY OF CONCORD, and the CONCORD REGIONAL AIRPORT, Defendants-Appellee. From: Cabarrus County, No. 03-CVS-2520, BRIEF OF PLAINTIFF-APPELLANT BARRY HULON HYDE, Robert A. Mineo, Mineo & Mineo, Corporate Plaza Suite 1201 333 Fayetteville Street, Raleigh, North Carolina 27601-ATTORNEY FOR PLAINTIFF-APPELLANT-BARRY HULON HYDE.

STATEMENT OF THE CASE

On June 1, 1998, the plaintiff blinded permanently, when the aircraft in which he was traveling as a passenger crashed in Virginia. The sole involvement of the defendant airport and the Defendant City of Concord in this action involves the Airport's commercial sale of gasoline to the Plaintiff's employer, a business located on the Defendant's airport property, for many months prior to 1 June 1998. On, 10 May 2001, the plaintiff herein brought his civil action against the pilot in command of the accident aircraft, the owner of the aircraft and the defendants, Concord Regional Airport and City of Concord. Thereafter, the plaintiff filed an Amended Complaint against the identical parties named in the original complaint, to correct his address to reflect his actual citizenship in Mecklenburg County. On six, August 2001, the defendants Concord Regional Airport and City of Concord Answered, denying the plaintiff's allegations and cross claimed against the pilot of the accident aircraft, the defendant Anderson.

Prior to the accident flight, the plaintiff had provided limited flight instruction to the pilot Anderson in a single engine aircraft, but was not providing such instruction to the pilot Anderson in the subject twin-engine aircraft on the date of the accident.

Although, Barry Hulon Hyde blinded in both eyes because of the aircraft crash, the plaintiff, prior to the filing of the original complaint, had permanently moved to Mecklenburg County to attend the University of North Carolina, Charlotte, as a full time student and to be near his treating physicians.

The Defendants further moved to transfer the action to Cabarrus County pursuant to N.C.G.S. § 1-83(1); and in the alternative, to transfer pursuant to N.C.G.S. § 1-83(2), for the convenience of the witnesses and the parties.

A hearing held on November 16, of 2001 in the Superior Court of Mecklenburg County before the Honorable Judge Marvin Gray, on the defendant's Motion to Transfer venue as a matter of right or in the alternative for the convenience of the witnesses and parties. The Court entered an Order on 8 January 2002, denying the defendants' Motion to transfer. On 10 January 2002, the defendants moved for reconsideration of Judge Gray's Order of 8 January 2002.

On 15 February 2002, another hearing held before the Honorable Judge Marvin Gray. The Court then denied the defendant's Motion for Reconsideration. The defendants filed a Notice of Appeal on 8 March 2002. This Honorable Court heard the Defendant's appeal in April 2003, reversed the trial court's decision, and remanded the case transferred to Cabarrus County Superior Court.

Thereafter, eight depositions of fact witnesses, regarding the liability issues in this case taken, and filed with the Court. The defendant then moved for Summary Judgment against the Plaintiff. During this time, the Plaintiff further noticed the depositions of additional fact witnesses, those Federal Aviation Administration employees/investigators who were involved in the subject aircraft crash investigation. The Defendant then moved for a protective order to prohibit the depositions of the F.A.A. investigators pending the summary judgment hearing. Subsequently, the Plaintiff moved to quash the Defendant's Motion for Summary Judgment. The Trial Court denied the Plaintiff's motion. Plaintiff at this time also filed his Opposition to the Defendant's Motion for Summary, Judgment.

On 30 March 2004, the Defendant's Motion for Summary Judgment heard before the Honorable W. Erwin Spainhour, Senior Resident

Superior Court Judge for Cabarrus County. He was located at the courthouse in Concord, North Carolina. The Court found that there existed no genuine issues of material fact that related to the claims of the Plaintiff against the Defendant City of Concord, and granted the Defendant's Motion for Summary Judgment. The Plaintiff filed Notice of Appeal of this Order on 8 June 2005.

STATEMENT OF FACTS

On 1 June 1998, the Plaintiff's employer, Lancaster Aviation, Inc., requested that the plaintiff accompany the pilot Robert Anderson on a flight to West Virginia in order for Mr. Anderson to visit his mother. Mr. Anderson had rented a twin engine Piper PA-30 aircraft from Lancaster for the flight and had indicated to Lancaster that he wished to practice instru7ment flight procedures in simulated instrument conditions during the flight to West Virginia. In order to accomplish this, Mr. Anderson needed someone to act as a "safety pilot" during the time he was practicing instrument flight procedures because his vision during this practice would be totally obscured by a training device commonly referred to as a "hood". Lancaster asks the Plaintiff if he would agree to fly with the defendant Anderson on this flight and act as the "safety pilot" if the defendant practiced instrument flight "under the hood". The Plaintiff could not provide any type of flight instruction to any pilot in the subject PA-30 aircraft, as a specific condition of the aircraft's insurance policy that Lancaster Aviation held by being the aircraft owner. Lanny Lancaster was the only approved person under this policy allowed to provide flight instruction in the subject aircraft. A safety pilot's duties are limited to only acting as an additional visual lookout for the pilot during the time his impairment of his vision by the training hood and does not require any FAA pilot's license.

Although the Defendant Concord has continually attempted to confuse the issue of the Plaintiffs duties and responsibilities during the subject flight, it is clear that the Plaintiff was unauthorized under the aircraft's insurance policy to provide flight instruction at any time in the subject aircraft.

The plaintiff returned to the Concord Regional Airport on the afternoon of 1 June, finding the defendant Anderson already in the pilot seat of the accident aircraft with the left engine running. The Plaintiff boarded the aircraft and the pilot Anderson told the plaintiff that he had performed a preflight inspection of the aircraft and that the aircraft was full of fuel. The Plaintiff having only limited knowledge of the pilot, also knew from firsthand experience, and relied on the fact, that the defendant Concord Regional Airport had a duty to refuel the accident aircraft daily; and that the Defendant Concord had been providing this nightly fuel service to the Plaintiff's employer for over a year prior to this flight.

The aircraft departed the Concord Regional Airport and after crossing the Virginia boarder, the right engine ceased to operate. The pilot Anderson, with the assistance of the plaintiff, was not able to restart the right engine and shortly thereafter the left engine also quit. Found after the crash, both engines quit as the result of there being no fuel remaining in the right and left main tanks of the subject aircraft.

The cause of this accident is somewhat analogous to when an engine of an automobile quits due to the lack of fuel in the fuel tank, and the driver tries to restart the engine once added fuel is to the tank. The driver finds that the engine still will not start since it was initially run dry and there is now air in the fuel lines. In this case, fuel in an aircraft's auxiliary fuel tanks only work properly when the pilot realizes that the fuel in the main tank is low and switches to the auxiliary tank before the main tank runs dry. This allows the critical fuel flow to remain constant. If fuel to the engine stops the continuous flow, the fuel will not start again from the auxiliary tanks until air clears from the system. The main tank running dry and stopping the engines prevented the engine restart and caused the crash. There is testimony from both the Plaintiff and the pilot Anderson that they had absolutely no knowledge that the main tanks were running out of fuel during the flight. There is no evidence that the fuel gages of the subject aircraft operated properly on the date of the crash, and all fuel gages found inoperable after the crash. After both engines quit in flight, the aircraft immediately crashed.

The plaintiff received critical head injuries in the subsequent crash. These injuries resulted in the appellant blinded completely for life in both eyes. In addition, the losses to the plaintiff consist of any taste, smell odors of any kind, and will suffer seizures for the remainder of his life.

On 10 May 2001, the plaintiff brought a civil action against the Defendant Concord alleging that they had a duty to refuel the accident aircraft and that this duty contracted for and acknowledged by the Airport, and these known facts to the plaintiff. The plaintiff alleged that he had relied upon the Airport to accomplish this refueling duty on 1 June 1998. It was prior to the accident flight and had further relied upon the fact that there was fuel in the main tank of the aircraft because of the Defendant's nightly refueling during his assistance to the pilot in attempting to restart the right engine after it had ceased operation. Most significant is the fact that if the Plaintiff had known that the main tanks of the aircraft had not been refueled by the Defendant, then this knowledge would have certainly caused the Plaintiff to refuse to fly in the aircraft on the day of the crash before the main tanks were properly refueled by the Defendant. Thus preventing the subsequent crash entirely. Knowledge of the fact that the Defendant had not refueled the main tanks of the aircraft would have also allowed the pilot and Plaintiff to modify the engine restart procedure to take into Account that the engine was dry of fuel and that there was no mechanical problem with the right engine.

ARGUMENT
CHOICE OF LAW ANALYSIS

As discussed in the foregoing factual statement, the subject aircraft crashed and the Plaintiff became injured after departing the Concord Regional Airport in Cabarrus County,

North Carolina, as the airplane entered into the State of Virginia. This fact raises the question as to whether the law of Virginia or North Carolina should apply to this case.

While it is true that our courts typically follow the law of the state where the injuries occurred, our Supreme Court recognized in Leonard v. Johns-Manville Sales Corp., 309 N.C. 91, 305 S.E.2d 528 (1983). This lawsuit was where a party seeking to apply Virginia law in a North Carolina case can point to no differing provision of Virginia law, then North Carolina law should control. In the case at bar, the law controlling the legal issues involved in this appeal, do not differ from North Carolina to Virginia. Specifically the standard of review of summary judgment in both North Carolina and Virginia are virtually identical. In the absence of any Virginia law one way or another on an issue, the rule of lex loci delicti commissi does not apply. This Honorable Court has applied the same approach in both negligence actions and contract actions where there is no difference in the substantive law between states. In light of the above, the substantive law of North Carolina should apply. However, since choice of law questions may still arise during the Court's consideration of this appeal, the Plaintiff will cite both cases from North Carolina and Virginia when possible.

STANDARD OF REVIEW

The standard of review on appeal from summary judgment is whether there is any genuine issue of material fact and whether the moving party is entitled to a judgment as a matter of law. The summary judgment movant also bears the burden of establishing the lack of any triable issue. This burden may be met by a showing either that (1) an essential element of the plaintiff's claim is nonexistent; (2) the plaintiff cannot produce evidence to support an essential element of its claim; or (3) the plaintiff cannot surmount an affirmative defense raised in bar of its claim. In the case at bar, the Defendant has failed to prove any of these elements.

Finally, the evidence presented by both parties must be viewed in the light most favorable to the non-movant. Since summary judgment is a drastic remedy, the court must cautiously observe these requirements so that no party is "deprived of a trial on a genuine disputed factual issue."

THE TRIAL COURT COMMITTED REVERSIBLE ERROR WHEN IT RULED THAT THERE REMAINED NO ISSUES OF MATERIAL FACT AS RELATED TO THE CLAIMS OF THE PLAINTIFF AGAINST THE DEFENDANT CONCORD. BECAUSE of THIS DETERMINATION THAT THE DEFENDANT CITY OF CONCORD AND THE CONCORD REGIONAL AIRPORT WAS ENTITLED TO JUDGMENT AS A MATTER OF LAW AND granted SUMMARY of JUDGMENT.

ASSIGNMENT OF ERROR

#1. Numerous questions of material fact were at still at issue when the Trial Court granted summary judgment for the Defendant City of

Concord. The Plaintiff will address each of these remaining "Questions of Fact" as follows:

1. PROXIMATE CAUSE:

The Defendant contends that the failure of not refueling the main tanks of the subject aircraft could not be a proximate cause of the subject crash. Because some fuel remained in the auxiliary tanks of the aircraft after the crash and that the Plaintiff did not state in a "meaningful" way that he relied upon the Defendant Concord to refuel the aircraft. Further, the Defendant contends that the crash of the aircraft and the injury to the Plaintiff was not a "natural and probable consequence" of the Defendant's failure to refuel the main tanks of the subject aircraft and therefore the Plaintiff's injuries were not foreseeable. The Defendant's first contention is that the Plaintiff did not say in a "meaningful way" that he relied upon the Defendant Concord to refuel the subject aircraft. The Defendant thereafter attempts to support this contention by relating that the Plaintiff was a well-qualified pilot and had testified in his deposition that he never took off without checking the fuel "when flying alone". This contention by the Defendant is intentionally misleading since the Plaintiff has continuously testified that he never anticipated being the pilot of the subject flight. He was not the pilot of the subject aircraft, and that his practices and procedures for flying as the pilot in command of a flight were materially different from what he was required to do and actually did as a passenger on the day of the crash. The Plaintiff's preflight procedures, when he was to be the pilot in command of a flight, therefore did not apply to the subject flight where he was only a passenger. This fact, that the Plaintiff was not the pilot in command of the accident flight and was only a passenger, is the very reason that the Plaintiff relied so heavily on the Defendant's refueling practices. Before and during the accident flight. As his duties and actual knowledge of the condition of the aircraft was decidedly less than what he would have had if he had been the pilot in command of the subject aircraft, and had assumed the duties associated with the pilot position.

It is further well documented through deposition testimony that the Defendant had in place, for a significant period of time prior to the date of the crash, an outstanding order to refuel the subject aircraft nightly. (Hyde Deposition Vol. 4, T.p. 228 ln. 8). That the Defendant had actually performed this nightly refueling procedure to Lancaster owned aircraft, including the subject aircraft for this same period, and was supposed to have refueled the accident aircraft the night before the crash.

Finally, the Plaintiff stated that he relied, as a passenger in the subject aircraft and as an employee of Lancaster aviation, on the past practice of the Defendant to refuel the subject aircraft prior to the flight that resulted in the subject crash. (Hyde Deposition Vol. 2, T.p. 139 ln.21 through T.p. 140 ln. 5; Vol. 3, T.p. 192 ln. 6-11; R.p. 315, 317, 319, 320). This well stated detrimental reliance by the Plaintiff, on the Defendant's refueling practices, not only was a primary factor in his agreeing to begin the flight with the pilot Anderson, also contributed significantly in establishing the unsuccessful emergency procedure utilized to restart the right engine, and manage the fuel for the continued operation of the left engine, after the right engine ceased to operate during the flight.

Secondly, the Defendant contends that the failure to refuel the subject aircraft cannot be the proximate cause of the crash because the crash and injury to the Plaintiff was not foreseeable and a natural and probable consequence of the Defendants negligence. This conclusion by the Defendant requires a great leap of logic to support this finding of fact. One foreseeable and reasonably anticipated result of failing to refuel and "top off" the main fuel tanks of an aircraft is that the aircraft's engine might cease to operate as a result of exhausting all of the fuel remaining in the main tanks before the time anticipated by the pilot. This anticipated exhaustion of fuel might cause the aircraft to crash. The test of foreseeability does not require that a defendant must foresee the injury in the precise form in which it occurred. Only, that the Plaintiff prove in establishing proximate cause that in "the exercise of reasonable care, the Defendant might have foreseen that some injury would result from his act or omission, or that consequences of a generally injurious nature might have been expected." Although foreseeability of the injury still remains a question of fact. It appears that an injury caused by an aircraft crash due to fuel exhaustion resulting from the failure of the Defendant to refuel the main fuel tanks of the aircraft, meets the foreseeability test established by the Hairston Court.

Generally, the question of proximate cause is an issue of fact resolved by a jury, and a court should decide this issue <u>only</u> when reasonable persons could not differ in the outcome.

Specifically, the Supreme Court of North Carolina explained that "It is only when the facts are all admitted and only one inference may be drawn from them that the court will declare whether an act was the proximate cause of an injury or not. But that is rarely the case."

Friday, November 2, 2001, I talked with Tony about the case. He wanted me to attend a hearing in Mecklenburg County.

Thursday, November 8, 2001, Tony contacted me to tell us that Robert Anderson dropped the lawsuit against Lancaster Aviation and me. Therefore, the lawsuit consisted of me suing the city of Concord.

Tuesday, November 13, 2001, Tony contacted me to tell me to wear dress shoes, slacks, and a dress shirt possibly with a tie. Mom put my suit out to wear to the hearing on Friday, November 16. On Friday morning, Mom, Wayne Yates, Lincoln, and I went to meet Tony and Rusty Almond for breakfast at the Center City Hotel. We talked a lot during breakfast, then we went to court at the Mecklenburg County Courthouse. We were there until 2:30 p.m. that afternoon. We found out how the hearing went on December 7 when he told me about the court date scheduled for October 14, 2002. He explained that he spent two days in Austin, Texas, to see Rusty and Popidaekus, who were both working on the case. Tony shared with me on December 12, 2001, that he wanted depositions from Misty Smith, John Crosby, and anybody else needed.

Letter Sent Out

During October of 2002, a letter from Tony Meneo was sent to Discover, First North American National Bank, and Chase Visa. This letter informed them to stop calling me due to the litigation going on. The document shared about the plane crash.

Christopher Thomas Marlowe

October 18, 2003, my close friend Christopher Thomas Marlowe was shot and killed by either his wife or his wife's stepfather early that morning. They shared a son together named Cameron after the Duke Blue Devils' basketball stadium. Early that morning, he was walking up their driveway, and she or her stepfather shot him.

Ferrell James II

On December 30, 2003, four years to the day of losing my father, my cousin wrecked his Harley Davidson. The motorcycle was a 2000 model Road King, and Ferrell crashed it off the exit of Webb Road off Interstate 85 that evening just after dark. The motorcycle cut half of his right shin off, and he took off his belt and used it as a tourniquet to stop the bleeding. He crawled up to the side of the road, and someone saw him and called for help. Help came, and he eventually was airlifted to the Baptist Hospital in Winston Salem in North Carolina. Todd, Terri, and I went to visit him early in January 2004. He now wears his prostheses and gets around really well.

More bad luck for my cousin took place on September 5, 2005. He had a battery explode in his face. Therefore, for his forty-fourth birthday, he had patches over both eyes.

Depositions

During the spring of 2004, the law required us to give our deposition about the crash. The pilot, Robert Anderson, gave his deposition first at Robert Potter's office, the city of Concord's lawyer, about all the lies and untruthful admissions recorded here. Next, I gave my deposition, and it lasted four and a half days. The attorneys asked me everything from how much sleep I had the night before the crash to if I had anything to drink that night. They deposed my mom, brother, the boss of the flight school, and the city of Concord employees.

Graduation

One very big accomplishment I achieved was finishing my bachelor of arts degree in history. I graduated from the University of North Carolina at Charlotte December 18, 2004, in the Halton Arena. Lincoln and I walked across the stage to receive the certificate, and we received a standing ovation. Mom, TC, Todd, Terri, Lauren, Austin, Tony Meneo and his wife, Athena, and Lorna Felts attended commencement.

After graduation and the celebration of doing so, my family and I went to the Thoroughbred Lounge, a bar in Charlotte, North Carolina. Misty Smith worked there as a manager, and she worked it out to have our party at the bar. A live band played that Mom's husband invited to play. We had a good celebration, and it was a good time. People I remember who were present were Mom, TC, Todd and Terri Hyde, Kendra and Sharon Harrington, Mike and Jackie Cook, Ken and Lisa Long, Dayton and Regis Mclean, Wayne Yates, Elaine Query, Renee Ritchie, Larry Morris, Randy Hyde and his ex-wife Ginger, Jeremy Miles, and Conway Kessler.

Charlotte Observer

On Sunday, December 19, 2004, David Pearlman wrote an article about Lincoln and me. In addition, a woman named Heather with the CBS Morning News saw the article, and she wanted to do a story on us as well. Unfortunately, the tsunami in Sri Lanka occurred, which killed over 250,000 people as well as other big news, so they could not do a story on us at that time. However, another article came out about Southeastern Guide Dogs Incorporated, Lincoln, and me on January 5, 2005.

This was posted on Sunday, December 19, 2004 on the *Charlotte Observer*, front page of the local and state section

> At UNCC, a walk to remember Crash survivor, now blind, builds new life by DAVID PERLMUTT | STAFF WRITER
>
> Thirty-seven minutes in the air, the right engine quit on the Piper Twin Comanche. The twin-engine plane was bound for West Virginia from Concord. There was no panic in the pilot or Barry Hulon Hyde of Kannapolis—on that 1998 flight, the safety pilot if the pilot needed to fly on instruments. The pilot tried several times to restart the engine. Then 10 minutes later, the left engine quit over Floyd, Virginia, and the plane slipped off Roanoke's radar. The plane went down abruptly, and the two pilots collected themselves into a ball and prepared to crash into a stand of trees. Both of the pilot's legs were broken. A medic got air to Hyde's lungs and paramedics airlifted Hyde by helicopter to a Roanoke hospital, where he was DOA—dead on arrival. So, the emergency doctors thought. Saturday, Hyde, 32, was one of 2,200 UNC Charlotte students in cap and gown during winter commencement exercises. His bachelor's degree is in history, yet he plans to continue teaching pilots as the first blind person to have ground instructor licenses by the Federal Aviation Administration. That he was even there Saturday—guided by his dog, Lincoln the Navigator—is all the more miracu-

lous. Dozens of injuries after emergency doctors revived Hyde at the hospital; they performed an inventory of all his injuries: 14 broken bones, both lungs collapsed. Four teeth were missing and his bottom jaw was broken in four places. The impact displaced the roof of his mouth from his face; a big hole replaced where his nose was previously located. The impact removed his left eye. His forehead had several cracks leading up to the hairline. Damage to the right eye's optic nerve was severe, and a cataract quickly developed over the retina.

He was in a coma.

The hospital chaplain contacted his parents in Kannapolis and told to come and identify him. When his father, walked into the hospital room and saw his son in critical condition, he fell to his knees and passed out. Barry remained in the coma for the next 20 days.

"They tell me I woke up on Father's Day and said to my dad 'happy Father's Day,' then went out again," Hyde said.

An affinity for flying

Regarding his family and friends, it was no surprise Hyde developed a desire to be a part of aviation.

At 12, Hyde started working for a cousin, Ferrell James Sr., helping restore and maintain James' rental houses while James flew Boeing 767s for US Airways.

James' son, Ferrell II, was a pilot, too, and often took Hyde flying.

"It was like being on top of the world," Hyde said. "He did spins and loops and that drew me more to flying. I thought I wanted to be just like Ferrell Sr., fly big jets and have a few rental houses on the side. "I thought teaching people to fly would be a great job."

That is what he set out to do. He learned to fly at Catawba Valley Aviation at the Statesville Municipal airport, and after graduating from Rowan-Cabarrus Community College with an associate's degree in business administration; he decided to sell a house he restored to go to flight school at American Flyers in Addison, Texas.

Returning to Kannapolis, he went to work teaching people to fly for Lancaster Aviation at the Concord Regional Airport.

His mother, Brenda Carpenter of Kannapolis, was a flight attendant for U.S. Airways Express, a commuter service, and got him an interview for a pilot's job, scheduled the second week of June 1998.

The evening before, he agreed to fly safety pilot with a man who had rented a Piper Comanche. In the afternoon, they took off from the Concord airport and at 4:20 p.m., Hyde made radio contact with the Roanoke airport.

Moments later, the plane crashed between two houses. Hyde said he could not talk about the reasons the engines quit because of litigation he filed.

A woman near the crash called 911. Paramedics converged on the crashed plane.

"The medic saved my life," said Hyde. "I was that near death."

New path for flight studies

Hyde remained in the hospital for three months. He remembers nothing but his dreams about the doctors with nurses and beeps with buzzes of the medical devices keeping him alive. "It was horrific," Hyde said. "When I started coming to, I couldn't see anything, which made it scarier. The sight I received was unclear and distorted. My brain wasn't accustomed to me not being able to see."

For the next two years, he underwent surgeries and learned the required skills for the blind to function and keep their independence. He went to the Rehabilitation Center for the Blind in Raleigh, NC and was taught to walk with a cane (a leg was broken in four places) and learned to guide his way with a pointer cane.

Therapy filled—cognitive, occupational, speech, mobility, and physical.

On Dec. 30, 1999, Hyde was home for the holidays when his father, a retired rodeo performer, died of a heart attack.

"We were very close; Dad was my hero," Hyde said. "I went back to the school in Raleigh, but didn't stay long—I wanted to be back home with my mom."

Therefore, he came home and began to study for the FAA's advanced ground instructor and the instrument ground instructor licenses. He passed both in 2000 and has the licenses to teach flight fundamentals in the classroom.

At the same time, Hyde recalled learning of blind people using guide dogs and he began checking into getting one for himself.

He found the Southeastern Guide Dog School in Palmetto, Fla., and that is where he and Lincoln, a sixteen month old black lab, became a team.

After 26 days of learning how to use Lincoln, the two came home in July 2000.

Having passed the FAA tests, he realized his brain functioned well enough to retain knowledge and he decided he wanted to get his college degree at UNCC.

A year later, Hyde enrolled in a summer session, and he and Lincoln moved into an apartment near the campus.

"This is something he really wanted to do," said his mother. "He was so bad with the head injuries and his short-term memory, that once he started school I never thought he'd make it. I prayed to God, if Barry's going to be blind, let him get his brain back."

He and his mother counted and mapped out the 1,800 steps one way from his apartment to the disability office on campus. For the next 3 and a half years, Hyde and Lincoln made the trip except during bad weather, when his mother drove them.

Times in his apartment did get a little lonely.

"There were times when I wished Lincoln could talk," he said. "I talked to him all the time; but I'd lean over and touch him and feel his body personality and knew what he was thinking. I couldn't have gotten this far without him and my mom."

Further schooling planned

On Saturday, with Brenda and other relatives in the audience, Lincoln, his tail wagging, led Barry across the stage at Halton Arena to collect their diploma. The assembled gave them warm applause.

He is applying to a master's degree program at Embry Riddle Aeronautical University in Florida.

"After being sighted for 26 years and blind for six years and six months, I am just making an effort to live day to day," Hyde said. "It is valuable for other people to see we all face our own issues every day. Some people have problems and some have real problems.

"I enjoyed school and participating in class and learning from others. It is stuff no one can ever take away from me."

Delta Gama Sorority

Sunday, January 9, 2005, Nance, Lincoln, and I went to the University of North Carolina at Charlotte to attend the Delta Gama Sorority Division of Blind Services event. I spoke for about ten minutes after they fed us dinner. I gave a description of the accident, my training with Lincoln, my education, and my future goals. Eleven guide dogs with their users were present.

Fox Morning News

Monday morning, January 10, 2005, Lincoln and I were on the Fox Morning news and were interviewed by John Wilson. Wilson said he read the article written about me in the *Charlotte Observer*. They interviewed me, and I spoke of how Southeastern Guide Dog Incorporated helps people, such as myself. We helped promote Pet Resort in Pineville, North Carolina, as well.

Lions Club

Tuesday evening, January 11, Lincoln and I went to a presentation to represent Southeastern Guide Dog Incorporated, in Welcome, North Carolina, to the Arcadian Lion's Club meeting with Nance Riedel and Jackson. Nance worked for Southeastern, and we attended meetings together to help raise awareness and money to sponsor Southeastern. We gave a presentation representing Southeastern Guide Dog Incorporated, and we showed the club where their donations were going.

Rotary Club

Tuesday at lunch, January 25, 2005, Nance, Lincoln, and I spoke at the rotary club. We ate lunch at the Speedway Club at the Charlotte Motor Speedway in Concord, NC, and then Nance and I did a presentation on how donations help Southeastern Guide Dog Incorporated, which then help people like me.

Touring Embry-Riddle Aeronautical University

Friday morning, January 28, 2005, Nance, Lincoln, and I toured Embry-Riddle. During this time, I had a seizure that lasted for about five minutes. I found out that I would be awarded a $12,000 scholarship from Embry-Riddle, and I found that out from Kim Clary and Bill Hampton, both from the Office of Human Services. In addition, Nance, Jackson, Lincoln, and I went to Southeastern to pick up a couple of dogs to bring back to North Carolina.

Barry & Lincoln at ERAU campus

Presentations

On February 7, 2005, Nance, Lincoln, and I went to an elementary school outside the university place in Charlotte. We gave another presentation representing Southeastern Guide Dog Incorporated on February 8, when we went to a Rocky River Preschool in Concord, North Carolina. Nance and I gave a presentation on how to treat guide dogs, and the kids were really taken with Lincoln and Jackson. February 10, Nance, Lincoln, and I went to a Latin School in Charlotte, and they donated dogfood, toys, and towels. We saw Anna Brock, a music teacher I had while attending UNCC, and her daughter attended this Latin school.

Court

Monday, February 14, 2005, Tony Meneo, my attorney, Mom, Lincoln, and I went to the Cabarrus County Courthouse in Concord, North Carolina, for the lawsuit. While we were present, you could tell that everyone was against us. They wanted me to settle out of court for $100,000. I could not put a dollar amount on what my injuries were valued at: sight, taste, smell, fourteen broken bones, and being pronounced dead on arrival.

Walk-a-Thon

On March 6, 2005, Nance, Jackson, Lincoln, Barbara, Charlotte, and I attended Southeastern's Guide Dog Incorporated Walk-a-Thon in Bradenton, Florida. This walk-a-thon was a fund raiser for Southeastern Guide Dog Incorporated. This is a three-mile walk with lots of people, dogs, and guide dog users.

Lion's Club

Monday evening, March 14, 2005, Nance, Jackson, Lincoln, and I attended the Jackson Park Lion's Club meeting at the Western Sizzlin' Steakhouse. I spoke for a few minutes and thanked the club for their donations to Southeastern Guide Dog Incorporated and shared with them how their donations were helping the school. On March 16, Nance, a dog named BJ, Lincoln, and I went to the Lion's Club in Salisbury, located at the Holiday inn Express. The sharing of one more presentation took place here.

Summary of Judgment

In the month of April, 2005, was the summary of judgment. In May, we found out that my case had been pushed until possibly June.

Lion's Club in Jacksonville

Monday morning, April 11, 2005, Nance, Jackson, Lincoln, and I went to Jacksonville, North Carolina to give a presentation to the Lion's Club. Monday evening, we shared dinner with the Lion's Club in Onslow County and on Tuesday, we ate lunch with Services for the Blind with about seventy people in attendance from the surrounding counties. We represented Southeastern Guide Dog Incorporated and shared training in regards to Lincoln and the accident details. Nance provided information and advertisement as well. On our way back to Kannapolis, we stopped in Raleigh at the school for the blind. I visited Ken, who was my mobility instructor when I was there. In addition, I visited Barbara McGinnis and a couple of other instructors, such as Kim. After leaving there, we went by the attorney's office and met his secretary, Judy. As we were leaving, Nance pulled over to look at a map, and Tony and his wife, Athena, snuck up on us and scared us by beating on the van. We spoke with him for fifteen minutes. When we came through Salisbury, we stopped at the Genesis Nursing home to see my grandma Hyde.

Mt. Pleasant Lion's Club

Monday evening, April 14, 2005, Nance, Jackson, Lincoln, and I gave a presentation to the Mt. Pleasant Lion's Club. We spoke of Southeastern Guide Dog Incorporated. They fed us dinner, and I met a pilot. We spoke of some flying characteristics.

UNCC Presentation

Friday, April 15, 2005, Nance, Lincoln, and I went to the University of North Carolina at Charlotte to give a presentation to Stacey Cuntsman's class. The presentation covered the disability, the blindness, guide dogs, and how Lincoln is helping me.

Court Case

On Monday morning, May 9, 2005, Mom took Lincoln and me to the Cabarrus County courthouse, where we met Tony Meneo and Nance. The case was not heard until 12:30 p.m. I could not believe how the judge kept cutting Tony off and would let the city attorneys talk for an hour. The judge was unable to make a ruling on the case, and he said he would contact everyone the next day with his ruling.

Enochville Elementary School

Wednesday afternoon, May 11, 2005, Nance, Lincoln, and I went to my niece's and nephew's school for a presentation on the guide dogs. The presentation was for the third graders, and Lauren's class was present. I visited them before they boarded the bus, and we visited them after they came home. At the school, the principal was my ninth grade basketball coach and the physical education instructor. We spoke to each other and had a nice visit.

Last Facial Surgery

Monday, May 16, 2005, Dr. David Matthews performed my last facial surgery. He removed a few pieces of metal, some screws, and used more bone from the cranium to replace the areas where he removed the metal in my face. He smoothed the area in the cranium where he removed bone. The bone was placed on my forehead and temples. Dr. Matthews stapled me back together across the top of my head with thirty-five staples and plastered my face and forehead in places. He resized my eye and moved it over to the left to help center it. I wish I could see how good of a job that he really did. Uncle Rudy stayed with me and aided me. Pastor Ken came by and prayed with me, and the nurse Nicole Mead was very helpful as well. Nance called me and gave me her blessings as she attended her sister's memorial service in Maryland. The nice people from Concordia Lutheran Church brought by meals after I came home from the hospital. On Monday, May 23, Mom took me to Dr. Mathew's office, and a nurse named Cheryl removed all thirty-five staples and bandages.

Westford Methodist Church

Tuesday, June 14, 2005, Nance, Jackson, Lincoln, and I went to Westford Methodist Church to give an oral presentation on Southeastern Guide Dog Incorporated. We had lunch and received a standing ovation. A couple of women stuck forty dollars in my pocket.

National Federation of the Blind

Monday, May 2, 2005, I was contacted by the National Federation of the Blind, and they told me I was one of thirty finalists that had been chosen out of five hundred people. It was a scholarship valued at $3,000, and it could increase. Nance, Lincoln, and I attended the National Federation of the Blind Convention in Louisville, Kentucky, over the week of July 4, 2005. We drove there on Friday, July 1, and we came back Saturday, July 9. As we were driving home on Saturday, we came through Frankfurt, Kentucky, the capital. Nance took a picture of Lincoln and me standing in front of the Rotunda. We also had our picture made with lookalikes of Abraham Lincoln and Mary Todd Lincoln.

Dr. Marvin Smith, Academic Adviser

Tuesday, July 26, 2005, at 10:48 a.m., Nance, Lincoln, and I were sitting in Dr. Marv's office on campus at Embry-Riddle Aeronautical University, and as we were discussing my classes, the *Discovery* space shuttle launched from Kennedy Space Center. In addition, we met the lady in the office of disability services. We met several people in the office in Division of Blind Services in Daytona Beach.

Donation as Scholarship

Sunday, August 7, 2005, I received a donation valued at $1,000 from Concordia Lutheran Church. This donation was a blessing, a huge surprise, and was signed by Frank Overcash. On Monday, Nance helped me write a thank-you letter to Concordia, the members, and Frank Overcash.

Going Away Party at the Cooks

Saturday, August 13, 2005, Mike Cook threw a party for me at his parents, Dale and Ann Cook's, in Kannapolis. I saw people I had not seen in a long time, such as Franky Reynolds, Scott White, Chris Reid, Brandon and Holly Beaver, Heather and Braxton Beaver, Scottie Stewart, Jeremy Miles, and Brandi Honeycutt. In addition, I visited with Deric Harrington, Randy Hyde, Bet and Ferrell James, Dale and Ann Cook, Mike, Jackie, Stephanie, Madeline, and Larry Cook. Philippe and Cricket Bonnatoe came as well. I spoke with Conway Kessler and Chris Beaver, who were unable to attend. Earlier that day, I visited with Rudy and Grandma Hyde, as well as Grandma Absher.

The Drive to Daytona Beach

Sunday, August 14, 2005, Lincoln and I drove down in the car with Mom. TC drove the U-Haul, and he followed us. Randy Hyde, Todd, Terri, Lauren, Austin, and Gene Goins saw us off, and I talked with Kendra and Nance en route. On Monday, Mom and TC moved all my stuff into the apartment I rented previously, with Nance's help, at Countryside Apartments.

People Assisting Me

As my life continued, God provided me people that assisted Lincoln and me in all issues I faced. For example, Nance helped me with schoolwork, helped with dealing with meals, and let me use her as a reference for the apartment. My uncle Rudy helped with revisions to papers as well. Dr. Marv helped me by being my adviser at school. Sheila Norris helped me by fixing me something to eat at the student activity center before or after school. Megan Osbourne worked with Lincoln and me on our mobility travel around the apartment complex, walking back and forth to the bank, and walking around school. Votrane picked Lincoln and me up and took us to Embry-Riddle and then brought us back home after class. In addition, most of the professors were exceptional and worked with me. Some favorites were Dr. Marv, Sid Mcguirk, Dr. Metscher, Don Hunt, Dr. Ester Forsyth, and Dr. Don Maccahrella. August 28 was the first day of class, and Heidi and Karen from Southeastern Guide Dog Incorporated came and walked around campus with Lincoln and me as well.

Mary, my next-door neighbor, would bring me dinner sometimes as well as busy bags, and she took me shopping a time or two. She would also check dates on things like my milk. The manager of the apartment complex we lived in helped me sometimes as well. She brought me milk, instant breakfast, and some bread at times. Walt Reedy, a man from church, would pick Lincoln and me up and take us to Hope Lutheran Church. Friends assisted me from school, such as Sandra Mora and Andrew Coffman. Both were in some of my classes, and Andrew even took me flying. Sandra and I had lunch with Lincoln, her mom, and Nance at a restaurant on the side of the Miami International Airport. I listened to air traffic control and pilots being cleared to land. Really awesome!

Master of Science in Aeronautics Degree

In the summer of 2005, Lincoln and I began our first class on August 28 to begin studies on my master's degree. The first class was the aircraft accident investigation class with Don Hunt. The second class was an aircraft transportation system class.

Presentation

Tuesday, September 13, Andrew Coffman, Lincoln, and I had dinner at the student activity center, and then we walked to the auditorium. Phil Boyer, the president of the Aircraft Owners and Pilots Association, gave a presentation to a group of several hundred people. It was a real interesting presentation, and I am glad I attended. Lincoln, Andrew, and I sat on the front row.

Cessna 172 Flight

On November 12, 2005, Andrew Coffman took me flying in a Cessna 172. We went out of a fixed based operator, Epic Aviation, located on the Daytona International Airport. The flight in the newer model 172 was great, and this flight made the seventh time I flew on a general aviation airplane since the accident. Andrew let me do some turns, climbs, descents, and talk on the radio. Andrew practiced some commercial maneuvers like chandelles, lazy eights, eights on pylons, as well as some ground reference maneuvers. I felt nauseated a few times.

Kendra's Passing

One more very large loss in my life was the passing of Kendra Ann Harrington on November 19, 2005. It was a Saturday afternoon, and she was at the dialysis clinic and went into cardiac arrest. We had spoken the Thursday before, and everything seemed perfect. I was very fortunate to attend her memorial service during Thanksgiving weekend. Mom, TC, Todd, Terri, and I attended the service and listened to her brothers Ryan and Jason speak. I met her dad, Ken, whom she was named after as well.

On January 5, 2006, my cousin Ferrell James II and I took her ashes up in his dad's Piper J-3 Cub and released some of her ashes over my house and over Kannapolis lake, where her mom could see them being released from the airplane. Kendra became my angel and follows me everywhere I go, I feel. I know she has gone to a better place, and I know she is with my dad. I miss her.

Brandon Beaver's Wedding

Thursday, December 1, 2005, I flew home with Lincoln. We flew from Daytona Beach on a Canadair Regional Jet into Atlanta on US Airways. A ticket agent walked us over to the gate to board an Md-80 to Charlotte. The Friday before the wedding, they rented out the *Catawba Queen*, a boat ride that lasted several hours, and they served alcohol and appetizers. There was a good amount of people on the boat, and it was a nice time for all.

The next day, December 3, 2005, Brandon Beaver married his sweetheart Holly Heidenworth. They were married on Lincoln's seventh birthday. Lincoln and I flew home on US Airways on a Boeing 737 from Charlotte to Atlanta, then on a Canadair Regional Jet, 700 series into Daytona Beach. Brandon asked me to be a groomsman, and the wedding took place at his church in Mooresville, North Carolina. This church was previously the #3 ex-race car driver, Dale Earnhardt's church, where he was a member. Afterward, we took the limousine to the peninsula on Lake Norman, where the party took place. The wedding reception was like a class reunion.

Greater Miami Aviation Association— Batchelor Aviation Scholarship Foundation

In May of 2006, Stephanie Henderson, Sarah Irvin, Lincoln, and I drove to Miami and were interviewed for a scholarship from the Greater Miami Aviation Association and the Batchelor Aviation Scholarship Foundation. The interview took place at the Tiami, Miami, airport. We were all from Embry-Riddle, and all were awarded scholarships.

Gallbladder Surgery

Tuesday, November 8, 2005, I found out I had gallstones. Patty at Dr. Waykin's office on campus shared the news with me. During August of 2006, I had my gallbladder removed and surgery performed at the Florida Hospital Ormond Memorial. The surgeon told us prior to the surgery that I should have several hours in recovery, and then I would be free to go home. Unfortunately, the recovery did not go as planned, as I was waking up I was suffering from severe sharp pains between the incision on the right side of my belly and the belly button. I was put in a room, and as I went back to sleep, Nance went back to our town house to feed Lincoln and Jackson. Nance and Lincoln came back and spent the night in the room with me.

Court of Appeals

On June 13, 2006, Tony Mineo emailed me to share with me the lawsuit details.

> Barry:
>
> I just received notice from the Court of Appeals whereby they AFFIRMED the Trial Courts Summary Judgment. They completely disregarded our legal claims based on your reliance on the past actions of the city and held that since there was no WRITTEN Contract to refuel the aircraft, and a written contract was necessary for a city to be held under a contract, the trial court's summary judgment was proper. This is the most simplistic view anyone could utilize and does not take into account years of case law on detrimental reliance and implied contract. The Court only applied the statutory law that would protect the city and refused to consider anything else.
>
> I am sorry my friend, but we did everything that we could and took every appeal that was available. Since the Court of Appeals decisions were unanimous, we have NO Appeal to the N. C. Supreme Court and this ends your case. Reliance on N.C. Statutory law that was written solely for the protection of cities was the choice the Court of Appeals made.
>
> Please give me a call so that I can discuss this with you more fully. I am sending you a copy of the Court decision and a bill from the court for costs that they taxed against you for the appeal. I have paid $507.50 to them on your behalf at the beginning of the appeal, but they billed you

an additional $266.50 for costs. <u>Please pay this directly to the Clerk of the Court of Appeals.</u>

Again, I am disgusted and angry, but there is nothing else we can do as far as the court system provides.

Tony Mineo

Air Traffic Control Association Scholarship

September 18, 2006, I was contacted by Miguel Vasquez, who worked for the Air Traffic Control Association. They awarded me $2,500 and invited me to the banquet in Washington, DC. On October 30 of 2006, Nance, Mom, Lincoln, and I flew to the Washington Dulles Airport. We then took a shuttle over to the convention at the Wardman Park Marriot. The ATCA Convention took place downtown Washington, DC.

We met the President of ATCA, Pete Dumont. In addition, we met the Chairman, Neil Planzar, Cindy Castillo, Becky Umbaugh, all are on the scholarship committee and the Air Traffic Control Association Scholarship board. In addition, visited with Larry Fortea, who is the chairman and president of the board, and a great friend, Miguel Vasquez. We also visited with Sid Mcguirk, Dr. Marvin Smith, and Dr. Don Metscher. These gentlemen met my mom and Nance while I sat on stage with Lincoln beside Cyndi Castillo, and next to her was Pete Dumont. Cindy shared with us when she did her presentation,

The efforts of reviewing and selecting the scholarship recipients for 2006. As we sit up here, year after year talking about the scholarships and it all begins with the contributors. All of you, our membership and all witness the generous contributions and giving year after year. The commitment to sponsoring just as many of you have given donations. We would not be a program that is expanding into giving more scholarships and in numbers, and amounts. We really appreciate all of the contributors for this year, the previous years, sponsors for the golfers, and other ways we get people to participate. So, thank you for that, where that begins. To start, what the scholarship fund is, it is a program that we get to recognize through the performance and excellent contributions for students, for employees, and for children of Air Traffic Control Specialists. These students are excelling, who are continuing their education, and do have a financial need, and do have things they want to accomplish in their life and career. We get to learn a lot about them thru their story, what it would mean to you, how you are going to make a difference in Aviation and Air Traffic Management. We have the cream of the crop that we want to share with you. The process started out with over 500 applications sent down to a lot of the FAA universities and schools. After two filtration processes, down to 12 scholarships given out. I do want to recognize those who have been involved in this process. The leadership, not only Larry Fortiea, but Cass Castlebury, who has been instrumental in his efforts on the Aviation education committee. But, without that connection with the scholarship board and the scholarship committee, there is so much effort that starts like looking through the applications and making sure they actually qualify. The process of great grade of Cass's thinking is that the committee has got it down to around 50 applications to choose for the four categories. Here is what we ended up with, the scholarship recipients for 2006.

Cindy introduced the separate categories, told the background of the winner and how much the scholarship was valued at, and introduced the recipients. Three recipients were present to receive their scholarship in person.

I spoke in front of nine hundred people, thanked ATCA for the scholarship, and told my story to everyone present, including ATCA and military members as well.

Cindy introduced me,

The next recipient is Barry Hulon Hyde. The amazing information up here is that Barry is the first blind student to ever attend Embry-Riddle. Also, the first person to hold certifications as an Advanced Ground Instructor and Instrument Ground Instructor. As we were sitting here, I don't know if you saw under the table the dog, but that is my good buddy, Lincoln. He licked my face and gave his mom a kiss as well. I wanted to bring him up on stage and his only job is to take care of his dad. So, I wanted to recognize Barry, have him say a few words, and also give his perspective and Barry welcome.

The crowd applauded for seven seconds. I stated,

Wow, good afternoon, everyone. Man, this is an awesome experience to be here, and I want to thank ATCA, of course. Wow, I want to thank my Guide Dog, Lincoln, who I call Lincoln the Navigator. The crowd laughed. I said, he has been a tremendous help, he has been a large inspiration, and a large motivation for me as well, and he has helped me get to where I am at today. Let's see, eight years, four months, and 29 days ago, my life changed dramatically. Of course, I wanted to be a commercial pilot and I was a commercial pilot, but I wanted to fly for an airline or fly corporate, possibly for a race team. Unfortunately, that day, June 1, 1998, my life so dramatically changed, and it shattered my dreams, but life goes on. Therefore, I put my emphasis on becoming the first blind Advanced Ground Instructor and the first blind Instrument Ground Instructor in the world for the FAA. I thought that was a large accomplishment.

I thought I wanted to go back to school and become something when I grow up. So, I thought I would check into attending Embry-Riddle and they accepted me. I said well shoot, if I can go to Embry-Riddle, maybe I can be the first blind student to graduate from there. So, that is where I wanted to graduate from with a Master's of Science in Aeronautics with dual specializations, Aviation Safety and Aviation Operations on May 7th of 2007. Man, that would be such a blessing and I am so thankful to be a part of life. God left me here and I am so thankful to be standing here talking to everyone. Thank y'all for providing me the scholarship and helping me to achieve what I am left here to do and that of course is to graduate. Thank y'all so much, once again. I really appreciate it.

The crowd stood and applauded for thirty seconds. Cindy said,

Thank you to the three scholarship recipients that joined us here today. The message that Barry laughed with me and joked broke my heart, but you don't look back, you look forward. What you don't have today and I can create and be a part of tomorrow. In just talking with Barry, the short time we had today, I really have a lot of respect for him. So, thank you all three recipients that are here today to spend your time with us. Again, this is about you, helping us and giving us a perspective on what we do. Keep it up and we look forward to seeing you again here next year.

Greater Miami Aviation Association and Batchelor Aviation Scholarship Fund

Saturday evening, November 17, 2006, Nance, Lincoln, and I attended the Gala for the Greater Miami Aviation Association and the Batchelor Aviation Scholarship Fund at the Parrot Jungle Island in Miami Beach, Florida. The chairman of the scholarship committee Bill Rivenbark was the presenter in front of over three hundred people. Bill Rivenbark introduced several previous scholarship winners, and three of us were present to pay thanks in person for this year's scholarships. Stephanie Henderson, Sarah Irvin, and Lincoln and I stood up at the podium as Bill begins by stating:

> Many of us in this room, me included are fortunate that we had parents that were able to help us through College. Then we were often fortunate enough, to add decent jobs and pursue advanced degrees if we wished while we were still working. Many in this room are most noticeably, are scholarship recipients that did not have it that easy. Every one of our recipients that you have met thus far this evening struggled to make ends meet and struggled to get to where they are

today. They often incurred tremendous debt in the way of student loans, they often worked two jobs while going to school, several had families and they raised their families while working and going to school. But knowing our recipients as I do, I know they would be the first among us to say their difficulties have been minor compared to what Mr. Barry Hulon Hyde has endured. In June of 1998, Barry was involved in an aircraft accident or which he was not at fault, which cost him his eyesight and nearly his life. Barry was operating as a Flight Instructor and at the moment in contention for a position with a regional Airline. For most of us such an experience in the weeks would detour us from pursuing Aviation as a career. Barry not only recovered from his injuries, he learned to master and handles his handicap. He gained the status as the only blind FAA licensed Ground School Instructor in the United States and probably the world. He is now pursuing a Master's Degree in Aviation Safety and maintaining a 4.0 average in the process. I would like to let Barry continue with this story.

The crowd applauded for 12 seconds. I began by saying,

Good evening everyone. Oh man, this is an awesome experience, and I want to begin by thanking the Greater Miami Aviation Association for the scholarship, as well as the Batchelor Foundation. I am very honored and blessed to receive this scholarship. I am like Bill said, maintaining my 4.0 grade point average at Embry-Riddle Aeronautical University. My specializations in the Master's of Science in Aeronautics are in Aviation Safety, which I feel that is rather ironic considering I lived through a plane crash, and also Aviation Operations. I learned about the scholarship through Dr. Marvin Smith, who was my academic advisor there at Embry-Riddle. He sent me the email and I applied for it, and these wonderful people accepted me. They interviewed me, took me in, made me feel more confident, and more at ease. Once again, I feel very blessed and thankful to be here, standing in front of everyone talking. It is such a honor once again. What can I say, the whole scenario is miraculous! I lived through something that I always told my friends that if the airplane crashes and it is my time, then, it is my time, obviously, it was not my time yet. That day, eight years, five months, and 16 days ago and about five hours, I lost my smell, taste, and my sight. As well as 14 broken bones, both collapsed lungs, my left eye, my nose was knocked off, sinus cavity destroyed, four teeth knocked out, jawbone broken in four places, the roof of my mouth was knocked loose from my face, and two cracks in my cranium. My goodness, my right leg was broken four times, and now I have a metal rod in my leg, still have metal plates in my face where the bone grew over them and they could not be removed, but hey, I think they did alright." The crowd clapped for eight seconds. "I would also like to say something about my career, I don't know what I want to be when I grow up although I know I do want to stay involved in Aviation. I would like to teach ground school, hopefully, for Embry-Riddle. I want to be involved in Aviation, some way, shape, or form, possibly going to work for the

FAA. I want to thank everyone once again. This is such a blessing and such an honor. I did not introduce my Guide Dog, Lincoln the Navigator.

The crowd applauded for seven seconds. I gave a treat to Lincoln, and then we walked from the podium. The crowd stood and clapped for twenty-five seconds. Bill took the podium and said, "Barry's time has not yet come. We have gone over our alotted time, and I apologize for that, but I hope you will agree that the story of Barry's scholarship is worth hearing."

Ninety-Fourth Air Squadron

Saturday, November 18, 2006, Nance, Jackson, Lincoln, and I met Sandra Mora and her mom at the Ninety-Fourth Air Squadron for lunch. We had our picture made in the yard in front of a DC-10. The air squadron had earphones to listen to the approach of the airplanes talking to air traffic control. Sandra and I attended and graduated Embry-Riddle together.

White Cane Awareness Walk

Nance, Lincoln, and I participated in the White Cane Awareness walk and made the news. We participated with the Daytona Beach police chief Mike Chitwood and the mayor. I met Traci from the Hog Radio Station and Taric Minor from the Channel 6 News. The Walk was advertised because a blind person and his guide dog were hit by a car, and we went and participated in making cars and trucks aware that humans have the right of way.

Discovery Liftoff

On December 9, 2006, Nance, Jackson, Lincoln, and I went to Kennedy Space Center or Cape Canaveral to witness the *Discovery* liftoff. The *Discovery* space shuttle lifted off at 7:40 p.m. at night. The astronauts were on a mission to the International Space Station. Nance said the liftoff lit up the sky and the horizon. The loud audible sound that lasted for thirty seconds was like nothing else I have ever experienced. The sound was the most patriotic sound and most exhilarating sound that I have ever encountered. The vertical climb could be heard for over five minutes.

Titanic Museum

Monday morning, December 11, 2006, Nance, Lincoln, and I went to Orlando, Florida to the Titanic Museum. The tour lasted for one hour, it was very historical, and was very interesting. I found out 703 people lived and 1,500 people lost their life. It was a huge ship, over five football fields in length, and ten stories high.

Gift Certificate

Saturday evening, January 13, 2007, Nance, Lincoln, and I went to the Outback restaurant to have dinner. An older man sitting beside us finished his dinner, and as he stood up to leave, he came over to me and offered me a gift certificate that someone gave him for Christmas. We told him thank you and he did not have to do that. He said that he wanted to, and he said he would give us what Jesus Christ gave him if he could. He patted me on the shoulder and said, "Have a great dinner." We told him thank you. We looked at the gift certificate, and it was valued at fifty dollars.

Daytona Beach International Speedway

Monday, January 15, 2007, Nance, Lincoln and I went to the Daytona International Speedway. A woman named Roxy, who was the assistant manager at the Countryside Apartments complex I lived at previously, saw us and came up and started talking with us. She talked us into taking a guide, who was a driver of the tram. It was a historical time, and we went to victory lane and made pictures. On the outside of the speedway, I had my picture made with my hand on Dale Earnhardt's handprint below his statue. I did the same for Dale Earnhardt Jr.'s handprint. Nance took Lincoln and my picture in front of the Dale Earnhardt's statute.

Flight Training Tutor Lab

Wednesday, January 23, 2007, a young man named Chuck was a flight instructor for Embry-Riddle, and he worked in the Flight Training Tutor Lab. He asked me to consider coming to work. Another flight instructor named Justin Johnson contacted me and said he wanted me to come to work for them as well. January 29, 2007, I met Bill Baker, who managed the Flight Training Tutor Lab, and on this day I met with him to fill out paperwork for the job. February 1 was the first day Lincoln and I went to work in the Flight Training Tutor Lab. On February 5, Bill contacted me and told me I was officially hired. I signed papers after taking my birth certificate and student identification to Student Employment Services. He had me sign a confidential document and two other documents.

Surprise Birthday Party

Saturday, February 3, 2007, Nance put together a surprise thirty-fifth birthday party for me. That afternoon, Walt Reidi showed up at five o'clock. Jack and Kathy Ottoson, Travis and Terra Brock, Travis's mom and dad, Michelle, Sandra Mora, Dan, Karen, Drew, Dr. Marv, Andrew Coffman, Scott Kegley and his wife Anna; their son Chris, Ruth and Dick Brown, Valerie Rogers, Mike and Letty Kolb, and Letty's son Dennis all surprisingly showed up. Travis and Terra gave me a nice baseball hat and a Dale Earnhardt Jr. Budweiser shirt. I got a nice card from Jack and Kathy. Valerie gave me a fifty-dollar gift certificate to Olive Garden. I spoke with my brother, his wife and kids, Brent Ross, Mom, Grandma Absher, Margie Norman, Tommy and his wife, Ruth Hyde, and Davida Courtney—all who wished me a happy birthday.

Air Traffic Control Association Journal

On February 5, 2007, the *Air Traffic Control Association Journal* arrived in the mail. Lincoln and I are on the cover with Pete Dumont, the president of ATCA. In addition, a picture of a Boeing 787 Dreamliner and a picture of the FAA Administrator Marion Blakey was on it as well. On the inside of the journal were details about the scholarship recipients.

Avion Newspaper Article

Tuesday, February 6, 2007, the *Avion* newspaper came out. The author was Kelly Billings, a student at Embry-Riddle, and she wrote for the campus newspaper. She wrote a very good article, and the pictures were really good on the cover and inside. Here it is.

A New Meaning to 'Flying Blind'

by Kelly Billon

Pronounced dead on arrival, doctors worked vigilantly to revive the lifeless body airlifted in from a plane crash site. Both engines on the aircraft had failed over trees. The swollen face was unrecognizable. The jaw was broken in four places, the nose was shattered and the left eye was missing. Coupled with a severely injured head were a spine fracture, collapsed lungs and a broken leg. Doctors hesitated to operate, as there was little hope in saving him. Family and loved ones waited in the ICU center of Roanoke Regional Hospital. Sitting on the operating table in a comatose state was 26-year-old Barry Hulon Hyde.

After a 12-week stay in the hospital, Hyde returned home. Though he had a miraculous medical recovery, he was left without his sight, taste and smell. Life had presented new challenges for Hyde, but he worked through each of them one day at a time. He sighed as he recalled his time in recovery.

"It took me awhile to accept. I was as mad as could be." He also vaguely recalled his surroundings. "I remember my dreams, and in my dreams I had my sight. In my dreams, I remember the doctors and nurses."

Hyde began his recovery by relearning how to walk, but now gets around by counting steps and using a pointer cane. Two years after the accident, Hyde was introduced to a godsend. He spent 26 days in training with his assigned dog, Lincoln. They trained together walking through revolving doors, up and down escalators, and crossing streets. Lincoln, a black Labrador, serves not only as his eyes, but also his companion. Hyde, with a hand on Lincoln's head and a smile on his face explained, "Lincoln is the smartest and greatest dog I have ever been around. He is the inspiration that has allowed me to carry on living and the greatest set of eyes I will ever have now. Lincoln is worth 40,000 dollars, but I wouldn't take all the money in the world for him. I love him."

His educational goals were always a priority. Preceding the accident, he had received his commercial pilot's license and associate's degree in Business Administration. Following the accident, he completed his bachelor's degree in History while pursuing his passion: aviation. In 2000, Hyde became the first blind person to receive his advanced ground instructor and instrument ground instructor's licenses.

"The FAA didn't know what to do with me. The examiner had never given an oral test for these certifications. I passed and he said I did better than he did when he took the test. It's funny though, the examiner received a certification of achievement for testing me orally, and all I got was a license," he explained with a smile and laugh.

Hyde had Embry-Riddle in his future plans for years. With his passion for aviation, ERAU was the place for him to continue his master's in Aviation Science and Aeronautics. He moved to the area in August of 2005, and began school.

"It has been a dream come true, I never thought I would be able to continue with my aviation career. It has been an awesome experience."

Hyde has maintained a 4.0 GPA with plans to teach part time in the flight training lab on campus. While teaching new pilots, he wishes to pursue his doctorate.

"I didn't think it was possible, but I'm here and I'm doing it. I know God has a purpose for me."

Hyde sits in the crowded University Center with other students and faculty. Lincoln wags his tale under the table as he enjoys his lunch. A friendly, lively dog, Lincoln sets his head on welcoming laps. Barry is told what is on his plate by clock positions. The time is told to him by holding a button on his watch. He talks with a smile and has jokes on hand. When asked about the cold weather, he explained that he enjoys the Florida sunshine; the cold weather is difficult due to the metal plates throughout his body. Despite all of the medical trauma and challenges he has faced, Hyde has a wonderful outlook on life and is an amazing individual.

Eight years, eight months and five days ago, Hyde was pronounced dead; he recalls the date to this accuracy. Six years ago, he became the first blind person to receive his advanced ground instructor's license and instrument ground instructor's license. Today, he continues to follow his dream, living life to the fullest.

Nance picked up several copies of the newspaper. That afternoon, after arriving back home, there was a message on the voice mail from a news writer with the *Daytona Beach News Journal*. I contacted him, and we planned on meeting on Thursday in the Flight Training Tutor Lab where he interviewed me. Afterward, we went outside and the photographer took pictures of Lincoln and me.

The Daytona Beach News Journal
February 13, 2007

Blind man's aeronautical dream
no flight of fancy

By MARK HARPER
Education Writer

DAYTONA BEACH—Sometimes a tear will creep down his cheek, though not because of any particular sadness or joy. Barry Hulon Hyde just has a face that works differently.

Barry Hulon Hyde, right, shares a laugh with Bill Baker, left, manager of Aeronautical Science Laboratories, in the College of Aviation lab at Embry-Riddle Aeronautical University recently.

Since a plane crash almost nine years ago, he cannot see or smell and has very little ability to even taste. Sometimes fluid forms a tear that randomly drips down his cheek because it is blocked from entering his reconstructed nasal cavity.

Other times, he cries because of sorrow. He felt those emotions when his father succumbed to a heart attack in 1999, and again when his girlfriend died two years ago. More often than before his accident, Hyde gets angry and impatient. But that humanity, that hunger to better himself, has also propelled him forward.

Just two years after his accident, he became the Federal Aviation Administration's first ever fully licensed, blind ground instructor.

Now 35, Hyde is the first blind student ever to attend Embry-Riddle Aeronautical University. He wants to someday become a professor there, teaching others to fly safely.

"Probably the best student I have," said Dr. Donald Metscher, an assistant professor of applied aviation sciences. "Working in academia, I think he would do excellent."

Yet he's proud of his good ol' boy roots, too. The son of a rodeo champion and a flight attendant, Hyde grew up in Kannapolis, the western North Carolina birthplace of NASCAR drivers Dale Earnhardt and Dale Earnhardt Jr. He first became interested in aviation when his uncle and cousin, both pilots, started taking him skyward about the time he was 10.

"Flying was my favorite hobby of all. I'd rather have done that than anything, man," Hyde said in an interview last week. "Fishing, flying, and chasing pretty women, and not necessarily in that order."

By age 26, Hyde had more than 1,600 flight hours and worked as a flight instructor. His dream to pilot a race team seemed within reach, as he once served as co-pilot in an airplane that flew NASCAR Chairman Brian France from Cape Cod to Concord, N.C.

Hyde's mother, Brenda Carpenter, helped land him an interview for a pilot's job at a regional airline, U.S. Airways Express. That was scheduled for June 8, 1998.

A week before, on June 1, Hyde agreed to accompany a less experienced pilot on a flight from Concord to Lewisburg County, W.Va., in a rented twin-engine Comanche. thirty-seven minutes into the flight, both main fuel tanks ran dry, stopping the engines. A preflight check by the pilot should have recognized the shortage of fuel in the main tanks, Hyde later contended in a lawsuit against the pilot.

The Comanche crashed in a thicket of trees near Floyd, Va. Both the pilot and Hyde were hurt, Hyde worse. He broke 14 bones, including nine in his face. Both lungs collapsed. He lost four teeth.

"The doctors, when I got to the hospital, asked the paramedics to go back to the scene to locate my (left) eye," Hyde said. But that wasn't necessary. A doctor later found the eye behind Hyde's cheekbone.

When Hyde emerged from a 20-day coma, vision in his right eye was very poor, and it got worse, as a cataract developed, blocking virtually all light from his detection. He is considered legally blind, but holds out hope that he will someday be able to restore some vision when the cataract can be safely removed.

After nearly a decade and a failed lawsuit, Hyde remains bitter about the accident, but his prevailing moods more often involve gratitude and wonderment. He is thrilled at the recognition he's been getting, including being featured in the Avion student newspaper and on the cover of a trade publication with the FAA Administrator Marion Blakey.

He's had help. His mother, he says, was especially important after the accident, coaching him and encouraging him through rehabilitation and learning living skills at the Rehabilitation Center for the Blind in Raleigh.

He dated Kendra Harrington until the diabetes that took her sight later took her life in 2005. She supported him through his undergraduate days as a history major at the University of North Carolina at Charlotte.

More recently, Hyde has been living with girlfriend Nancy Riedel, who does all of the cooking and cleaning. Riedel also helped him get acquainted with another important figure in his life, Lincoln, his black Labrador guide dog.

"I still have a very large desire and I want to be a part of aviation," Hyde said. "I want to teach other people and make sure what happened to me does not happen to them. Maybe that's the reason God left me here."

As a graduate student, he's researching preflight safety. After earning his master's degree in May, Hyde plans to stay in Daytona Beach, teaching at Embry-Riddle while doing his doctoral work online.

Marvin Smith, a professor of applied aviation sciences at Embry-Riddle, wrote in a letter of recommendation: "(We) marvel at his positive attitude, determination, and most of all—his resourcefulness." Because of his blindness, Hyde has developed a study technique that's more effective than most students'. He records his professors' lectures, then listens to them a second time at home while he types notes into his computer. Later, he reviews his notes using a screen reader. He also uses the screen reader to review his textbooks, most of which don't come in Braille.

The approach has helped Hyde maintain a perfect grade-point average of 4.0. It's enough to bring a few tears—not just his own—at graduation.

Eddie Money's Concert

In early February of 2007, Nance, Lincoln, and I went to Eddie Money's concert in Daytona Beach. This concert was a couple of weeks before the Daytona International 500 Race. Eddie Money and his band put on a great concert. He sang one song he wrote about Dale Earnhardt. A couple of favorite songs he performed were "Shakin'" and "Two Tickets to Paradise."

VIP on Air Radio Interview

Friday, February 16, 2007, Simon from Glasgow, Scotland, contacted me. The radio station is in the United Kingdom, and they are going to do a telephone interview with me on Tuesday at 10:00 a.m. on February 20. Simon called me again on February 19 and said they would be in contact Tuesday morning at eleven o'clock. Tuesday morning, February 20, 2007, I interviewed with the radio station, VIP on Air. In addition, this day is the birthday of my father, and he would have been sixty-three years old.

VIP on Air Radio

Tuesday, February 20, 2007, a woman from Glasgow, Scotland, contacted me with the Visually Impaired on Air Radio. The Scottish woman put me on hold, and I listened to a song playing, then she handed me off to the announcer. He said, "Next, we are going to applaud for our Daytona Beach News. This is the safest place for various kinds of travel. Daytona Beach News Journal, in Florida, USA, recently published an article about a blind man named Barry Hulon Hyde, 'Dream of No Flight of Fancy.' Since a plane crash almost nine years ago, Barry Hulon Hyde cannot see, nor actually can he smell, and has very little taste ability. Sometimes, fluid forms and a tear that drips down his cheek because it is blocked from entering his reconstructive nasal cavity from a very serious accident. Nearly two years after that, he became the Federal Aviation Administration's first ever fully licensed blind ground instructor. He is thirty-five, and he is the first blind student to attend the Aeronautical University, and that is Embry-Riddle Aeronautical University. And once he is in, he wanted to become a professor there, teaching others to fly and fly safely. Barry is on the line." I say hi.

"Hi, Barry, and thanks for joining us."

I said, "Yes, sir, hello, how are you doing?"

"We are good, how are you?"

"I am very well, thanks for asking, sir."

"Thanks for asking. Barry, we just read a little about your story there. Maybe you could tell us a little about the accident that changed your life."

I explained, "Yes, sir, June 1, 1998, I boarded the airplane as a passenger, and we crashed thirty-seven minutes later. I was pronounced dead on arrival at Roanoke Regional Hospital. I was in a coma for twenty days, my goodness. I had fourteen broken bones, both collapsed lungs, left eye knocked out, and severe head trauma. I had several metal plates put in my face, a metal rod in my leg. Goodness, man, I was in the hospital for, I guess probably, three months. My jaws were wired shut for ten weeks. As I said, it was a lot of trauma."

The radio interviewer said, "Barry, those were such horrific injuries. How did you manage to recover from it relatively quickly, by your story?"

"Wow, I guess my faith in dear God and the support of my family, my mother, my brother, my loved ones, and everyone around me that allowed me to carry on and giving me the support that I needed. Then, my guide dog, Lincoln, came through, and he provided me the motivation and inspiration that I needed to carry on."

The radio announcer asked, "Was flying always in your blood, and was that a dream to be a pilot?"

I answered, "Yes, sir, I had two cousins that were pilots, and they owned a grass strip there in Kannapolis, North Carolina, where I am originally from, and they provided me the drive that I needed to carry on and become a pilot. They showed me all the rewards that came from being a pilot as well as the work I needed to do to be able to become a pilot in that fashion. They had a lot of things that I learned from, and this helped me to become the pilot that I wanted to be."

The announcer stated, "After the accident, you mentioned that your family was a great support to you. Did you have a determination to get involved in aviation again?"

I explained, "Yes, I never wanted to leave aviation. That was my life before the accident, and I wanted to continue in some way after the accident. Of course, I wanted to prove to my case and to everyone else that the negligence that had occurred caused me the injuries that I attained and suffered from. I felt that I needed to carry on, and I wanted to carry on and I wanted to be involved in aviation."

The announcer stated, "To get back into aviation, you obviously encountered some obstacles and problems you had to overcome, and do any of them stick out in your mind?"

I explained, "Yes, one for example, in aviation, there are not any textbooks in an audible format—a legible format that blind people in an audible sound or on tapes to listen to or learn from in aviation—because they have never had any blind folks to pursue Aviation."

The announcer said, "You obviously conquered that. You changed their minds. What were people's reactions to you wanting to get back into aviation and you wanting to be an instructor again?"

"Well, people opened the door for me, and I just learned the material in the best way that I could. That was repetitiously learning the test questions to pass the written test, and the FAA had an examiner named Rich Burns. He gave me the test orally for the first time in the FAA's history. They had never given a test in that format. They always gave it in a written or computer format, and someone with vision would take the test. I had to have the examiner orally read me the test and ask me the questions. He did so, and I passed the test and I was very proud to do so. He says that I scored higher than he did on it."

We laughed, and he said, "That is a plus point. Tell us about this course that you are qualified through the Federal Aviation Administration and you are able to instruct from the ground."

I explained, "Yes, sir, the FAA tells me I am the first blind advanced ground instructor and instrument ground instructor in the world. I feel that is a large accomplishment, and both tests were given by the same examiner, Rich Burns, who worked for the FAA. He orally asked me the questions, and then he would type in the answers on the computer and we would go through the test questions until I answered them all."

The announcer inquires, "What would you be actually doing instructing a student or pilot?"

"I would help them pass the written test, I would teach them all the different sections and parts whether it would be for a private, instrument rating, commercial, flight instructor, or airline transport pilot license. Any of those I can teach on the ground, and I can teach them the parts, procedures, regulations, whether it be airplane procedures, general operating procedures. Any of the stuff that can be done on the ground, I can teach it. I can sign them off to go and take the written tests when I feel they can pass that written test."

The radio announcer stated, "It is remarkable, and also, you will be completing your master's degree."

"Sir, I will graduate May 7, and the master's of science will be in aeronautics and the specializations will be in aviation safety. How ironic since living through a plane crash! And then the other specialization will be in aviation operations." The announcer said, "Now, Barry, I am a guide dog owner myself. I have a Lab retriever cross. He makes quite a difference to my life, and does Lincoln do the same for you?"

I explained, "Yes, sir, he has opened doors for me that would still be closed. I mean, with a white cane, I would not be where I am at today, but with my guide dog, he has provided me the eyesight that I needed to carry on and continue living in the way I wanted to. Not really the way I wanted to, but in the next best way. He is such a lovable companion like no other. You know, I would not take all the money in the world for that wonderful animal."

The announcer said, "Yes, Barry, we chatted with a man called Miles Hilton Barber, and he is blind himself. He flies and is about to undertake a flight from London to Australia in microlight. Can you see yourself perhaps doing that? Would you like to try that?"

"Yes, sir, that would be awesome, I would love to experience something like that."

The announcer said, "Barry, it has been a pleasure talking to you. Good luck with the rest of your studies, and thanks for joining us today."

"You are more than welcome, sir, and best of luck to you!"

He said, "Thank you, Barry," and I said, "Yes, sir, God bless!"

"Boeing" Presentation

Tuesday, February 20, 2007, I participated in a group presentation on Boeing. The presentation was for the leadership class for Dr. Metscher's MSA 616 class. The slides shared with the class were about William Edward Boeing and how he built the company Boeing.

B-24 Liberator Witchcraft

Sunday afternoon, February 25, 2007, Nance, Lincoln, and I went to the Flagler County Airport in Florida to see the bombers that airplane rides were offered on. The B-24 Liberator, the B-17, Flying Fortress, and the B-25 Mitchell were offering rides. I bought a ride on the B-24 Liberator Witchcraft for $425 for a flight that lasted for about thirty-five minutes. The airplane used four 1,200 horsepower Pratt and Whitney radial engines with 14 cylinders a piece to power the airplane. One aspect I remember is the airplane had a pole stuck under the tail, so it would not fall down onto the tail and cause damage. When the engines start and run, the prop wash sent enough lift over the tail to keep weight off the tail. It was a try-cycle gear, but the rear of the airplane was heavy. In addition, I met the pilot, and he was a graduate from Embry-Riddle in 1959.

Associated Press

Tuesday, February 27, 2007, Mark Harper, the news writer with the *Daytona Beach News Journal* contacted me through email. He shared with me about the article with the *Associated Press* being in the Jacksonville paper and in the Sarasota paper. He stated someone from Indiana contacted him, and Mark passed that person's email to me. That person wanted to discuss some blind issues with me. A friend of Ferrell James, Tom Hornsby, told him that he read about me in the Miami Herald.

Division of Blind Services Presentation

Wednesday, February 28, 2007, we went to the Division of Blind Services in Daytoana Beach, Florida. Mary Ann West worked there, and she came and picked Lincoln and me up and drove us there to the rehabilitation center. I spoke in front of thirty people about the accident I lived through. I shared with them the accident, the people who helped save my life, my rehabilitation, my education, my will to live, and my dreams for the future. A friend, Pete Scirello, worked there, and he is a member of the National Federation of the Blind as well. Mary Ann brought Lincoln and me home in the school van.

Aircraft Owners and Pilots Association (AOPA)

Monday, March 12, 2007, I found out that Alisha Miller wanted to interview me on Wednesday afternoon at 2:30 p.m. AOPA found out about my story through the *Lakeland Newspaper* in Florida. The article in the newspaper they read was the same article that was in the *Daytona Beach News Journal*. However, it did not have the pictures of the crash and of me that were in the journal. The *Lakeland Newspaper* had a picture of Lincoln and me as well as the Bill Baker and the article had a different title. On Wednesday afternoon, I spoke with Alisha who worked for AOPA, and she interviewed me for forty minutes. She told me that the article should come out in E-Pilot in the next week or two. Alisha said that there was a chance it would come out in the AOPA magazine. In addition, that evening Wednesday, Nance helped me pick out the pictures to send Alisha, and Nance mailed them the pictures the next day. Monday, March 26, Linda with AOPA contacted me through email and the note said over 410,000 AOPA members received the E-Pilot.

AOPA ePilot online newsstory - Volume 9, Issue 12 • March 23, 2007

Severe accident redirects pilot's life

A serious accident in a Piper Twin Comanche in 1998 changed Barry Hulon Hyde's flight plan for his future. The accident left Hyde legally blind, yet he still pursued his love for aviation. In 2000, he became the first blind person to receive FAA advanced ground and instrument ground instructor licenses, and now he's the first blind student at Embry-Riddle Aeronautical University's Daytona Beach, Florida, campus. He is set to graduate in May with a master of science in aeronautics and specializations in aviation safety and aviation operations.

But it's been a turbulent ride getting to this point. In 1998, at the age of 26, Hyde had logged about 1,600 hours of flight time, was a certificated flight instructor in single- and multiengine aircraft, and was on his way to becoming a regional airline pilot.

On June 1 that year, one week before he was scheduled to interview for a regional airline pilot position, he was critically injured in a Piper Twin Comanche accident. Hyde was riding along on a flight from North Carolina to West Virginia when the aircraft ran out of fuel in its main tanks and crashed in Virginia.

With two collapsed lungs, multiple broken bones in his face, and a broken leg, Hyde fought to stay alive. He lost his left eye in the accident and damaged the optic nerve in his right. A cataract also grew over the right eye, leaving him legally blind.

Yet Hyde still pursued his love for aviation. In 2000, he became the first blind person to receive FAA advanced ground and instrument ground instructor licenses.

Later, he decided to continue his quest in the aviation world at ERAU. Because most aviation materials, like textbooks, don't come in Braille or on audiotapes, Hyde must record class lectures, listen to them at home, type notes on his computer, and then use a screen reader to review them.

All that work seems to have paid off though, he carries a 4.0 grade point average.

"In aviation, there are zero ways for a blind person to have something to read," Hyde says, later explaining, "I hope to teach the blind that there is technology that is available for the blind and that it will help in the learning of all aspects of aviation."

In June, Hyde hopes to begin teaching at ERAU while simultaneously pursuing his doctorate in business administration. His goal is to become a full-time professor at ERAU or to work for the National Transportation Safety Board or the FAA (he hasn't ruled out shooting for FAA administrator).

Ultimately, Hyde wants to prevent pilots from encountering the same fate as him. That's why he tutors students at ERAU's flight training lab, helping them prepare for their FAA written, oral, and flight tests.

While he's only gone flying with fellow pilots about a dozen times since the accident, he says it's "still just as fun to go up" now as it was when he could see. He hasn't given up hope that someday he'll be able to fly PIC again, whether aviation technology develops to the point that pilots can fly blind or he finds a procedure that can restore sight in his right eye.

"I miss seeing and living the normal life I lived for 26 years," Hyde explains. "But I'm blessed to be where I am."

Greater Miami Aviation Association and the Batchelor Aviation Scholarship Fund

Tuesday, April 3, 2007, Bill Rivenbark with the greater Miami Aviation Association and the Batchelor Aviation Scholarship fund emailed me to let me know that they were considering me for another scholarship. He shared with me in the email that since I was being considered for the scholarship, I did not have to drive down to Miami for the interview. The email stated that if I was chosen as a scholarship recipient, I would be invited to the luncheon on May

9 and to the gala in November. I took the email to mean that I had that one in the bag.

Florida Council for the Blind Scholarship

Monday morning, April 16, 2007, Barbara Grill contacted me and shared with me about being chosen for a $1,500 scholarship. She congratulated me, and she contacted me on Tuesday to share the details and reservations of the conference in Tallahassee, Florida.

Presentation on Marion Clifton Blakey

Monday afternoon, April 16, 2007, I gave a presentation on Marion Clifton Blakey to Don Metscher's MSA 616 leadership class. I began by stating, "Good afternoon, class. Today, I will be presenting Marion Clifton Blakey." Dr. Metscher read the PowerPoint slides beginning with the history, review of leadership qualities, and summary of her background. I explained she was from Gadsden, Alabama, and born in 1948. She is married to William Ryan Dooley, and they have one twenty-year-old daughter. I asked Dr. Metscher to read the next slide. He began, "Her history, background, and education are a bachelor's degree, which came from John Hopkins, and she attended the University of Florence, Italy, although she did not get a degree from there."

I asked him to continue. He said, "Let's see, background, sworn in on September 13, 2002, as the fifteenth administrator for the FAA. She was the second woman to hold this position, responsible for regulating, advancing safety of airways, operating the world's largest aviation system."

I stated, "With her becoming the fifteenth administrator, therefore, she became the second female administrator. Does anyone want to tell me the first woman?" Several classmates answered, "Jane Garvey."

I continued, "You are correct. Okay, moving on."

Dr. Metscher continued, "Leadership positions held—four previous presidential appointments, two of which required Senate confirmation. She served as a Commerce education national endowment of humanities, the White House, and the United States Department of Transportation."

I stated the four presidential appointments held began with Reagan. She began with Reagan, then Bush Senior, Clinton, and now Bush. Originally, on September 13, 2002, she received appointment a year and two days later after 911 that she came into office. She originally declined President Bush's first offer. She accepted his second time he offered the position to her.

Dr. Metscher continued reading the slide, "From 1992 to 1993, administrator of the Department of Transportation, National Highway Traffic Safety Administration. She held the national leading highway official, was instrumental in reducing deaths, injuries, and economic losses resulting from motor vehicle crashes."

I stated, "These are huge deals, and this is where her safety process began in this whole role here in the early nineties—the Highway Traffic Transportation, the DOT, if you will. Beforehand, she was the chair of the NTSB.

Dr. Metscher stated, "I did not know that she came from traffic safety."

"Yes, sir."

He continued, "Leadership initials, NTSB Chairman. She worked to improve NTSB accident reporting process, increased industry and regulatory responsiveness to the NTSB safety recommendations, managed key accident investigations including the crash of American Airlines Flight 87 in November 2001."

I explained, "Now, does anyone remember anything about that plane crash? This plane crash was the second largest and deadliest crash in the United States and killed five people on the ground. I think it shows her surveying the tail, if you will."

Dr. Metscher said yes. I began by stating that 911 occurred two months prior to this accident, so everyone thought it was a terrorist activity. "Therefore, everyone was paranoid about the terrorist activity but come to find out it was an engineering problem in an Airbus A300."

Dr. Metscher said, "Okay, next slide. Review of leadership techniques and abilities. Directive—how to implement safety and participative with the US Airways captain."

I asked him to stop right there, and I said "Directives, sir. Now, we know her being such a safety-oriented type of woman and specializing in safety. She is giving her directions what she feels needs to be in place, and everyone under her is following what she wants. Therefore, to me, that is how I feel she is being directive. Next is participative, about her following. Therefore she is not a pilot, and she has upper level management skills required for her position. So therefore, the participative part that I have included here in is that she flew with US Airways pilots up and down the East Coast to figure out how or if things were occurring in the airway system and how to go about fixing those things. She went and put hands on declaration on what is occurring in our airway system by flying with pilots. I thought that was extremely beneficial to her role in safety. Next, we have her being charismatic. She has a large amount of education. She has a large role in safety as the fifteenth administrator."

Dr. Metscher explained the next slide, "Summary of analysis of leadership. Successful leaders Marion Blakey works creatively with—there is a list here."

I interrupted, "This is where I want to say something about Aircraft Owners and Pilots Association and Phil Boyer, the president of AOPA. Phil Boyer said she had a very studious process working with the Republicans, Democrats, and the Congress. He said the half dozen administrators that he has dealt with, she is the most studious of all of them. I thought that was a large compliment coming from Phil Boyer. However, he is opposed to several of her beliefs."

Dr. Metscher continued to read the next slide, "Marion talked forth and creatively with the FAA, NTSB, NBAA, AOPA, ALPA, ATCA, NATCA, and ICAO. There is a picture, and it shows her commissioned as a new runway in Atlanta, Hartsfield. The new runway, 10/28, costs $1.28 billion, expected to reduce delays by increasing the airport's capacity to handle more flights."

I stated, "Definitely, I agree with that, and I feel once again, she is very participative and charismatic. She is there with hands-on approach to the FAA or the safety of the airway system and airports."

Dr. Metscher explained the next slide, "The FAA is doing what it has always done, following the leader, then change comes. The list shows 911 then price of fuel."

I stopped him and said, "Let me interrupt you there, sir. I want everyone to understand where this came from. She gave a presentation on February 28, 2006, to the Commercial Aviation Forecast Conference. Marion was talking about when a snowstorm that came through and she began talking about a snowplow situation. A man went to pick up a package, came out with this package, and loaded it into his car. He saw this snowplow, and the visibility was almost zero. Marion began talking about this man driving the car, and she said he thought he could fall behind the snowplow and follow him and get to where he is going. As this man is following this snowplow, about thirty minutes went by, the snowplow stops. He came back and tapped on the guy's window and asked, 'Where are you going?' The guy driving the car answered, 'I am going up to Morgantown,' and the snowplow driver said, 'You would not get there going this way.' He said, 'I am plowing a parking lot.' Marion told us about following the leader. Not all of these years the FAA is following the leader and come to find out it is not working anymore. All of this time, the FAA did everything correctly and has worked by pilots and controllers. Next, the fuel price issue came. She talked about the Joe Blow aviator and the trickle-down effect. An example wants a seventy-cent tax on a gallon of fuel. This tax will surely affect aviation. Next are user fees. You would not go to Hartsfield Airport in Atlanta or come to Daytona Beach International Airport and pay the user fees. You can go to an uncontrolled airport to buy fuel and not pay for the user fees. One more factor, when Reagan fired controllers during the PATCO strike in the early eighties, now this is playing part because these people are reaching retirement age. The age requirement for pilots increased from sixty to sixty-five. Well, for me, they are going to change the age requirement for pilots for them carrying passengers but not going to change the age requirement for air traffic controllers watching the airways. I asked, 'What is going on with these people?' You would think they would be decreasing the age requirement for pilots and increasing the age requirement for air traffic controllers."

Dr. Metscher continued sharing the slide information. "On 911, price of fuel, user fees, age of pilots, and retirees for air traffic control need to be replaced. ICAO paralleling the US for pilot's age increased. Then, at the bottom, it says all of a sudden, 'follow the leader' does not work anymore. An employee says, 'I love my boss.' The administrator position is a political appointment. I believe she will be gone when her term is up. I see her job as providing direction at the corporate level whether a pilot or not. She is at the top of a business where management skills will be more important. Marion Blakey is a terrific leader. Any questions?"

I said thank you, and the students applauded for five seconds. Dr. Metscher said, "Very good. Regardless of what you personally think of Marion Blakey, she is a good politician because she does not really have an aviation background. You have shown that, and yes, she has learned the vocabulary necessary to be a leader in that position. You are going to face this as leaders no matter what job you go into, even if it is in aviation. As you move from one department to another and every time you move, there is a whole set of acronyms and things to learn. For example, what you want to do is what she did, ride with pilots and surround herself with people that are knowledgeable and made sure they educate her very quickly. You have to learn the language of the department you are in and at least be able to speak intelligently about the main subjects that are involved in that department, and that all comes down to leadership skills. If you are going to be working for the FAA, it is nice to have some aviation experience, but she has proven that you do not have to depending on the job. You just have to have good leadership skills."

Who's Who in Universities and Colleges

Thursday, April 19, 2007, I found out that I became a Who's Who Student in universities and colleges. I became a member of Who's Who, and there is a chance that I would be selected as Chancellor's Pick or the student chosen from Embry-Riddle.

Presentation on Pratt & Whitney

Tuesday afternoon, April 24, 2007, I gave a presentation in a suit and tie on Pratt and Whitney to Dr. Don Metscher's production and procurement class. Dr. Metscher introduced me and stated that I was going to speak about Pratt and Whitney, the added technology company. He said, "That was the opening slide with a jet engine on it."

I began by stating,

> Yes sir. Good afternoon everyone, this is Barry and Lincoln the Navigator once again. We will be discussing Pratt and Whitney. Once every five seconds somewhere throughout the world, a Pratt and Whitney engine powers the aircraft. I will begin with an overview, the history of the company, the engine development, and then the summary of analysis. So, let us start with the company beginning. Francis Pratt and Amos Whitney began in 1860 during the civil war. They worked for the Colt manufacturer assembling pistols. I asked if everyone was familiar with Eli Whitney of the cotton gin, the cousin of Amos Whitney. In early 1900, Edward Deeds buys the rights to the Wright Brothers name in 1915. Deeds invented the National Cash register and I assumed this was what came up with the amount of what you owed when

145

purchasing something. In addition, he came up with DELCO, which was Daytona Engineering Laboratories. In 1918, Edward Deeds sells out to Mack Trucking. I thought that was historical, since I did not know that Mack Trucking began in 1918. Historically, the president of that company was Frederick renchelor and his role is important because he and Boeing come together further down the road. In 1924, the board does not want to follow what he wants to do in engineering and developing of airplanes. The government's request if you will, so by 1924, Renchelor gets out of the company and by 1927, he and Boeing get together and the airmail industry begins. Boeing puts together the Wasp engines to power a 40-model airplane. In 1928, Boeing and Renchelor bought Pacific Air Transport and in 1928 merged with Hamilton and Vought, the engine manufacturer. Vought, a big engine manufacturer, and everyone is familiar with the Corsair that was a very awesome single piston engine airplane and powered by Pratt and Whitney engines. In 1932, Donald Douglas introduced the new Curtiss Wright cyclone engine and it was in direct competition with Pratt and Whitney. Pratt and Whitney supplies four airplanes, beginning with the Hell-Cat, Corsair, Curtiss Commando, the bomber, B-24 Liberator and I rode in this airplane a couple of months ago. That was one of the most awesome rides I have ever been a part of in my life.

Dr. Metscher says, "That is a beautiful looking airplane, isn't it? They really restored that well."

I have to say that airplane has four Pratt and Whitney engines on it. Each engine has 14 cylinders per engine and has 1,200 horsepower on each one of those engines. You can just imagine what it felt like for me on takeoff, I was like oh gosh, I just held on. The decibel level was 110 decibels and that loudness was the reason I did not take Lincoln. Next World War II comes about and 129,000 engines produced. They came out with a license and this allowed them to produce another 234,000 more engines. The next part of history was the engines for the F-100 for the Blue Angels. This particular engine was in the F-100 that recently crashed. Pratt and Whitney are in direct competition with General Electric's F-104. The man I spoke with who worked with Pratt and Whitney for 33 years said he spoke with a blue Angel pilot. The pilot quoted to him that was the most responsive engine that he had ever flown. The pilot told him that none of the pilots had ever turned the engines wide open. They never had to go there for maximum performance. There were restrictions that would not let them take the engines wide open. Next, brought us to 1951 and 1952, I asked, was anyone familiar with the atomic engines. Does anyone know anything about the atomic engines? There were two atomic engines built, one by Pratt and Whitney and another built by General electric. The two are located in Atomic city, Idaho on display. I never knew anything about them or knew of their existence. These two engines were in place by the political system at the time because they could run for 60 years without stopping to refuel. The engines powered by the ums: Plutonium, lithium, columbium, titanium, magnesium, and others. The metallurgists that I interviewed that worked for Pratt and Whitney that I discussed this presentation with the 1962 president, John F. Kennedy shut that system down. Simply, because it was so explosive and had so much power and you know what a pea looks like and you could drop one of the ums the size of a pea on the ground and it would blow a whole the size of 6 foot square crater in the ground. He said they would heat these ums up to 5,000 Fahrenheit and then flake them off to produce the power for these engines. In 1971, the summary of analysis, how much money the company is making and how much they are worth. In 1971, Pratt and Whitney sales were only valued at two billion dollars. In 1982, their sales were over 13 billion dollars. In 1990, their sales were over 21 billion dollars. In 2006, their revenue is over 11 billion dollars. The slides show the engines may be Boeing, Airbus, and military. In addition, Pratt and Whitney engines are in the F-15 eagle, the F-16 Falcon, the F-22 Raptor, and the F-35 Joint Strike Fighter. I did not realize they built such magnificent engines. In closing, 38,442 employees supply over 9,000 companies in over 180 countries throughout the world.

I asked, "Any questions?" Dr. Metscher stated, "I worked the F-15 Eagle that had the Pratt and Whitney F-100 engines. The F-16 I worked had the GE engines. The companies put out similar engines, and the government tries to make sure they both stay in business and they both have the same type of engines. The F-15, I thought with the Pratt and Whitney motor in it, was a very forgiving engine. The GE engine I worked with was on the F-16 being a single engine aircraft. I do not think it was as forgiving, and I worked several incidents and accidents involving flameouts of the GE aircraft engines. The F-15 with two engines—I can remember pilots coming back and complaining that they had multiple after-burner blowouts and different problems, but the engine never really quit. So I think even the pilots seem to like the Pratt and Whitney over the GE. Although, the pilots said the General Electric was more powerful, and they were tweaked just right, but they were not as forgiving." The students clapped about four seconds. In addition, I scored a 97 on his final written exam.

Letter from United Captain

Tuesday, April 24, 2007, I received a letter from a United Captain. The man sent the letter from California to the office of Dr. John Johnson, the President of Embry-Riddle. The office sent the letter to me. That man thought it was great how I continued on after my misfortune. The pilot thought it was great that I was recognized by ERAU.

Greater Miami Aviation Association and Batchelor Aviation Scholarship Fund

Wednesday, April 25, 2007, I received an email from Bill Rivenbark, the chairman of the scholarship committee. He emailed me with the details that the Greater Miami Aviation Association and the Batchelor Aviation Scholarship Fund awarded me a second scholarship. The value of this scholarship was worth $7,500. They invited Nance, Lincoln, and me to their luncheon on May 9.

Embry-Riddle Aeronautical University Senate

Friday afternoon, April 27, 2007, Nance, Lincoln, and I went to the Hampton Inn in Daytona Beach. We met Buddy Counts and quite a few of the faculty senate of Embry-Riddle. They fed us lunch, and I stood up with Lincoln and spoke for around five minutes. I discussed the accident, becoming the first and only advanced ground instructor and the first and only blind instrument ground instructor in the world for the FAA, the scholarship from Embry-Riddle, and the degree I was seeking. In addition, I shared with them about my future goals of wanting to work for Embry-Riddle, the FAA, or the NTSB. I told them thank you, and I felt very blessed to have been asked to speak in front of them.

Embry-Riddle Aeronautical University

The next great accomplishment in my life was graduating from Embry-Riddle Aeronautical University with my master of science degree in aeronautics. I graduated with distinction, which is a perfect 4.0 grade point average. My master's degree in aeronautics has two specializations: aviation safety and aviation operations. This achievement was accomplished on May 7, 2007.

The spring semester of 2007, I taught at the Flight Training Tutor Lab on campus. I taught students and pilots about airspace, taught the safety aspects of general aviation, and Federal Aviation Regulations, parts 61, 91, and 141. As well, the pilots and I worked on filling out flight plans, receiving a weather briefing, covering the operating handbook of the airplanes at the school, and discussing visual meteorological conditions versus instrument meteorological conditions.

Achievements

In addition to graduating, during the month of May in 2007, I received three scholarships: the National Federation of the Blind Florida state chapter, the American Council of the Blind Florida state chapter, and the second one from the Greater Miami Aviation Association (GMAA)—Batchelor Aviation Scholarship Fund.

Graduation details of that awesome weekend included Lincoln, Nance, Jackson, Mom, TC, Mom's brother, Wayne Absher, Todd, Terri, Lauren, Austin, Ferrell, Bet, Ferrell II, Tammy, Taylor, Doug, Donna, Douglas, and Brandon, who fell in the pool and received five staples in his head. My best friend Deric Harrington and his date Heather Barringer; Carol Blake, who was Lincoln's puppy raiser; Tony and Atthena Mineo also went. In addition, those who attended the party were Mike, Letty, and Dennis Kolb, Ron and Marylin Deteau, and Sid McGuirk and his wife. Andrew Coffman, Dr. Marv, Scott Kegley, Jack and Kathy Ottoson, and Terra Brock also went.

Lincoln's promotion was to Lincoln the aviator. The hooding ceremony was an experience of a lifetime, and I was glad to share it with those people who were present. Dr. Marvin Smith hooded me. Nance and I hooded Lincoln, and we had pictures made with Dr. Marv. We received a standing ovation as we walked across the stage in the building on campus of ERAU in Daytona Beach.

NASCAR USA was where one party took place after the hooding ceremony. That evening was a great socializing time for the family and me. The family participated in driving the simulators and watching videos made from previous races. Very historical to be a part of!

Graduating from Embry-Riddle Aeronautical University

Graduation took place on May 7, 2007. That morning while waiting for the program to start and making pictures with classmates, the president's wife Maury Johnson came and gave Lincoln an Embry-Riddle bandanna to wear that she ordered from the Prescott campus. As Nance, Lincoln, and I crossed the stage and we shook hands with the president, Dr. John Johnson and the Dean, Tom Brady. We had our picture made with the diploma certificate in hand. As we sat in the crowd of all the graduates, there was a picture made from the back of the coliseum, and Lincoln was very visible in the aisle on the left of me. Degrees Conferred for Spring 2007 for the Daytona Beach Campus: Associates: 0; Bachelors: 370; and Masters: 45. It took several hours for 415 graduates to receive their certificates.

Second GMAA Scholarship

Embry-Riddle provided one of their pilot instructors and a Cesna-172 airplane on Wednesday, May 9, 2007, to fly us roundtrip to Miami to receive the second (GMAA) Batchelor Aviation Scholarship award. The trip on the Hobbs meter totaled four hours and forty-eight minutes round trip. The Airport Marriot held the award program. The pilot's named was Jamie. She did a fine job and even let me talk on the radio to air traffic control. One thing in particular I remember is when there were many fires occurring and everyone was talking about how hazy and close to being IFR it was.

During this luncheon, William Rivenbark began by stating, "The fact that the overriding mandate of our scholarship is to finan-cially assist those who need it the most. Many of you will remember Mr. Barry Hulon Hyde from last year's award luncheon and at the gala. I am pleased to announce that Barry is a repeat recipient, and he continues to be an inspiration to us all. We are pleased to have Barry, Lincoln, and Nancy to join us today."

The crowd applauded for eight seconds. Bill explained,

> Barry was on the verge, for those of you who may not know the story, Barry was on the verge of being hired by a regional carrier, nine years ago when he was in an aircraft accident to which he was not at fault. His injuries were both serious and dramatic. However, the most serious of all was the loss of his sight, which to any of us would have been traumatic, and life altering enough. However, which as you can imagine to a pilot is

absolutely unthinkable. Most people in such a situation would come to grips with being sightless less and learn to deal with their disability. They would most likely and understandably be on disability the remainder of their lives and then get by and we would be accepting and understanding of this collectively. Barry was not accepting of this. Barry stands before us today, having been awarded a Master's of Science in Aeronautics from Embry-Riddle with a specialization in Aviation Safety and Aviation Operations.

The crowd clapped for six seconds. Bill continued to explain,

In June, Barry will begin work on his doctorate at Northcentral University in conjunction with Embry-Riddle in business with a specialization in Aeronautical Safety. Barry maintained a 4.0 at Embry-Riddle when he graduated earlier this week and his diploma noted with distinction, which is Embry-riddle's highest academic level. This past April, Barry was listed in Who's Who among students in American Universities and Colleges. It is not hard to believe that Barry is Embry-Riddle's first blind student in their 81 years of existence considering what Embry-Riddle specializes in. However, what is even more impressive is the fact that Barry is the only FAA Advanced and Instrument Ground Instructor in the United States and in the world.

The crowd applauded for five seconds. Bill continued, "Barry hopes to teach possibly at Embry-Riddle. Whether or not he ever holds a formal teaching position, he has already set an example these past few years for all of us to help deal with adversity. We are honored to have been able to assist you again, Barry. It is great to have Lincoln here again." The crowd clapped for five seconds. Nance and Bill helped Lincoln and me to the podium, and I began by stating,

Wow, good afternoon everyone. Oh man, this is really a dream! I would like to thank some people beginning with the Greater Miami Aviation Association as well as the Batchelor Foundation for recognizing Lincoln and me, for giving us the opportunity to carry my life on. Wow, I am so amazed, so thankful, so blessed, and I want to praise God and thank him every day for allowing us to carry on and to meet our goals. To allow Lincoln to serve my needs and as my guide and as my navigator, but since I graduated I am now calling him the Aviator. The crowd laughed momentarily. I would like to thank the GMAA and the Batchelor Foundation once again, and I am so blessed to graduate from Embry Riddle Monday. It is very awesome for me to be a part of history. Considering my Bachelor's Degree was in History, people ask what did you get a degree in history for? I asked how many people you know that lived through a plane crash. I figured since I lived through a plane crash that I made history, so I thought I would get me a degree in history, so I did. The crowd laughed at that statement. That degree opened up the door for me to carry on and come down here to Florida to go to school at Embry-Riddle. Phenomenally, I attended for one year and nine months for the master's degree, and how I pulled it off, which is beyond me, as well. The crowd chuckled. Man, thank God and thank everyone involved with the whole aspect. I am just so blessed, once again, thank you.

The crowd applauded for ten seconds.

Keynote Speaker for the Schepens Eye Research Institute

Wednesday, May 9, 2007, the Schepens Eye Research Institute of Harvard asked me to be a keynote speaker for their fund-raising event, Flight for Sight. Nance, Lincoln, and I flew directly out of Orlando, Florida, on Jet Blue on Saturday, June 9, 2007. This was my first flight on an Airbus A320 with Jet Blue, and it took us directly into Logan Field in Boston, Massachusetts. We flew up at an altitude of 39,000 and came home at an altitude of 41,000 feet. Bob Schepens owned the plantation and held the fundraiser and its name called Flight for Sight. A lady named Melanie Saunders who worked for Harvard picked Nance, Lincoln, and me up at the airport and drove us to the plantation. We met Mr. Collins, his wife, and many other people. The hangar was full of eighty antique cars from A-model to T-models to the limousine of Al Capone. In addition, he owned twenty-one classic airplanes like the B-24 bomber, the Liberator, Witchcraft, I rode on out of the Flagler County Airport, however only eleven were there. The eye research group asked me to speak about my love of aviation and how important it would be for me to get my eyesight back. Annmarie Ware with Harvard drove us back to the airport Sunday morning.

Florida Council of the Blind

Friday, May 18, 2007, Nance, Jackson, Lincoln, and I went to Tallahassee, Florida, to the Florida's chapter of the American Council of the Blind. Saturday morning, I was awarded the scholarship, and I spoke for five minutes. I was one out of eleven recipients awarded.

National Federation of the Blind in Florida

Over Memorial Day weekend, May 26 through 28, 2007, Nance, Jackson, Lincoln, and I attended the National Federation of the Blind of Florida scholarship convention. We had a fun time and met lots of nice people. Nance helped me to the podium, and I accepted a $1,000 scholarship check, and I spoke for five minutes. The recipients included three sighted individuals, and two of us were completely blind.

Beginning the Doctorate Degree

June 1, 2007, was the first day of beginning my doctorate degree at Northcentral University. The first day of June is the anniversary of my accident in 1998, as well it was the day I graduated high school in 1990. I have done well in my first class and passed it with an A minus.

Northcentral University Volume 1, Issue 2 June, 2007

We are proud of Barry Hulon Hyde who has taken lemons and made them into lemonade. Barry was involved in an accident in a Piper Twin Comanche aircraft in 1998. This accident changed Barry's flight plan for his future. The accident left Hyde legally blind, yet he still pursued his love for aviation. In 2000, he became the first blind person to receive FAA advanced ground and instrument ground instructor licenses and is the Federal Aviation Administration's first ever fully licensed, blind ground instructor. He has maintained a 4.0 grade point average in his academic career. Hyde is pursuing his doctorate in business administration at NCU. He tutors students at ERAU's flight training lab, helping them prepare for their FAA written, oral, and flight tests. Today, he continues to follow his dream, living life to the fullest. We are delighted to have Barry as part of the NCU family as one of our Learners.

Atlantis Liftoff

The night of June 8, 2007, at 7:38 p.m., Nance, Jackson, Lincoln, and I went to Kennedy Space Center and witnessed the space shuttle *Atlantis* lift off. The audible sound, the rumble, and the feeling was intense for forty-five to fifty seconds. The liftoff was awesome and successful!

American Institute of Aeronautics and Astronautics Scholarship

On June 15, 2007, I was informed of being awarded the American Institute of Aeronautics and Astronautics scholarship. This scholarship was awarded to me in Reno, Nevada. I presented my Graduate Research Project (GRP) that I did for ERAU and the Master's degree. I presented it orally in front of around 30 people.

Insight Radio

Monday, June 18, 2007, the Insight Radio out of the United Kingdom did a telephone interview with me. Jill Daly said, "We will talk with a blind flight instructor. We are talking about partially sighted people today, with very unusual jobs on the daily lunch, and very shortly, we will be speaking with a blind flight instructor, believe it or not. That is coming up right after this. Now today, we are talking about blind and partially sighted people with very strange jobs. They don't come any more strange than Barry Hulon Hyde. Now, Barry, you are a flight instructor, I just don't believe it!"

I said, "Yes ma'am."

Jill said, "Well, listen, how did you actually lose your sight in the first place, Barry?"

I explained, "Yes ma'am, it was in a plane crash on June 1, 1998."

"My goodness, so you actually lost your sight in a plane crash? What made you decide to go on and become a flight instructor?"

"Well, aviation was my dream, and after the plane crash, the only way to continue my career was to become an advanced ground instructor and an instrument ground instructor for the Federal Aviation Administration. That was the goal I set for myself during my rehabilitation. That was to study that material to get those licenses, and that is exactly what I did. It was my dream before the plane crash to be a part of aviation, and now it is continuing to be a part of my life."

"Most people would probably be terrified with the fact that you lost your sight in an airplane crash to begin with, and you have gone on to become an instructor. But you were not actually flying the plane, were you?"

"No, ma'am, I was a passenger, and I feel that aviation is the safest source of transportation there is, and the accident I lived through should have never happened. I still feel safer there than I do anywhere else."

Jill asked me to tell her the time between the plane crash and the time of going for my instructor licenses because there must have been a lot of time in between where I had to recuperate, come to terms with the loss of my sight, and rehabilitate.

I answered, "Yes, ma'am, there was. I felt with me working on my rehabilitation, I needed something to do to get my brain back working. The way for me to do that was to get involved in school-work and homework to help improve my short-term memory. My long-term memory was not affected too badly, but my short-term memory was in really bad shape. Going back to school was the best thing I could do for it, I felt at the time, and I feel now it was the right time to go back to school. Working on those ground instructor licenses, I felt that was the best way for me to continue my aviation passion."

"So what did the authorities say then when you actually went back to them and said, 'Okay, I have my commercial license, I am blind now, but I want to become a Flight Instructor'? I mean, people must have been a bit puzzled. Did they not sit and scratch their heads for a while?"

"Yes, the examiner had given me the actual written test, which was off the computer, so I had to have someone help me to read it audibly. The FAA had never given a blind person a test, so they first had to figure out how to test me. The examiner Rich Burns with the Federal Aviation Administration called the FAA out in Oklahoma City, and he explained that 'we have a blind person here, how do I administer his test?' They contacted Washington and then finally figured things out and told Rich just ask him the questions off the computer. 'You administer them, and we will do it that way.' Sure enough, that is the way they did it. He asked me the questions, and he would read the choices as well, and I would give him my answer. Then, when I finished the first test, he said, 'Darn, Barry, you did better than I did. How did that happen?' We will take it as long as I passed, and certainly, I did. I passed the first time."

Jill congratulated me and said, "How do people actually cope, and how do people actually feel when they get into an airplane with you? Do they not think, 'Oh my goodness, this guy beside me that is teaching me is blind.'"

"I think a lot of people feel that what I have to offer is a great deal of education, and I can pass along what I knew previously before going blind. When you say flying with student pilots, they are not students. They are pilots, but they are not students with their license. They are not necessarily students, but they are trying to improve their license, meaning they are already a private pilot, and I could help them get their commercial license, but I cannot do certain things like sign them off for certain certificates because you have to be a sighted flight instructor."

"I used to be nervous and I have very vivid memories of how the skies look and how the horizon looks when you are up above the clouds, and sometimes when I am sitting in a commercial flight, I will think about that. I will think I am so glad I saw that. I know the captain saw that, and it looked differently from the way I saw that from the window of a plane. Because it is almost panoramic and it is a most wonderful vision, and it is that something, which keeps you going when you are up there?"

"Yes, ma'am, I do miss seeing those wonderful visual images as well as being able to reference an airplane to the horizon. Seeing the sun set or sun rise, and I miss those things. But life goes on, and so do Lincoln and I."

"Now, Lincoln is your guide dog?"

"We used to call him Lincoln the Navigator, but when I graduated, we call him Lincoln the Aviator."

We laughed. Jill continued, "Wow, I have to say, I know exactly what you are talking about with the sunrise and the horizon and those things I would not have missed for the world, so I am very grateful for those memories. I am sure you are too, and Barry, it has just been fantastic talking with you today. I take my hat off for you, and I think what you have done is absolutely incredible."

"Thank you."

"Thank you very much for joining us."

"Yes, ma'am, and thank you so much for including me on your wonderful presentation, ma'am."

Jill closed by saying, "It was a pleasure."

I said, "Yes, ma'am, likewise."

Jill continued on the radio by saying, "There you go, that is Barry Hulon Hyde. We have been talking about blind people with unusual jobs today, and Barry Hulon Hyde, certainly an exception to the rule. He is honestly so incredible I am speechless. We are going to a track now. It is the Kinks, with 'Sunny Afternoon.'"

Visit to Nascar's Hangar

Sunday morning, June 24, 2007, Nance, Lincoln and I went to church and spoke with Travis Brock. He is a pilot for Nascar, and he asked me if I wanted to go and see Nascar's airplanes. Of course, I accepted the offer and Nance, Lincoln, and I went and met Travis and his wife, Terra Brock, at the Nascar hangar at the Daytona Beach International Airport. Travis let me board the Beechcraft Hawker and sit in the cockpit. Nance took our picture standing outside the Hawker as well as the Cessna 310 that was inside the hangar as well. The Hawker is the nicest airplane that I have ever sat in the cabin and cockpit of. The hangar floor was clean enough to eat off of.

Scholarship from Pastor Larry Bost

Wednesday afternoon, July 4, 2007, I received another scholarship. This one was from the reverend Dr. Larry Bost, and he is the associate pastor at the church I attend, Concordia Lutheran Church in China Grove, North Carolina. He presented this nice gift to me at my mom's home in Kannapolis. The scholarship was a check valued at $2,000.

ERAU Summer Program

Friday, July 27, 2007, Nance, Lincoln, and I gave a presentation on safety to the Summer School Academy at ERAU. Pam Peer was the director of the Summer Academy, and she invited me to share my story with the students. The students' ages were twelve to eighteen.

I shared the following:

> About June 1, 1998, my life changed dramatically. I knew I wanted to be a pilot and fly for somebody whether it was for an airline or a

race team. Then after the accident that took my eyesight, that goal changed. The role changed for me to be involved or stay in Aviation. I knew I wanted to stay involved in aviation but I did not know how.

I began studying for my Advanced Ground Instructor license. I began studying and did the application to receive Lincoln. I needed Lincoln because walking with a pointer cane is so much different than walking with a sighted animal or a sighted person. I mean when you get to a certain point, that cane does not tell you which way to go where as the animal or person will make the turn for you. So, I thought to myself, throw that cane away, I do not want that sucker. I don't know which way to go when I get to a turn. Therefore, I did that application to receive Lincoln. Now, as I return back to the month of June, the 6th, 2000, I became the first blind Advanced Ground Instructor for the FAA in the United States or in the world. I thought that was awesome.

Next, June 12, 2000, six days later, I came here to Palmetto, Florida, which is over on the west side of Florida. I began the program at Southeastern Guide Dog Incorporated to receive Lincoln. I was there in training with him for 26 days, and on June 12, they brought him into my life. I call him a God sent because he has given me more motivation than anything since going blind. After coming back home with him in mid July, I was sitting around and I thought what do I do now? It came to me to begin the Instrument Ground Instructor studies for that license. I contacted Rich Burns and told him what I wanted to do and he told me to call him when I was ready. I began studying for that test and I took it orally from Rich in October of 2000. I passed it and became the first and only blind Instrument Ground Instructor in the FAA's history. I began considering what to do now, since I had all of this time on my hands.

In May of 2001, I began working on my Bachelor's of Arts Degree in History at the University of North Carolina at Charlotte. Well, mom and I rented me an apartment and moved to Charlotte, North Carolina by myself with just Lincoln. The school was one, 800 steps one-way from my apartment. Lincoln and I walked this journey five days a week for three and a half years. I graduated in December of 2004 with my Bachelor's of Arts Degree in History. Some people ask me why did I get a degree in History. I answered, well, since I lived through a plane crash, I feel I made History so I thought I might as well get me a degree in it. The students laughed. After I attained that goal, I thought to myself, what do I do now? I knew I still wanted to continue my future in Aviation. I was learning all the History I was interested in, but I wanted to continue something involved in Aviation. Therefore, Nance, her retired guide dog, Jackson, Lincoln and I came here to Daytona and Nance said that she used to work for the guide dog school where Lincoln and Jackson came from. We came here in January of 2005 for an evaluation, which was to show everyone that if I did attend Embry-Riddle, what would I need, and the accommodations I would need. We found out everything that would be feasible for me to attend and Nance stated because you are the first blind student to attend ever. I stated I am the first blind student to attend in their 81-year history. I thought that was miraculous as well. I moved down here in August of 2005 to begin school in August. Next, I graduated May 7, 2007, with my Master's of Science Degree in Aeronautics with specializations in Aviation Safety and Aviation Operations. Nance reminded me to tell what I graduated with and what my GPA was. I graduated with distinction and that is a perfect 4.0 Grade Point Average. Next, June 1, came and can you guess what happened on this date. I began my doctorate at Northcentral University on-line and they are out of Prescott, Arizona. So, blessed am I to begin that degree. Many memorable things happened in the month of June for me. Yes, June 1, 1998 was a rough date for me, living through a plane crash is beyond me. Especially everyone here when you see the crash pictures, you all are going to be in for a surprise and I cannot wait to share with everyone what happened and why it happened. Nance said tell them the new saying you picked up from President Jack Hunt, of the University. I stated everyone is familiar with the Jack Hunt library, right. Maybe not, let me familiarize you with it. The Jack Hunt library, called that after him, and his saying to most people is "The sky is the limit, but for those who love Aviation, the sky is home". Yes, I love that saying.

Some of you may be wondering why I am sitting rather than standing. I have one broken vertebra, number 5, a degenerative disc between the shoulder blades; my right leg has a titanium rod in it because of it being broken in four places. Those are the reasons I cannot stand for long periods. Now, I will ask Nance to begin the slides for the presentation. First off, if anyone has questions you have to say hey blind man or raise your hand so we can address them, okay. I like to have everybody interact and ask questions and that way everyone gets to learn and participate. Nance says do not wait until the end, just shout out if you have questions. Please feel free to interrupt at anytime.

Nance begins by asking, "Do you want to explain the airplane that is on the slides with you and Lincoln?"

I replied, "Yes, that airplane is a 1930 model Waco. That airplane belongs to cousins in Kannapolis, North Carolina. They owned Piper J-3 Cubs and a grass strip. I rode in the Waco twice since the accident in 1998. I have been flying probably sixteen or seventeen times since the accident. I went flying in Jets, the Waco, Piper J-3 Cubs, a Cessna 172, a Cherokee 180, and a Canadair Regional Jet. We rode in our first airbus, A-320, ride on June 9 up to Boston, Massachusetts. I would like my next flight to be on the Boeing 787 Dreamliner. Let's get to the slides."

Nance said, "Since he cannot read them, I will." I checked my watch, and the students laughed. And so I played it again, reading the time.

I said, "Let me start with a joke first. Is everyone familiar with a biennial flight review? It was time for Santa Claus's biennial review."

Nance said, "We have a groaner back there. Jamie Ohaira used to be one of the instructor pilots here. We had to go to Miami back in May, and Chancellor Connolly was very kind to Barry, Lincoln, and me. At the school's expense, they flew us down to Miami for the day so Barry could speak to the Greater Miami Aviation Association. He has received two scholarships from GMAA. Therefore, Chancellor Connolly gave us a Cessna and an instructor pilot to take us to Miami for Barry to speak on behalf of Embry-Riddle. Therefore, while we are flying along, I am in the back of a Cessna with Lincoln, and Lincoln was continuing to push me over. Jamie was talking to us during the flight, and Jamie now is with one of the regional airlines out of Georgia. She is no longer an instructor here at Riddle, and she is the one who told us this joke. One of the guys in the back of the class is there going, 'Yes, he is doing the Santa Claus joke.' This joke is a compliment of a former instructor pilot here at Embry-Riddle, and Barry loves the joke."

I began by telling the students, "Santa went in front of the examiner and said, 'Sir, I would like to get my biennial flight review. The examiner said, 'Go on out and begin the preflight, and in a few minutes I will come out and we will get started.' Santa Claus went out and started checking the sled, the reindeer, and he made sure to check all the hooks. Here came the examiner carrying a shotgun, and Santa ran over to him and asked, 'What are you going to do with that?' The examiner said, 'Well, we are going to have an engine out on takeoff!' He was going to shoot one of those poor reindeer on takeoff. Remember, if you students will cut the wood, I will pile it!"

Nance and I began the presentation. Nance asked me if I wanted to give the call sign or the N-number of the airplane. I asked if anyone was familiar with what the *N* stood for on airplanes. The *N* stands for nationality. The *N* number on the airplane I crashed in was N7794Y. Nance begins reading, "It says at the top of the slide N7794Y accident investigation. The header slide includes the history, what happened, why N7794Y crashed, recommendations, and analysis. Beginning with the history and the airplane information: a 1965 PA-30 Piper Twin Comanche, all maintenance records were current and up to date. It was a four-seater. It had two 160-horsepower Lycoming engines and a total fuel capacity of ninety gallons of which only 84.5 gallons were useable. More history, do you want to explain that you were not the pilot in command?"

"I was a pilot, but I was not the pilot in command or an instructor of that airplane that day. I was a passenger and the FAA, NTSB, and the insurance stated that I was not the pilot."

"Next, pilot in command information on Robert Anderson: He was a commercial pilot with single-engine land and multi-engine land instrument airplane, and his total hours were 801, with 168 hours of multi-time, so he had more multi-engine time than you did. This is information about you as the passenger. Also listed you as a safety pilot, and do you want to tell them why this could be?"

"Yes, that was my role that day, which was to fly with him as he flew under the hood. So to meet the Federal Aviation Regulations to fly under the hood, you have to have a safety pilot on board."

"Pam is saying that they do not know what that is at this point."

I explained flying under the hood is what the pilot wears, which are foggles, a hood, or something that will prevent you from seeing over the instrument panel.

Nance continues, "Your credentials state you worked as a CFI, certified flight instructor, for twenty months and four months as an MEI, multi-engine instructor. You helped eight students attain their private pilot license. You trained several private pilots in addition of their instrument rating. You helped a few attain their commercial license, and you helped two commercial pilots attain their certified flight instructor license. You worked seven days a week and accumulated over 1,200 hours' flight time to give you a total of 1,560 hours. You were one week away from a job interview with a US Airways Express chief pilot in Charlotte, North Carolina."

"My mom was a flight attendant with US Airways Express, and we crashed on Monday, June 1, 1998. And I had an interview scheduled for the next Monday. I was that close to going to work for an airline even though I wanted to fly for a NASCAR race team.

What happened was the next thing we discussed. Nance continued, "Monday afternoon, June 1, 1998 at 1632 the Pa-30, Piper Twin Comanche went off Roanoke's radar in Virginia thirty-five minutes into flight. Serious injuries occurred to the pilot and the passenger on board. Visual meteorological conditions prevailed. A beautiful spring day existed in Floyd, Virginia, the site of the crash."

I explained, "I boarded the airplane at five minutes to four that day, and we went off Roanoke's radar at 16:32. If we converted that to normal time, it is four thirty-two that afternoon. That is thirty-seven minutes after I boarded the airplane. Does anybody have any idea what happened thus far?" I asked why an airplane would crash thirty-seven minutes after takeoff. Someone answered, "Not enough fuel."

I stated, "Out of those ninety gallons that was supposed to be there, almost sixty gallons were missing. I will explain what is going on. You will see why it happened the way it did. Also, you will be able to tell every time there is a crash, and everybody heard about the NASCAR plane that crashed into those houses, right? What was the big thing that happened? Big fire, right! You will not see a fire in the crash I lived through. So keep that in mind that anytime there is a crash and there is not a fire, chances are there is no fuel to burn. That might be an indication that the engine that was not developing power upon impact, that there is nothing to start a fire with, like sparks from the magnetos arking, and the props were not turning."

Nance continued,

> The airplane crash was due to engine failure. The right engine failed first at 9,700 feet. The pilot assumed it was engine failure, and the pilot conducted emergency restart procedures. Approximately ten minutes later, the left engine quit. The aircraft crashed into a stand of trees next to a home. The impact with the trees knocked off the auxiliary fuel tanks.
>
> Next, are some pictures from the crash. Does that look like a Piper Twin Comanche? Does that even look like an airplane? No, you can take that home in a lunch bag. Do you see how mountainous it is there? They were near the Virginia Mountains when they went down. Barry was sitting on this side. He was sitting on the right side of the airplane. Do you see how the right seat is leaning forward?
>
> The breaking of the seat is part of the reason his injuries were so extensive. When his parents got to Roanoke Regional Hospital, they lived out-

side of Charlotte, North Carolina, and as his plane was coming down, his mom's flight was taking off from Greenville, North Carolina coming back to Charlotte. When they arrived at the airport, they told her there was a family emergency. When his parents finally got to the hospital, the paramedics already brought him back to life even though the doctors pronounced him dead on arrival after they air lifted him from the crash site to the hospital. When his parents arrived at the hospital, they talked to the doctors after assessing his injuries. The doctors put his X-rays on the lighted board so his mom and dad could see his skull; his mom said you could not even tell you were looking at a face. The doctors said if you were to take a raw egg and drop it on the concrete, the egg would go splat and that is what his face would look like. That first picture you saw with Barry and his cousin with all those catfish and those photographs was one that his family had given to the doctors when they started reconstructing his face. However, the reason he had so many facial injuries came from the red seat you see leaning forward. His seat broke on impact and that forced him into the dash of the airplane. Back in one of the slides, it showed you that the airplane was a 1965 model airplane. That airplane did not have a shoulder harness, only a lap belt. I asked him once, what was his last memory? He said, as they were coming down the pilot in command freaked out and was not doing well flying the airplane. Barry tried to keep that airplane aloft, especially with that one engine running, trying to keep it from turning and rolling, just trying to keep it in level flight. His last memory, both feet were on the left rudder pedal and the control yoke turned all the way to the left during impact. The control yoke left an imprint in his chest and collapsed both lungs. He remembers tightening that lap belt really tight and on impact the seat broke.

I explained, "For a 1965 model airplane, it was not mandatory for the airplane to have a shoulder harness. The FAA did not require shoulder harnesses in airplanes at that time. If a shoulder harness were in place, then I would not have suffered the injuries I did. Even if the seat had broken, the shoulder harness would have kept me from hitting the dash and the control yoke. I had my sunglasses and my headset on, and I hit that dash so hard that it knocked my left eye completely out. Does anybody want to guess where the doctors found it? The doctors found it behind my cheekbone."

Nance said,

The emergency room doctors when they brought him back to life and he was fighting like a mad dog to stay alive, only 26 years old and very healthy. They had him on life support, he had a tracheotomy, and that is what saved his life. All the county medical emergency personnel were having a group meeting about five minutes down the road at the fire department. One of the pictures that you will see is how close they crashed to a house. They were aiming for a softball field in a distance. The airplane came up short and hit a stand of trees between two houses. They knew they were short of the softball field and were trying to avoid the two houses. As you can tell how close, they were to that house around 4:30 that afternoon. The woman that lived in that house was home, she heard this noise, and she thought the noise was her husband coming home from work by opening the garage door. She thought why my husband is not coming in the house. She went outside and saw this airplane in her yard. She dropped to her knees and said a quick prayer. She ran inside and called 911 and the paramedics were just minutes down the road and they all converged on the crash site. The medic that reached Barry first saw he had the worst injuries. The pilot only had both broken legs and was conscious. The medic placed a tracheotomy in him and inflated his lungs to save his life. However, by the time they airlifted him to the hospital, he died again. Do you see anything significant with part of the airplane you see?

Some students answered no tail. Nancy continued,

You will see some pictures later showing where the tail is at after impact. She explains a picture of the inside of the airplane and how it is not too recognizable. The next picture is of Barry in the hospital. The blue tube coming out of his neck is a respirator that was helping keep him alive. Do you see the gauze on his face, what you do not see that the gauze is covering is the hole where his nose used to be.

Barry is six foot two and his father was six foot four. His dad was a rodeo cowboy and won many titles in the Southern rodeo Association district. When his parents finally got the call from the hospital chaplain, and said your son is in serious condition and you really need to get up here. His parents and brother went to Roanoke several hundred miles from Kannapolis. When they got to the emergency room, his left eye was knocked out and when the doctors figured out that he was going to survive, then they began assessing his injuries. His left eye socket was sunken in because there was nothing there to support it. The doctors at the hospital actually sent the paramedics back to the airplane to look for that eye. The doctors talked about trying to find a needle in a haystack and they did not find the eye, however when they started reconstructing his face, they peeled his face down and found the eye behind the cheek bone. When his dad saw him, in the emergency room, his dad passed out and his head hit the floor. His mom knew at that time he was going to be blind for the rest of his life. The left eye socket was closed and sunken in because nothing was supporting the eye lid, but the right eye was looking straight ahead and covered in blood.

I stated not only did I lose my sight, but I also lost my taste and smell. Nance explained, "Yes, his whole sinus cavity was destroyed. Therefore, don't ever assume you are going to get on an airplane that you are always going to have a good flight."

Nance asked if anyone had any questions. A female student asked how long it took to reconstruct my face. I answered that my last surgery was in May of 2005. "What they had done originally, they took bone out of my head, the top of my cranium on the right side, and the doctors left it real jagged from the first surgeries. The last surgery they smoothed out the bone and took more to use in rebuilding my face. I still have cracks that you can feel." I showed a crack in my jaw and told them that was where one of the big breaks was located in my jaw.

Nance explained, "Why did N9974y crash? Multiple factors contributed to the crash of this airplane. Factor 1 is the pilot in command did not do a proper preflight. This plane crash is the primary reason why one of the specializations he received here in his master's degree was aviation safety. He was a very safe pilot before the crash, and if he had been the pilot in command, the airplane would have never crashed."

I added, "The graduate research project I did for the master's degree, titled *The Proper Execution of the Preflight Checklists to Ensure Flight Safety.*"

"Factor two, the pilot said the airplane was full of fuel, but he forgot to check the oil. The passenger entered the terminal and charged two quarts of oil to take on the flight."

I spoke up and said,

> Let's rewind right there. We crashed on Monday; now let us go back to Friday. On Friday, the airplane flew back from Greensboro, North Carolina, and that was a 30-minute flight or 30 minutes of fuel burned out of the main tanks. Therefore, out of those 60 gallons of fuel: 30 minutes of fuel is gone. If we say that airplane burns 15 to 18 gallons per hour, then we could say 9 gallons burned out on each side already. The airports job was to provide a service to our flight school because we had 13 airplanes on-line, and the airport service workers were to top off our airplanes every night. All the flight school airplanes accept the Champ and an Arrow received fuel each day or night. Sunday, we flew the Comanche, 2. 4 hours and that is two hours and twenty-four minutes. Including that 30 minutes already gone, now we have almost three hours of fuel gone. I figure we should get three and one half hours out of those main tanks. Now, the airport has not fueled that airplane. Before the fuel in Greensboro, records show that the Concord regional Airport had not fueled that airplane for

two weeks. That Monday we crashed, we took off at five minutes to four and we went off Roanoke's radar at 4:32 that afternoon. I said we already had two hours and fifty-five minutes burned out, and then we crash thirty-seven minutes after takeoff on that Monday. Now, when the first engine quit; guess what the pilot said, we are full of fuel: what is going on. Well, if the airplane had been full of fuel the engine would have never quit. It took a while for us to figure out what caused this accident. I had never flown with a lying pilot. Has anyone ever flown with a lying pilot? That is the reason we do pre-flights, and a pilot has to make sure things are correct and even if the gas gauge is inaccurate, we visually check to see how much fuel is in the tanks. That day the pilot was telling me we were full of fuel and I did not believe the fuel gauge because of what the pilot was telling me. He said I did the preflight, I know how much fuel is in the airplane.

Nance continued, "Factor number three is the airport service workers on the ground did not do their job correctly. Documentation proved the last known fuel came from another airport four days earlier. The owner of the aircraft and the flight school stated the previous day that he would have the airplane topped off and put back online."

I stated that we flew 2.4 hours on that Sunday, and when the flight was over, I came into the office that evening around five o'clock. The guy I worked for told me to go on home, that he would take care of the airplane. He would have it fueled and put back online and it would be ready to go tomorrow. I went home and came back the next morning, and the boss was not there. I dated the girl behind the desk, and I asked her to make sure the airport service workers fueled the airplane. I worked with all the line guys for twenty months.

Nance explained, "A copy of a memorandum came out 22 days after the crash. The last line highlighted that ASW's are not topping off Lancaster Aviation airplanes at night. This checklist performed every night or at least checked to see if the airplanes need fuel. That girl Barry was involved with gave this document to his family.

"Factor number five, the first engine started failing approximately twenty-five minutes after takeoff. The pilot stated at this time the airplane was full of fuel."

I said, "Let's talk about the first engine that quit. Now, I am perfectly aware that you students are not multi-engine students yet. As a multi-engine operator, when an engine quits and it is starving for fuel and you continue to start while sucking air into the lines, do you think you can ever get that engine started back?

"Factor number six—the pilot's decision not to land at the closest airport when the failure first occurred. The pilot wanted to land at Roanoke because he was sure he could rent a car at that airport and drive. The pilot also thought the airplane could be checked by maintenance on the ground at Roanoke. People, anytime something happens on the airplane, get it on the ground, then ask questions. Get the airplane on the ground and then try to do restarts and distinguish what is going on. Do not wait for another situation to arise in the airplane while you are still in the air. While that one engine was still operating gave us enough time to land that airplane and get that airplane on the ground, then we could have done a proper flight safety checklist and found the problem. Then I could have put the pilot on the spot more so. He is on the spot and lives with what happened every day."

Nance said, "The reason Barry put this as factor number six is we actually have a tape of the air traffic control of their conversation and distress call. The call made to the tower that one engine was out, and they were trying to get it restarted. We have it on the tape recording that the ATC controller had suggested to the pilot in command of the aircraft that there were three closer airports between Roanoke and where they were, Roanoke, Virginia, where he wanted to land to get a rental car. The pilot in command of that aircraft chose not to land at those closer airports. The pilot made the conscious choice not to land that airplane sooner. Of course, they did not think that second engine was going to quit either."

I explained, "We still think it is mechanical, not due to fuel exhaustion."

"Factor number seven," Nance spoke, "the pilot alternated switching the fuel selectors back and forth from the main position to the auxiliary position."

I stated,

> Okay, we are now sucking air into the lines in the main position. Then when we go to the auxiliary position, where there is fuel we get a bunch of blue smoke coming out of the exhaust almost as if we have a fire. We think something mechanical is going on, we switch the selector back to the main position. You have to understand that it states in the pilot's operating handbook or the (poh), the airplane flew only in the auxiliary position during straight and level flight. We are flying along at an angle because the right engine is out and we are preventing the airplane from wanting to roll towards that dead engine. That sounds crazy but the left engine is developing power, rotating clockwise and it wants to roll because of that torque and propeller slipstream. Therefore, I am turning the yoke into the good engine and I said that a while ago the imprint of the yoke went into my chest with a full turn to the left. Now, thinking why we cannot get a restart in the auxiliary position, we are at an angle. We thought we could not get fuel to flow to that engine and we were still speculating. We go back to the mains, we do a couple more restarts, and we were thinking it is not

starting and what is going on. Therefore, we go back to the auxiliary position and we get more blue smoke and we think what is going on: are we starting a fire. We now know when the first engine quit and we would have gone to the auxiliary position and never touched it again, then we may have got a restart. However, each time we went back to the main position, a restart would have never occurred because we were starting on empty tanks. We may have to land the airplane, refueled before we could have got a restart on the right engine. We will never know because we never got the airplane landed.

Nance continued, "If the pilot and his passenger would have known the airplane was low on fuel before takeoff, then the airplane would have been fueled before takeoff."

I added, "Factor number eight, the pilot explained we were full of fuel, and he was asking me what is going on? If there would have been fuel in the main tanks, failure of the right engine then the quitting of the left engine would have never occurred. As all restarts of the right engine failed, the left engine lost power ten minutes later. The airplane was already getting low in altitude. Ten minutes—that is plenty of time to get to an airport and land. In addition, you have to understand that a Lycoming 160 horsepower engine is not enough horsepower to help in maintaining altitude. Guess what? As we lost the engine at 9,700 feet mean sea level, we were losing 100 to 300 feet per minute in altitude before the crash occurred. Possibly more than that at times, you have to keep the airspeed up to keep from stalling."

"Factor number nine, best glide was 110 knots, and the airplane glided like a rock, approximately 128 miles per hour," said Nance. "The pilot and his passenger impacted the airplane into a group of trees next to a house. They were attempting to land on a softball field that was nearby the crash site."

I said, "110 knots is a fast glide speed and those trees did not give an inch."

Nance said, "Moving on to recommendations. Recommendation number one, teach the importance to the ground crew at the airport of how one party's failure can turn into multiple failures if their job is not done correctly. Have three checklists to follow for airport chores—morning, afternoon, and night. Have an airport employee manually review this checklist periodically to see if the airport service workers follow directions. Did you want to tell them about some of the accidents you investigated for your graduate research project (GRP) and the maritime accident?"

In addition, the Graduate Research Project I did for my master's degree titled "An Examination of Properly executed Preflight Checklist to Ensure Flight Safety". I investigated six plane crashes and the failure of the preflight led to those accidents. One was mine in the Comanche. One was the Comair flight because those pilots did not notice taking off on an unlit runway. Why were they not aware of the closures or the construction on the AWOS or ATIS? I do not understand why they took off on an unlit runway when there is a lighted one nearby. Next, I investigated a Beech Baron that took off in Dallas, Texas. This pilot did not remove the control lock and that mistake killed everybody. Six people killed instantly because the pilot did not remove the control lock. The airplane lifted off the runway, went straight up, stalled, and crashed upside down. Would you not think when you were taxiing down the taxiway and you could not move the yoke, do you not think you would reach down and remove the lock. Next, I did the accident of a Fokker, f-28 in Dallas that took off in 1992. This

accident killed 28 and was due to deicing procedures. The next two were Birgin Air and Aero
Peru. Everybody is familiar with the Pitot tube
and the static port systems. One of the accidents
was due to bugs that built a nest in the Pitot tube.
These bugs blocked it enough that the airspeed
indicators were erroneous. Now, in jets: you have
three airspeed indicators: the captain's, the first
officer's, and the standby. On the climb out, the
pilots were receiving two alternate readings, but
the standby was never checked to see what it was
indicating. The Aero Peru Flight had tape over
the static ports and maintenance placed tape
there. It was the job of the maintenance to put
tape over the static ports when washing it and
they failed to remove it after they did their job.
When the pilots did their walk around, they did
not check it. Therefore, human factors will bring
you down every time. All of you are sighted and
all you have to do is walk around and look. Has
any students failed to check something or not
remove anything while doing their preflight? I
know I did when I was instructing. I caught a student every time and I wanted to instill to them if
they do not check things properly, then they may
get into trouble. You have to carry the checklist
around with you every time you preflight an airplane because it is part of the flight. You have
to untie the wings, remove the chocks, remove
the control lock, untie the tail, right, which that
is just standard policy. An airplane that you fly
every day and it is always parked in the hangar,
then you may not have to check things so closely.
However, if the airplane is parked outside and

birds build a nest in it, then you will be glad you did a proper preflight on it when you find a nest.

Nance explained,

> One of the things he investigated while doing his graduate research project is there is lots of industries that have checklists. Obviously, Aviation has checklists, nuclear plants have checklists, and so does maritime, things with boats. One of the accidents he investigated did not have to do with Aviation; it had to do with sailing. A professor who teaches here, Dr. Don Metscher, a wonderful friend of ours and he is one of Barry's best friends here on campus, since he started. Dr. Metscher was his advisor on his GRP in the last semester, and one of the accidents that he wrote about had to do with a ferry that crosses water and carries cars with it. I forget how many cars it had on board in Belgium during the 1970's and Dr. Metscher was in Belgium at this time. One week after this ferry sank, he was on a ferry and they did not know why the ferry sank yet. He said they sailed by where the ferry sank and he never went into the cabin of the ferry and he stayed out on the rim of it, in case he had to jump out into the water. Investigations later proved that hundreds of people lost their loved ones in this ferry sinking. The cause of the sinking ferry was due to the ramp not being raised because the man in charge of raising it was asleep. The captain of that ferry never checked to make sure someone raised the ramp. When the ferry started moving, immediately, it started filling with water and hundreds of people lost their lives. The ones that survived were injured. Dr. Metscher knew all along

what the ferry, the Herald of Free Enterprise was about and he knew it half sunk. It was not until learning of the GRP approval by the higher ups of the College of Aviation that he was there when that happened. He has pictures of the Herald of Free Enterprise half sunk because it actually hit a sandbar when it turned over and capsized. So you talk about people not doing their jobs.

I said, "Negligence, which that is all I can say about it."

Nance read, "Recommendation number two. Remember Barry was talking about the biennial flight review with Santa Claus? Well, that is one of his suggestions. Reinforcing proper preflight procedures to the pilot during his biennial flight review, which may need implementing. The FAA may revoke his or her license if the pilot cannot follow checklists in the airplane." She asked me, "What happened to the pilot of your airplane accident?"

"The FAA grounded him by taking his medical and license."

Nance continued, "The pilot of his airplane crash will never fly again as pilot in command. The FAA has revoked all of his licenses. The NTSB, when they did the investigation of his plane crash, included a lot of inaccuracies in the report of the plane crash. One example—ATC said they could hear a warning horn going off in the cockpit, and they mistakenly identified what the horn was. Barry said whatever the NTSB report said was false, that aircraft did not have that type of warning horn. The NTSB spoke with him during his brain injury recovery in the hospital."

I explained that the horn was the gear-up warning horn to remind you to put the gear down when pulling the power back so far. "We did not want the gear down. We wanted the least amount of drag we could have on it."

Nance continued to read, "Recommendation number three and perform interviews on passengers involved in accidents. Recommendations number four, bring the pilot up to speed and increase training on the proper preflight of airplanes in biennial flight reviews. Next is the probable cause. The NTSB determined the probable cause of this accident as follows and comes word for word out of the NTSB accident report. The pilot's improper position of the fuel tank selector resulted in fuel starvation of both engines."

I stated, "There is a lot more to it than just that way. How many times did the pilot lie to me? So much negligence occurred that this accident should have never happened."

Nance asked me what my favorite saying is. "Life goes on and so do we!"

A female student asked a question about the pilot in command and his instrument skills. I explained that he was supposed to wear a hood or foggles to bring his instrument skills up to speed or become current. However, he never put the hood on because we were filing a flight plan. When Greensboro handed us off to Roanoke, the right engine up and quit. He had 168 hours in a twin, and I only had seventy hours.

Nance said,

> We now have some slides with what Barry and Lincoln have been up to since the crash. The first one shows in the top left that Barry graduated from Embry-Riddle on May 7, 2007.
>
> That is Barry and Lincoln receiving their diploma from Dr. Tim Brady, who is the dean of the College of Aviation here, and Pam's boss. The middle picture on the top is when we were in Miami, twice now; Barry has received scholarships from the Greater Miami Aviation Association and the Batchelor Foundation. Both have helped him fund his education at Embry-Riddle and he was just down there in May, two days after graduation. We flew down there with one of Embry-Riddle's pilots and a Cessna 172. The GMAA kind of used Barry as one of their spokespeople for their program and they have

given him a scholarship towards his doctorate degree. In the upper right corner is a photo from Washington D.C. last fall. Barry received a scholarship from the Air Traffic Control Association and we flew up to Washington, so he could speak and receive it in person at a convention of over 800 attendees, Aviators, Air Traffic controllers, people and instructors from Embry-Riddle. ATCA was very touched from Barry's story and his situation, so they wanted to recognize him with a scholarship. The man in the middle is Pete Dumont, who is the President of ATCA, and he loved Lincoln. We have pictures of Lincoln shaking hands with Pete Dumont. One of the photographs of Barry, Lincoln and Pete Dumont were on the front cover of the ATCA journal last fall along with the FAA administrator, Marion Blakey who was at the convention, and heard Barry speak. Barry spoke and received a standing ovation. Air Force Colonels came up to Barry and shook his hand and they said they could not believe his story. On the bottom left, Barry rode the B-24 bomber, the Liberator. He rode it out of the Flagler county Airport back in February and a 1959 Embry-Riddle graduate flew the airplane. When he came off the airplane, he said that was the most fun I had wearing clothes!

The crowd laughed. Nance continued,

On the bottom right when we rode our first Airbus A320, an eye research institute asked Barry to go up to Boston and they actually think they may have some procedures that might be able to restore some sight to his right eye. His left eye was lost in the crash and now it is a glass eye. The right eye suffered severe optic nerve damage from swelling and his lens has a 100% fully matured cataract on it. In June, they had a fundraiser called Flight for Sight. The man that owned those historic bomber airplanes, lots of vintage aircraft, and classic cars opened their home up to this event. We had dinner in their hangar, and Barry was the keynote speaker at the Flight for Sight.

Lincoln is the first service dog to ever attend Embry-Riddle. When Lincoln and Barry graduated in May at the Ocean Center, I was with him and Letty. Pam Peer played a big part in graduation as well. As we were waiting to walk into the commencement hall, 15 minutes prior to doing so, the president's wife of Embry-Riddle, Maury Johnson found us and the silk scarf you see on Lincoln's harness was a gift from the president and Mrs. Johnson, the official scarf of Embry-Riddle. She said Lincoln had to have one of these scarfs, since he is the official spoke dog. So, when he does stuff at Embry-Riddle, we make sure he is wearing his silk scarf that Mrs. Johnson gave him.

A female student asked about how I felt about aviation now that I lived through a crash. I said, "It is still the safest source of transportation there is. Once again, that accident should have never happened. Aviation was my love before the accident and continues to be so today. Although in a different aspect, it is still my favorite thing to do. I feel safer in an airplane than in a car. Therefore, I would rather fly in an airplane than ride in a car."

Hope Lutheran Church Presentation

Sunday, August 19, 2007, I shared the trials and triumphs of my life with Hope Lutheran Church. This presentation was at the chapel at Embry-Riddle, and Pastor Jack Ottoson held the service with the help of Sandy Thompson. Nance did the children's sermon, and I began by thanking God, Nance, Lincoln, and everybody else that helped me get to where I was at today. I began by sharing the trials and triumphs of my life that began after June 1, 1998:

> That day changed my life significantly and dramatically. At 4:32 that afternoon, we went off Roanoke's radar and crashed into a group of trees between 2 houses, and about 100 yards away from a softball field. The trees did not give much as they demolished the airplane and God blessed us in several ways. First off, the house close to where we crashed, it was close to 5 o'clock that afternoon, and the lady that lived there thought her husband was home from work and she thought the noise she heard was the garage door opening. She came outside to greet him and saw the closed garage door. She looked in the yard, saw the airplane, and heard us grieving and sighing. She panicked if you will and she dropped to her knees and said God, what do I need to do. It dawned on her to go inside and call 911. Unbelievably the paramedics were right up the street on a weekly or monthly meeting. That was a blessing or the angels that came forward to save my life. I do believe the woman that was home that called for help was the beginning of saving my life. Out of all the places to crash, we crashed in someone's yard and close to where a fire station was located. I feel the paramedic that saved my

life was a woman that intubated me at the crash site and got air to my lungs. When the call came across the radio, the paramedics were just leaving the fire station and the woman paramedic was one of the first ones there to the scene. She and a couple of others pulled me out of the airplane and stabilized me, and the woman dropped to her knees and prayed as well. This woman had never been able to intubate someone on the first try; it always took her two or three tries. She hit my airway on the first try. She was able to get air to my lungs on the first try and miraculously saved my life. However, I was not out of the woods yet, they pronounced me dead on arrival as they airlifted me in a helicopter to Roanoke Regional Hospital. That paramedic that got air to my lungs saved my life and that was a triumph. I feel those two acts of those two women were angels put into my life. I want to thank those people in person, but I have not been able to yet. This accident brought my family together in the hospital where I stayed in a coma for 20 days. The family tells about my cousin, Bet James giving me an angel figurine on the shelf over the bed and they said it had eyes that looked at you and followed you around the room. I did not have a clue what was going on, I was still really far out there. In addition, speaking of angels, the nurses gave me a bath and put on me a clean robe. When they gave me this robe, there was an angel attached to it. My brother asked the nurse where that came from. She told him she did not know that it was a clean robe. My family thought that the angel played part in me getting well. They thought this showed how this answered their prayers. The Lord was listening to all of our prayers. I told everybody about how the Intensive Care Unit was and how they let all of my visitors in the room with me along with cards and flowers as well as they played music for me on the CD player.

I was in the hospital at Roanoke until the end of the month of June, then Spitfire Aviation, which was out of Concord, North Carolina, flew me back there and the family drove me to the Charlotte Rehabilitation Center. In early July, I developed a staff infection from the facial surgery that I had done before leaving Roanoke and my spine was leaking spinal fluid. My injuries were so bad, I had 14 broken bones throughout my body, nine broken bones were in my face, four bones in my leg, and a broken vertebrae. My jawbone broken four times, roof of my mouth knocked loose from my face, my nose knocked completely off and this left a big hole in my face, three cracks in my cranium, and the left eye knocked completely out. The doctors at Roanoke sent the paramedics back to the crash sight to look for my eye and they later found it behind my cheekbone. I had both lungs collapsed. That first facial surgery in Roanoke consisted of putting seven plates in my face to rebuild it. A staff infection took place and they cut me from the top of my ear to the top of my other ear and peeled the skin down to the bottom of my jaw. They took all that stuff out and threw it away, and then went to my right hip and took bone out of it and rebuilt my face with that bone, more metal plates, and screws.

My brother and dad missed enough work and they had to return to work. So, when they went home the white dove was there and they noticed it. This white dove played part in my family's life as I was in the hospital. The dove lived in the back yard of our house. The dove was there the entire time I was in the hospital and dad would share the dove's presence with us. Believe it or not, when I came home from the hospital and began walking outside, the dove was still present. During September of 1998, the girl I was involved with at the time decided she could not take anymore of the trauma so, she hit the road. The next several months were blocked from my memory. I do not remember Christmas that year. Next, during July of 1999, I had another facial surgery. They removed plates and screws then took more bone out of my cranium and made me almost as good-looking as I am today.

In August of 1999, the doctors recommended that my family send me to the Rehabilitation Center for the Blind in Raleigh, North Carolina. So, I did go and I learned Braille, a computer program called JAWS (Job Application with Speech), and mobility. I walked with a support cane and a pointer cane to help me in figuring out where I was going. Then I came home for Christmas and we celebrated Christmas, then December 28, 1999, my dad had a serious heart-attack and died on the 30th. Losing my sight, taste, and smell did not compare to losing my dad, he was my hero and losing him was a heart breaker. In January of 2000, I went back to the Rehabilitation Center for a couple of weeks and they felt I was too upset to continue. I asked myself what I am going to do now. I was trying to figure out what I was going to do at this point in my life. So, I filled out an application to receive Lincoln from Southeastern Guide Dog Incorporated in Palmetto, Florida.

During this time in 2000, I began studying for the Advanced Ground Instructor License. June 6, 2000, I became the first blind Advanced Ground Instructor in the world for the FAA. I thought that was a large achievement, but that was just the beginning of achievements.

June 12, 2000, the big guy came into my life. That statement made the congregation laugh. After the presentation, we sang "I Love to Tell the Story" and then I spoke of the trials and tribulations after the accident. I shared with the congregation about receiving Lincoln. Lincoln was 86 pounds and his puppy raiser was Carole Blake and her boyfriend. Nance, Lincoln, and I are friends with her and we know she did a fine job raising Lincoln and giving him a lot of love that he has passed on to me. We are very thankful to God for that. I spent 26 days in training to receive Lincoln in Florida and met her and her boyfriend for the first time at puppy raiser day.

I came home with Lincoln and began studying for the Instrument Ground Instructor license. So, in October 2000, I became the first blind Instrument Ground Instructor in the history for the FAA.

In December of that year, I met Kendra Ann Harrington. Kendra was blind and very special to me. She had a kidney transplant from a 20-month-old baby and carried those kidneys for 10 years. In 2003, the doctors told her that they had to go in and remove them because they were producing toxins to her body. They removed them as well as her pancreas.

In May 2001, I began attending the University of North Carolina at Charlotte. Lincoln and I moved to Charlotte and lived by ourselves. After all of my injuries, I am still taking 1,500 milligrams of anti-seizure medication today and I have not had a seizure since January 2005. Lincoln and I walked 1,800 steps every day for three and a half years. How we pulled that off I do not know, but I thank God every day for that. I graduated December 18, 2004.

During January 2005, Lincoln and I came down here with Nance and toured Embry-Riddle. During May, I had my last facial surgery and I said taa-dah. The congregation laughed. They took out more metal plates, stuck more bone under my nose to raise it up more, and they took more bone out of my cranium. I said, I thought that it looked good, so I was happy with it I guess. I began school here in August of 2005. November 19, Kendra passed during dialysis on that Saturday afternoon. That was a real heart breaker.

In 2006, I had another surgery, which consisted of me having my gall bladder removed. That was painful, so I won't talk about it. Then, I graduated May 7, 2007.

Cub Scout Presentation

September 3, 2007, Nance, Jackson, Lincoln, and I went to Shirley James's house in Ormond Beach to give a presentation to her son's Cub Scouts' group. We presented how a blind man functions in society. We showed the Cub Scouts how a blind man folds money, identifies the color of their clothes, and showed how to use a money identifier to indicate a one dollar bill versus a twenty dollar bill. We showed and explained the Braille labeler and the Braille slate and stylists. I made a Braille label of each kid's name and gave it to him or her. In addition, I explained how Lincoln helped me as a guide dog, and how he helped me in my life.

Women in Aviation, International, Daytona Beach First Coast Chapter Presentation

Tuesday evening, September 11, 2007, I gave a presentation to the First Coast Chapter of Women in Aviation, International. Nance, Lincoln, and I gave this presentation, and it took place at the Daytona Beach International Airport in a conference room in front of about twelve people, mostly women and a few men. Most of the women were pilots, and one woman was Maury Johnson, the wife of the president of Embry-Riddle. Letty Kolb, the treasurer of the group, had her son Dennis video the presentation with his girlfriend, Dessie.

Nance introduced me, "This is Barry Hulon Hyde, and I get the honor of introducing him."

I said, "This is Lincoln the Aviator."

Nance said,

> This used to be Lincoln the Navigator. Once they graduated from Embry-Riddle with their master's degree, we promoted him to Lincoln the Aviator. Therefore, he is officially Lincoln the Aviator now. For those of you who do not know Barry, he was a pilot and was about a week away from starting his Commercial career with US Airways Express in Charlotte, North Carolina, close to where he is from. You will hear that Kannapolis twang in his voice and he was a pas-

senger in a Piper Twin Comanche that crashed. The doctors actually pronounced him dead on arrival from the accident. They brought him back to life and he is going to talk about the crash today, and his presentation about graduating from Embry-Riddle in May. He was the first and only blind student to ever attend and graduate in the 81-year history of the school. He received his Master's of Science in Aeronautics Degree with two specializations. The degree has one specialization in Aviation Safety and the other one is in Aviation Operations. Therefore, Aviation safety is very near and dear to his heart. June 1, 2007, he began his doctorate degree through the on-line program with Northcentral University in Prescott, Arizona. They are in partnership with Embry-Riddle, however, he was hoping to attain his doctorate with Embry-Riddle, but they do not have it in place yet. His advisor, Dr. Marvin Smith from Embry-Riddle suggested to him that he start with Northcentral. His joke is he wants to be Dr. Hyde in addition to Dr. Jekyll.

Everyone present laughed at Nance's comments. She continued,

Barry, Lincoln, and I will be traveling out to Reno, Nevada in early January. We found out that the American Institute of Aeronautics and Astronautics awarded him a scholarship. They are flying us out there for five days to their international convention and they have asked Barry to present his GRP, from Embry-Riddle at the convention. The GRP specialized in the preflight checklist to ensure flight safety. You will find out in his presentation about the pilot in command of the small aircraft flunking the preflight and that is what caused the airplane to go down. He is very big into Aviation Safety and this summer the Director of the summer academy asked him to speak to the students that attend the summer academy. Pam Peer, who is in charge of summer academy, said the kids were strutting around campus like Teflon. Here were 15 to 18 year olds on campus for a month or so, and they were getting a little cocky. During summer academy at the world's largest flight school where nothing could go wrong. Pam asked Barry and Lincoln to come in and speak to them in two different sessions. All the flight instructors sat through the presentation as well, and they saw an immediate change in the attitudes of the students. There was one student from Italy in summer academy, and apparently, he was emailing his parents back home about Barry's presentation. The parents actually came from Italy for graduation of the summer academy and the mother of this young Italian came up to Pam Peer and said, I do not know who the blind guy is, but that is all my son has talked about is what an impact he had on my son. Therefore, we are very proud of Mr. Hyde and Lincoln the Aviator! So, with that I am going to turn the presentation over to Mr. Hyde, and I am going to move the slides for him.

I began by saying, "Good evening to all, and I hope everyone is doing well this evening. I want to begin first by paying thanks to the Women in Aviation for allowing me to come and share my story. I want to begin with the history of the accident that I lived through. Why the airplane went down and share what has occurred since then."

Nance shared, "In Barry's crash, the seat broke on impact and what he will talk about is the airplane being a 1965 model airplane. The airplane only had a lap belt and did not have a shoulder harness. That is the reason he had so many facial injuries as well as a brain injury, because he hit the dashboard. We shared this picture with the Summer Academy, and this picture is one the doctors used to rebuild his face. He had nine broken bones in his face, and the doctors said if you took the egg and dropped it on concrete, that is how Barry's face looked like."

I said, "Ta-dah!" The females laughed!

Nance said, "He has two of the three favorite pastimes here tonight, women, aviation, and the third is fishing."

I said, "All right. Let us talk a little about the airplane that I lived through that crashed—N7794Y, a Piper Twin Comanche—and how ironic the American Institute of Aeronautics and Astronautics has awarded me the only general aviation scholarship they give that I will attend in Reno, Nevada, to receive. This scholarship is the William T. Piper Senior General Aviation Systems Graduate Award. I am very proud of that considering that I crashed in a Piper, and here AIAA is recognizing me after what I lived through, and I thought that was awesome. Back to the airplane. It had two 160 horsepower Lycoming engines, four seats, only had lap belts, no shoulder harnesses, and had four fuel tanks, which held ninety gallons of fuel."

Nance began reading the slides. "What happened? June 1, 1998."

I explained, "It was a Monday afternoon, and we went off Roanoke's radar at 4:32 p.m. that afternoon. We took off from Concord Regional Airport that day at five minutes until four, and we crashed thirty-seven minutes after takeoff. Carry on, Nance."

"The airplane crashed due to engine failure."

I said,

> Well engine failure, the airplane has two engines and both quit. That is odd, isn't it! I want to share with everyone what caused it and sev-

eral things led up to what caused the crash. I will go through more factors as she goes through the slides and there will be more detail. Now, anytime there is a plane crash and there is not a fire, what does that mean? Someone said no fuel. I said well yes, the main tanks were empty, and the auxiliary tanks had an undetermined amount of fuel in them. The impact knocked the auxiliary tanks off during the crash. We found this out months later after all investigations. We found out that two of four tanks were out of fuel. The airplane held 90 gallons of fuel and 84.5 were useable. It actually went 15 gallons in the left auxiliary tank, 30 gallons in the left main tank, 30 gallons in the right main tank, and 15 gallons in the right auxiliary tank. The two auxiliary tanks were knocked off outboard the engines. If the main tanks had fuel, of course, the engines would never have quit. Of course, if we crashed with fuel in the main tanks, then we would have burned. Since there was not any fuel on board, that was a blessing, but the failure of several negligent acts caused the accident. What do you have next, Nance?

Nance showed a picture of the crashed Piper Twin Comanche. Someone said, "Good Lord!"

She continued, "That is the airplane crash that he lived through. As you can tell, they were in mountainous terrain. They were about thirty-five minutes into the flight from Concord, NC. They were aiming for a softball field. They fell short of it, and they knew they were not going to make it to the softball field, and they went into a stand of trees between two houses. Barry always says those trees did not give much. However, that is the front end of the Comanche. This is Barry's side, and you can see how the seat is leaning forward.

His head hit the dash and that tore his nose off. Do you want to go through your injuries?"

I said yes, since we had time. "I will begin with the head injury. I had nine broken bones in my face, four broken bones in the lower jawbone, four teeth knocked out—two teeth in the lower jaw and two in the front of the upper jaw. The upper jawbone knocked off from my face, nose knocked off, sinus cavity destroyed, and three cracks in my forehead. The left eye knocked completely out, both lungs collapsed, and the right leg broken four times."

Nance said, "I asked him what his last memory was, and he said, 'Tightening the lap belt.' He said his last memory he had both feet on the left rudder pedal and cranking the control yoke almost all the way to the left, and he can still feel the imprint in his chest where the yoke went. He said the pilot freaked out and acted as if it was Barry's airplane. Barry was trying to keep the airplane from rolling."

I stated,

> If you can picture what is going on, we turned the airplane into the good engine, the left engine was the good one and the right one was out. We turned the airplane into the good engine by rolling to the left preventing it from wanting to roll into the dead engine. Now, let me explain what it says in the pilot's operating handbook of that airplane. It simply states, the only time the airplane operates in the auxiliary position is during straight and level flight. It is not during flying in the traffic pattern, not making turns, not practicing engine out procedures while flying at an angle because you are porting a fuel tank when flying at an angle. Once again, the pilot is telling me that he did the preflight and we are full of fuel, what is going on. The only thing I could do is help him keep the airplane straight and level and I did not know he was lying to

me. It is very upsetting and frustrating for me because hindsight is 20/20, I never put myself in that position or predicament. I never flew with someone that lied to me, so I never flew with a lying pilot. The pilot was a 55-year-old man with around 800 hours and had more multi-engine time than I did. He had 168 hours and I only had 65 to 70 hours. The accident happened because he flunked the preflight. To this day, he claims all four tanks were full of fuel. Well, 60 gallons of fuel, what happened to it, did it just evaporate or did the fuel tanks have holes in them?

When we hit the trees, the seat forced me into the dash and into the control yoke. I had on my sunglasses and my headset. I think the sunglasses cut the left eye out. The doctors sent the paramedics back to the crash site to locate my eye. I do not know what they would have done with it when they found it. Of course, the paramedics did not find it, but the doctors in the emergency room began assessing my facial injuries and they did find the eye behind the left cheekbone. The chaplain called my family from the hospital to tell them I had been in an accident, and they needed to come identify me. My mom was on a flight that took off from Greenville, NC on its way back to Charlotte. When they arrived at Charlotte, she received a message to report home and my dad was waiting to hear from her. Therefore, when she called, he told her what was going on and she rushed home. The family was waiting there with their bags packed to go to Roanoke Regional Hospital. Here was a 6'4", 220 lb, cowboy that came into the emergency room to identify me and he passed out because of the distortion and swelling of my face. My head looked like a basketball. The amount of swelling took my eyesight in the good eye. It damaged the optic nerve in the right eye. Occasionally, I will see light behind the cataract. I have a 100% fully matured cataract on the lens of the right eye. I am only 35 and I am hoping one day if it takes the doctors 30 years to bring my eyesight back, I will only be 65. If I live until age 90, then I will still get to see for another 25 years.

The crowd laughed. I asked Nance to carry on, and what was on the next slide? The next slide showed was how close we were to the house. A woman said, "Oh my god!"

Nance said,

I asked the ladies what do you find odd about the picture of this aircraft? The tail is gone and it sheared off and is in the trees way back. At 4:32 pm that afternoon, the woman was home in that house and she thought it was her husband coming home from work. She thought it was the electric garage door opening and when her husband did not come into the house, she went out to see what the noise was. There was this aircraft and blood everywhere and she dropped to her knees and prayed to God because she did not know what to do. That was the first thing to save his life and the next thing that led to saving his life Was the intubation he received. The paramedics were holding a weekly meeting five minutes up the road and they responded quickly to the emergency scene. The female that arrived to the scene first knew he did not have a chance with his collapsed lungs. This woman gave him a tracheotomy to and saved his life, which she told his family it normally took her two or three times. She prayed to God to help her incubate him, since it was so critical. The paramedic visited the hospital for weeks while he was in a coma. We are trying to track her down, however; we have not had any luck finding her.

More pictures Nance showed was like the one the family took of me in the hospital. Nance explained, "That gauze over his face covered his sinuses or crater that was in his face at the time."

I said, "The injuries were so bad that I am still on antiseizure medicine today. That is 1,500 milligrams or three peels a day, and I have not had a seizure in two and a half years."

Nance said, "The last time he had a seizure was in late January of 2005. He graduated from University of North Carolina at Charlotte and came here to tour Embry-Riddle and we met Kim Clairy. We roomed at the Ramada Inn, and this geared, tensed, and overwhelmed him so much that it gave him a seizure in the morning after his shower."

Next, Nance went to the human factors of why N7794Y crashed. She explained, "Multiple factors contributed to the crash of this aircraft. The pilot in command did not do a proper preflight checklist."

I said,

It is as simple as that, as I said, he is still saying the airplane was full of fuel. In his deposition and the lawsuit, I brought and let me confer on this issue, since I have mentioned it. Does anyone want to guess what I received out of this plane crash? Someone said an education from Embry-Riddle, Lincoln, and Nancy! I said I like the way you think. The insurance on the airplane just like the insurance on a car and you are hurt in your car the insurance pays so much. The insurance on the airplane was for $100,000. The attorney got 40% of what I received, so there is $40,000 gone. Medicare and Medicaid received $33,333.33 of what I received. We had to hire a private investigator and there is another $10,000 gone. I got the rest, a whopping $17,000. In addition, my mom took a leave of absence from her job for three years and she finally quit after her leave was up. His mom provided a lot of care for him. She gave him care such as taking him to rehabilitation, took him to speech therapy, cognitive therapy, provided home health care for him, and many other things. It was very disturbing as you can imagine I was 26 years old when I lost consciousness and then when I woke up I could not see. The head injury alone was very traumatic as well as trying to understand and accept what happened. Over time, things started coming back to my memory on what happened. When you hit so hard you knock an eye out, it takes a lot out of you. The doctor said part of my brain is still not working today, but obviously I do not need it, however, I am not that worried about that.

Everyone laughed, and Lincoln wagged his tail. Nance continued about the pilot flunking the preflight. She said, "Factor number two—the pilot said the aircraft was full of fuel, and he forgot to check the oil. You, as the passenger, entered the terminal and charged two quarts of oil."

I interrupted and said,

Let us talk about what my role was on the airplane that day. I was to be the safety pilot on board that day. I am sure everybody is familiar with what a safety pilot does. The role of the safety pilot is there to be a set of eyes to make sure the airplane does not fly into another airplane while the pilot flies the airplane under the hood or foggles blocking his sight over the panel. The only thing he can see is the instruments verses looking out the window. I never have to serve that role because I was filing a flight plan and 25 minutes after takeoff the right engine started giving trouble. As I filed the flight plan with Raleigh Flight Service Station and I helped him before Greensboro Approach handed us off to Roanoke Approach. Shortly, thereafter is when the right engine started giving trouble. As soon as this engine started giving trouble, we needed to land that airplane. However, the pilot wanted to go on to Roanoke to rent a car and to get the airplane worked on. He thought that this decision was better, since the three closest airports did not have rental cars or maintenance available. I look back and cuss, but I was not the pilot in command, I was the passenger. The FAA, the NTSB, and the insurance considered me as a passenger that day. I was a flight instructor with 1,600 hours, but that did not matter that day, the NTSB still considered me a passenger or a safety pilot. A woman asked what did the pilot rent the airplane to do. The pilot's mother lived in West Virginia, and we were to go visit with her. The pilot was instrument rated and he was getting instrument current. He was trying to get his six hours for his instrument currency. I was just in the wrong airplane to be honest. I just got my Multi-Engine Instructor license in February of 1998, and we crashed June 1, 1998.

Nance read factor number three. "The airport service workers on the field did not perform their job correctly. The documentation proves that the last known fuel on the airplane came from Greensboro, NC, four days earlier. Barry's boss the previous day told Barry that he would have the airplane topped off and put back online."

I stated,

> Let us go through the main tanks, the 60 gallons of fuel very quickly. The airplane flew from Greensboro on Friday for about a half an hour. If you figure one 160-horsepower, engine burns about nine or ten gallons burn rate per engine, per hour. Therefore, there is nine gallons gone. What I am leading up to is we had three and a half hours of fuel burned out of those main tanks when we crashed. The time the airplane flew from Greensboro was one half hour on Friday. We flew that airplane 2.4 hours on Sunday. Sunday evening the boss told me to go on home, he would have the line guys top off the airplane and put it back on line. Unfortunately, he did not. On Monday, we crashed 37 minutes after takeoff. Three flights that the Concord Regional Airport and the City of Concord did not do their job correctly. The City of Concord is the only City in the State of North Carolina that owns and runs an airport. They have the highest fuel prices in a 50 nautical mile radius of the airport.

Nance said, "Share with everyone how many airplanes were in the flight school."

I stated,

> We had 13 airplanes online at the airport and three of those did not receive fuel on a daily

basis. The other 10 airplanes were checked daily or nightly. The twin needed fuel on Friday, it needed checking on Saturday and we flew it 2.4 hours on Sunday. The fuelers did not top off the airplane either day or night. The fuel burned out 30 minutes on Friday, 2.4 hours on Sunday, and 37 minutes on Monday. That is the three and a half hours of fuel in the main tanks.

Nance continued,

> Factor number four was the pilot did not administer a proper preflight. The attorney and I concluded that the pilot only looked in the auxiliary tanks when he did the preflight. We think he only checked two of the four tanks and those were the auxiliary tanks. He never looked in the main tanks; he just assumed all four were full.
>
> Factor number five is not landing the airplane immediately after the right engine started giving trouble. ATC gave them permission to land at three closer airports. As Barry said previously, when an airplane is giving trouble, get it on the ground.
>
> Factor number six consisted of the pilot alternating switching fuel selectors back and forth from the main selection to the auxiliary position.

I stated,

> Let us briefly touch on that issue. The fuel selectors were located in the floor between the pilot and me. There were only a few fuel selector positions to place the selector. I feel if we just went from the main position to the auxiliary posi-

tion, and never touched it again, I feel confident about the restart of that right engine. However, each time we went from main to auxiliary positions and from auxiliary to the main positions, we sucked more air into the lines. The pilot continues to tell me we are full of fuel, then I think we have a mechanical failure of that right engine. Looking back on things and seeing all that blue smoke coming out of the exhaust in the auxiliary position, and that was because that is where the fuel is at. Well, we go back to the main position because we think that blue smoke is a problem like an engine fire or something. I did not know about what occurred because I had never run a tank dry. Hindsight is 20/20 or even 20/15. Once again, that accident should have not happened. In that, position was a first for me and the pilot should not have put himself in that position. All he had to do is a proper preflight and he would have found the problem before takeoff.

Factor number seven shared by Nance is about getting the airplane on the ground when the first thought of a problem is occurring. From the time the first engine quit until the second engine quit and we had almost 10 minutes to land that airplane. The airplane was already getting low on altitude. This airplane would not hold altitude on one engine. That is another reason we should have landed the airplane immediately. Instead, we went from 9,700 feet losing 200 to 300 feet per minute loss in altitude and I am sure this increased the closer we got to 5,000 feet. I can remember if we were just a little bit higher with a little more altitude, we would have made the softball field.

Nance read the recommendations. "Recommendation number one, teach the importance to the ground crew at the airport that one party's failure can turn into multiple failures if their job is not performed correctly. Train them to follow checklists—morning, afternoon, and night. Have a manager periodically check their work. The second recommendation consists of reinforce proper preflight procedures to the pilot during his or her biennial flight review. The FAA may revoke their license if they cannot follow checklists."

A woman asked if the pilot lost his license. I answered, "Yes ma'am, the pilot was grounded by the FAA for the rest of his life. It is ironic. The boss of the flight school I worked for, the crash was June 1, 1998, and he was out of business by December of 1998. The next year, he, of course, was an airframe and power plant mechanic, a commercial multi-engine instrument pilot. The FAA took all of his licenses and medical and grounded him because as he was selling one of the airplanes out of our flight school to a pilot located in Asheboro, North Carolina. During the takeoff, they crashed, and when the NTSB started investigating, they found he signed people's logbooks with an expired endorsement in their logbook. They grounded him for one year."

Nance continued, "Another recommendation is to bring the pilot up to speed and increase the training on the proper preflight of airplanes on the biennial flight reviews. The NTSB determined that the probable cause of this accident is the pilot's improper selection of the fuel position selector resulting in fuel starvation in both engines."

Nance read my favorite saying, "Life goes on, and so do we!"

Nance showed some photos of what I have been up to since June 1, 1998.

> He graduated from Embry-Riddle and Dr. Brady giving him his diploma. During 2006 and 2007, Barry is receiving two scholarships from the Greater Miami Aviation Association. They have also invited him to speak at their black tie gala in November. In the upper right is a picture with Pete Dumont, the president of the

Air Traffic Control Association in Washington. Barry received two scholarships from them and spoke at both events. Sid McGuirk, Dr. Marvin Smith, and Dr. Don Metscher were there along with lots of controllers and military people. The lower left is when he rode on the B-24 Bomber, the Liberator out of the Flagler County Airport. The bottom right is when we were in Boston at the Flight for Sight Fund Raising event. They learned of Barry's story and thought they may one day restore some sight back in Barry's right eye. The Collins Foundation owned the Bomber Barry rode on at the Flagler county Airport. Where Barry is standing is their hangar that holds their 24 Vintage airplanes and 80 Classic, Antique cars. They asked Barry to come and be their keynote speaker at their fund raising event.

A woman asked what year the Bomber was built. I said in 1941. Nance told them, "The pilot of the B-24 was an Embry-Riddle graduate in 1959. After the pilot found out that Barry was Embry-Riddle's first and only blind graduate, he then wanted to speak to him. In addition, the aircraft that Barry and Lincoln are standing in front of is a 1930 Waco. Barry's cousin tells him that there are only six of these left flying today. This airplane is not insured."

I said, "If anyone has any questions, feel free to ask me."

Someone asked me what I do during my time. I said,

Just work on my doctorate and that takes up most of my time. It is the hardest job I ever had. I thought the Master's Degree was hard but nothing compared to this doctorate. After the education, I hope to teach Master's classes or a ground school somewhere. A woman asked how I prepared for doing the assignments and how

I listened to lectures. I explained that I have a screen reader called JAWS (Job Application with Speech). It reads everything on the screen to me. I can go on the internet and find scholarly journals and JAWS would read it to me. I could arrow down for it to read either letter-by-letter, word by word, line by line, paragraph by paragraph, or page by page. I can stop the reading where I need to and make notes either on my tape player or on Microsoft Word. I repetitiously listen to my notes to help me study for an assignment, writing a paper, or taking a test. Everything for me is audible.

Nance said,

The aviation industry is sight dominated, so none of his textbooks were in an audible format or in an electronic version. We had to figure out what plan B was. Therefore, we had to buy new textbooks, and I would send them to North Carolina to Barry's uncle, who worked at a college. He would take them to work and cut the spines off, and I would stay up all hours of the night scanning chapters into Word. This scanning was then made into audible text so his screen reader could read it. I learned his professors like Sid Mcguirk, Dr. Marvin Smith, Dr. Dan Mackirella, Dr. Don Metscher, Don Hunt, Dr. Ester Forsyth and a few others that worked together to help him. I figured if I could do it from 500 miles away that I could do it better if I moved here. He is very fortunate that 36 hours from his master's degree transferred and was put towards his 81 required for his doctorate. I have been fortunate that since I work for Embry-Riddle that I can get a library loan, therefore, I can get a hard copy of the book.

Someone asked how many hours I have left. I shared that I have forty-two hours remaining plus the dissertation. The woman asked how I would do that. I said one day at a time.

"The past nine years, three months, and ten days—that is the way it has been. Life is passing one day at a time. Looking back on June 1, 1998, I do not wish that on my worst enemy. Not that I have any enemies, but I do not wish that on anybody to have to go through what I lived through. I was in the hospital for three months and multiple facial surgeries. I have a rod in the right leg going from my knee to my ankle, five or six metal plates in my face, and a couple of screws here or there."

A woman said, "Do you give airport security a hard time." Everyone laughed. I said, "Accommodations make it easy for me. Thank you all once again for allowing me to share my story with you."

The crowd clapped four seconds.

Embry-Riddle International English Class Presentation

On Saturday, October 13, 2007, Kim Hardaman emailed me to ask me to consider giving a presentation to her English class. Kim is an international English teacher, and she wanted me to speak to her students. I gave the presentation to her class on Tuesday, September 18, and most of her students were foreign students. In addition, I gave a presentation to another class she taught on Thursday. Kim is originally from Hong Kong, then she moved to France, Kim's father raised her while he worked for British Airways. On Thursday, she presented me a key chain that had nine eyes on it in thanks for the presentations.

National Federation of the Blind
Daytona Beach Chapter

Wednesday, September 17, 2007, I received an email from Sabrina Deaton, the vice president of the Daytona Beach chapter of the National Federation of the Blind. She asked if I would like to be on *Good Morning America*, so I called her to tell her yes in person. She talked about putting together some other packages and broadcasts with my permission to use my story and name. Nationally, Sabrina is over the NFB Newsline and the vice president of the Daytona Beach chapter.

Barry Hulon Hyde: Flying High
By Sabrina Deaton

Barry Hulon Hyde is flying high and making tremendous breakthroughs for the blind in an occupational field that to this point has been dominated by the sighted. Hyde is soaring toward a career in the field of aviation.

In 2000, According to the Federal Aviation Administration Hyde made history by becoming the first blind person to earn their Advanced Ground Instructor and Instrument Ground Instructor licenses. He continues to make history as the first blind person to attend Embry-Riddle Aeronautical University in Daytona Beach, where he has continually earned a 4.0 grade point average in their master's program.

By May 2007, he planned on completing his Master's degree with a double specialization. The specializations are in Aviation Safety and Aviation Operations. He doesn't plan on stopping there either. He will continue his aeronautical studies and pursue his doctoral degree from Northcentroll University through an online program.

Some could consider Hyde's accomplishments amazing—breaking into aviation as a blind person. However, what truly makes his accomplishments and determination amazing stems from the cause of his blindness: A plane crash.

On June 1, 1998, Hyde boarded a twin-engine plane as a fully sighted pilot and flight instructor. He was serving as a safety pilot for a fellow aviator who needed currency status on his instrument license. In other words, Hyde's job was to look out the window to make sure they didn't run into any other planes while the pilot flew by instruments only. Approximately 30 minutes into the flight, the right engine failed.

Both men immediately abandoned their original purpose and put their training to use and tried to restart the engine. Unbeknownst to Hyde, proper procedure had not been followed by the crew at the Concord Regional Airport in Concord, N.C. from where the pair had departed and the airport where Hyde had worked for 20 months. The crew had neglected to refuel the small craft. Furthermore, the pilot failed to check the fuel before takeoff, which is proper procedure for all aircraft pilots.

After tremendous efforts to restart the right engine, the left one failed. The pair braced for impact as the pilot aimed for a baseball field in their path. At 4:32 p.m. they crashed into a patch of trees in a residential area in Floyd, Va.

The trees were in the yard of a woman awaiting the arrival of her husband. Hearing the noise of the crash, she assumed it was her spouse opening the garage door. When he did not enter the house, she went outside to see what was keeping him. Instead, she found a grave scene. Frantic at first, she mustered the strength to call 911. Paramedics arrived almost immediately after receiving the dreadful call. According to Hyde, as luck or an even higher power would have it, the paramedics were holding a conference down the street from the crash site.

Once they arrived, they found Hyde was not breathing. Both of his lungs were collapsed. Immediately, a female paramedic gave him a tracheotomy. Later, he would learn she had never successfully performed that procedure on the first try until that day on him.

Now that he was taking in air again, he was airlifted to Roanoke Regional Hospital in Roanoke, Va. Upon reaching the hospital, he was pronounced DOA. Fortunately, doctors were able to revive him.

During that time, the hospital chaplain notified the Hyde family giving them very vague details of the accident. Hyde's mother, father and brother raced to his side. It was there they learned the extent of his injuries. The crash left him with 14 broken bones, which included three cracks in his cranium, a jaw broken in four places, a broken vertebra, a broken leg and four missing teeth. His left eye was knocked out—paramedics were unable to locate it at the crash site. In addition, the roof of his mouth was knocked loose.

"I was slightly injured," Hyde jokes. These "slight" injuries are what awaited his family. Hyde's father, a former rodeo cowboy passed out upon seeing his son. His brother cried at the tragic sight of his sibling. Mrs. Hyde, his mother, remained strong and intuitively knew that her son would be blind even before doctors informed her. His right eye is now completely covered by a fully matured cataract.

"My poor mother I probably took 10 years off of her life," Hyde laments.

The family stayed by his side while he was in a coma for 20 days. He remained in the hospital for 10 more days until being transported to The Charlotte Rehabilitation Center in Charlotte, N.C., where, among other things, he had to relearn how to walk; but this time without his sight.

Even with the tremendous love and help from his family, recovery and rehabilitation have been both long and hard; However, his determination has remained strong and focused. He has overcome many of his injuries and learned to work around others, learning the skills of blindness that allow him and so many others to live independently.

One aspect of his blindness training that has attributed to his independence and psychological well being is his guide dog Lincoln. The two were introduced in June of 2000 at Southeastern Guide Dogs, Inc. in Palmetto, Fla., where the black Labrador Retriever memorably gave him the first of many kisses.

"He has helped me build my confidence and has been my constant companion," Hyde said.

Despite his losses, which include the death of his beloved father only 18 months after the plane crash, Hyde sees a bright future for himself. In five years, he wants to be working as a ground instructor for a flight school or the FAA. In 10 years, his goal is to have 100 of his students earn their pilots licenses per year.

Respectfully, this North Carolina native believes he survived and overcame this tragedy for a reason.

"I do believe I was left here for a reason. I want to teach pilots how to avoid what happened to me," Hyde explained. "I don't know if they want to listen to a blind person, but I want to pass on my knowledge."

Ultimately, he hopes his story and his knowledge will not only have wealth in the field of aviation but to all persons, despite occupation, disability or social status.

"I want to be the one people look at and say, 'If he can do that, so can I.' I want to be an inspiration and motivation to people," Hyde said.

Barry realizes everything in his life - and life in general - boils down to determination.

"I've gotten to where I am because I want to be here," he explains.

Daytona Beach Community College

Friday, September 21, 2007, I spoke with Suzanne Amsel who worked for Daytona Beach Community College. She runs the disability services office, and she asked me if she could invite me to attend their gathering on September 22. I took a cab over to the school and met with her, and I took some articles and pictures of Lincoln and me. She placed them around the table that we sat at under a tent.

Contacted by the Air Traffic Control Association

Tuesday morning, September 25, 2007, Miguel Vasquez contacted me from the Air Traffic Control Association located in Washington, DC. He called me to tell me they selected me as a recipient of their scholarship, and their scholarship convention took place from October 28 through October 31.

Embry-Riddle's Business Management Presentation

Friday morning, October 5, 2007, I spoke with Tamilla Curtis. She wanted me to do a presentation to her business management class on Thursday, October 11. Nance took Lincoln and me to meet with her, and then we walked together to her class. After the presentation, Tamilla brought us home.

Contacted by ATCA

Thursday, October 11, 2007, Miguel Vasquez emailed Nance and told her Cindy Castillo came by and talked with him. She asked him about me speaking to the Air Traffic Control Association at the convention. He emailed her to pass along the information and the request to me.

White Kane Walk

Saturday, October 13, 2007, Nance, Jackson, Lincoln, and I went to the White Kane Awareness Walk in Daytona Beach. The walk included the National Federation of the Blind state and the state of Florida Council for the Blind. In addition, the American

Council for the Blind, national and state blind representatives, both sponsored the walk.

VIP on Air Radio Interview

Tuesday, October 16, Jill Daly from VIP on Air called me and asked me if I would consider a radio interview at 8:40 in the morning. In addition, Wednesday, October 17, 2007, I had an interview on Insight radio station out of Glasgow, Scotland. The song playing before Jill Daly interviewed me was "I Love a Rainy Night" by Eddie Rabbit. Simon Pauli lined the interview up, and Jill Daly interviewed me for three minutes.

Jill said, live on the air, "We are talking about blind people with mainstream jobs, and I am joined on the line now all the way from the states, Barry Hulon Hyde. Good afternoon to you, Barry."

I said hello, good afternoon.

"Good afternoon, it is actually morning where you are. What is it, eight forty in the morning?"

"Yes, it is, ma'am!"

"Thank you very much for getting up early and talking with us on the Daily Lunch today. We are talking about people in mainstream jobs, and what makes yours so particularly remarkable is that you teach sighted people how to fly, don't you, Barry?"

"Yes ma'am!"

"And you are completely blind yourself. Now, tell us how you lost your sight."

"Yes, ma'am. June 1, 1998, I was involved in a plane crash, and I lost my smell, taste, and sight. I had fourteen broken bones, both collapsed lungs, my left eye knocked completely out, and four teeth lost. Wow, it was a very traumatic experience. I was fortunate enough to pull through it. God does have a plan for me, I do believe."

"Barry, this line is incredibly bad, so here is what we are going to do. We are going to go to a track, and when we come back, we are going to try to get you on a better line. We are going to a track now, but we will be with you very shortly."

"Yes, ma'am."

"You are talking to the Daily Lunch. We are talking to people about mainstream jobs today. We will get Barry Hulon Hyde back right after this." They played "Freebird" by Lynrd Skynrd!

Jill Daly came back on and said, "Let us go there with 'Freebird.' You are listening to the Daily Lunch. We are talking to blind people in mainstream jobs, and we are trying to have a chat with Barry Hulon Hyde there. Barry Hulon Hyde is a blind pilot in the United States. He teaches sighted people how to fly. Now we have him on the line again, and, Barry, hopefully we have a better line this time."

"Yes, ma'am, it is better, good afternoon or good morning to you!"

"Well, good morning to you wherever you are in the States. It is eight forty in the morning there, and we do appreciate you getting up nice and early to speak with us. As for anybody that did not catch your story, can you recap how you actually lost your sight?"

"Yes, ma'am, nine years, four months, and sixteen days ago, my life traumatically changed. The plane crash occurred, and I lost my smell, taste, and sight. Wow, significant trauma if you will, and the doctors pronounced me dead on arrival from the crash site into Roanoke Regional Hospital, where they airlifted me. Miraculously, I survived."

"Well, as you say, it was completely miraculous because you were pronounced dead."

"Yes, ma'am."

"That is actually incredible. Now, at the beginning of this, Barry, we were talking about blind people in mainstream jobs today. After all you have been through and living through a plane crash, and I cannot imagine—it is one of my worst nightmares. How did you survive that? You want to be a pilot again, and you teach sighted people how to fly."

"Yes, ma'am, after the plane crash and getting over that obstacle, I wanted to continue my role in aviation. The love of aviation is kind of in my blood, if you will. I grew up around aviation, and it has been a large part of my life. I wanted to continue my role in aviation, so I wanted to become a ground instructor. In 2000, I began studying for that license, and I made history by becoming the first and only blind advanced ground instructor and instrument ground instructor in the world for the Federal Aviation Administration. Wow, that was a huge honor to achieve that goal."

"That is incredible, and when did you decide that you were going to take to the skies again and to try to teach sighted people?"

"During my rehabilitation and during 1999, once again, I wanted to do something involved in aviation. I did not know what it would be at that point in my life because I was still suffering from the brain injury. I knew I had to get involved in school again and studies to help me get my brain back working because it affected my short-term memory. Although my long-term memory was good. However, I improved the short-term memory by going back to school, studying, and learning and remembering, which helped me in continuing to share the knowledge of aviation that was already in my brain.

"Barry, I want to win the lottery, but it probably will never happen. Did you ever think at some stage, 'Yes, I want to teach people to fly, but this is not going to happen'?"

"No, ma'am, I wanted to put myself in a position to teach people if they ever encounter the situation that I did, how to handle it, what to do to make sure that they do not have to suffer through what I did. That was a blessing, if you will, for God to keep me here, for me to share my experience with other people and pilots. I feel that is possibly why God left me here, for me to be an example to other fellow pilots, to share my knowledge, ma'am."

"Of course, when you go to teach somebody that is sighted to fly, what is their initial reaction when you are introduced as the pilot for the day, the instructor for the day, and Barry, you are completely blind?"

"I have not received much feedback on what people think about a blind person trying to teach a sighted person how to fly an airplane."

Jill said, "Maybe they're too frightened to talk?"

"Yes, I think it rather intimidates some people, and others, it rather shocks them where they do not know what to say or how to approach me if you will. However, I am blind, and I am still the same person. I still have the same heart, I still have the same thoughts, and so forth. I just cannot smell, taste, or see if you will.

"So, Barry, do you have to give a pep talk when you get into the cockpit? Do you say, 'I am blind, I know what we are doing and I know how to use these instruments, I know what I am doing, do not worry, everything will be fine'? Do you feel you have to relax a little bit, or they do not seem to make any comment about that?"

"I try to instill in people's thinking that aviation is the safest source of transportation there is in the world. It is not that I am just saying that, it proves that Aviation is still the way to go. An automobile is safe, but it is very dangerous because there are many crazy people in the world today. I feel I would rather be in an airplane than in a car on the ground."

"Barry, you are a true inspiration, and it is an absolute amazing story. Now, unfortunately, because we had a problem getting a good line with you we won't be able to go on today, but we will have you on again very, very shortly. Thank you so much for telling us your amazing story."

"Yes, ma'am, thank you so much for allowing me to share my story, ma'am, and it is such an honor to be on your radio station!"

"It is an honor to speak with you, Barry, it really is, and thank you so much!"

"Yes, ma'am, thank you, Jill!"

"That was Barry Hulon Hyde there, a blind pilot and blind instructor. You are listening to the Daily Lunch with Jill Daly on Insight Radio!"

Daytona Beach Community College

Wednesday morning at 10:15, October 17, 2007, Lincoln and I went to Daytona Beach Community College. I was there until 1:00 p.m., and Nance picked us up. We attended their disability program, and Suzanne Amsal put us at a table under a tent. They had a live band whose members were blind, and their name was Out of Sight. October 24, Lincoln and I attended the Come Make a Difference program.

Lutheran News

October 23, Darlene Joy, a member from Hope Lutheran Church emailed me. She informed me that the Lutherans wanted to include me on their Faces page. She said that they wanted an article of four hundred words written about me.

Second Air Traffic Control Association Scholarship

On Monday, October 29, 2007, Nance, Lincoln, and I attended the Air Traffic Control Association (ATCA) International Convention in Washington, DC, at the Wardman Park Marriot, where ATCA awarded me the second scholarship in front of 1,600 people. We visited briefly with Cindy Castillo, Pete Dumont, and Becky Umbaugh. Cindy Castillo was the speaker and grand mistress of the event. At this great lunch, Nance, Lincoln, and I sat at the head table with Cyndi beside us and the FAA administrator Bob Sturgil at the table behind us. It was great meeting this leader and having our picture made with him. Cindy shared with the crowd about ATCA's scholarship fund and what it represents. The ATCA Scholarship Fund provides financial assistance to deserving students who have chosen to seek higher education in the science of air traffic control and other disciplines, including children of air traffic control specialists. Cindy explained the different categories and amounts of scholarships available to participants. Cindy introduced all seventeen recipients, and only four of us were in person.

Cindy Castillo stated,

> The last recipient who is here with us today,
> Barry Hulon Hyde, who is a previous scholarship
> recipient last year. Barry is the first blind student
> to attend Embry-Riddle and the only blind stu-
> dent to hold certifications as Advanced Ground
> Instructor and Instrument Ground Instructor. He
> graduated with a MS in Aeronautics and is cur-
> rently pursuing a PhD in Business Administration
> at North Central University. I would like to wel-
> come my friend, Barry and Lincoln up here to
> accept a certificate with help from Nancy. If any-
> body gets a chance, this man is an amazing man.
> I think he had all of us teary eyed last year so, the
> only thing I ask is, say a few words but Barry keep
> it clean.

Nance helped Lincoln and me get to the stage, and then Cindy
pointed me in the proper direction at the podium and to the microphone. I began by saying,

> Good afternoon everyone. Man, what an
> honor to be here, once again. First off, I would like to
> begin by thanking ATCA and the committee. First
> off, allowing us to come forward to receive the schol-
> arship last year. Man that was such an honor to grad-
> uate from Embry-Riddle with my Masters of Science
> in Aeronautics with specializations in Aviation Safety
> and Aviation Operations. This year, the scholar-
> ship will help me attain my doctorate in Business
> Administration with a specialization in aeronauti-
> cal Safety. Of course, everyone is wondering about
> Lincoln the Aviator. We originally called him Lincoln

the Navigator but when I graduated from Embry-Riddle, I promoted him to Lincoln the Aviator. The crowd chuckled. I continued,

Of course, I would like to thank the ATCA committee once again for awarding the scholarship to us this year. Man, it is such an honor to be here to share this experience with everyone. As you can tell, Lincoln wants a treat, so let me give him a treat first.

The crowd laughed once again.

June 1st of 1998, at 4:32 that afternoon, we went off Roanoke's radar. We crashed into a stand of trees and believe me the trees did not give, but the airplane was completely demolished. Miraculously, the paramedics saved my life. I do believe I have a purpose, I do not know what that purpose is yet, but I am going to make the best of what I have left to live for. I want to go to work for an organization, whether it is to teach safety, human factors, because all of us are aware that 75 % of all accidents come from negligence, human factors, or errors. Next, I began by speaking of studying for the AGI and taking the written on June 6, 2000 and I became the first blind Advanced Ground Instructor in the world for the Federal Aviation Administration. Following this accomplishment, I came to Palmetto, Florida to receive Lincoln after 26 days of training with him. I came home and I thought I wanted to continue my role in aviation. The next step was beginning studying for the Instrument Ground Instructor license. Therefore, in October of 2000, I became the first blind IGI in the world for the

FAA. I asked what I should do now. I decided to go back to school at the University of North Carolina at Charlotte to receive the Bachelors of Arts Degree in History. Fortunately, December 18, 2004, I graduated with a BA in History. I thought then I needed to continue my role in aviation. Therefore, I came to Daytona Beach, Florida and met Dr. Marvin Smith, who was my advisor and he became a terrific friend. He signed me up for classes every semester and I moved to Daytona in 2005 to begin classes in August, and I graduated May 7 of this year with the Masters of Science Degree in Aeronautics with specializations in Aviation Safety and Aviation Operations. I asked, what do I do now, June 1 came back around and this day was a very memorable day, and it changed my life and I am letting this day change my life a little more, so that is the day my doctorate began at North Central University. Eventually I will achieve this goal and by December of 2010, I would like to become Dr. Hyde instead of Dr. Jeckyl. The crowd laughed once again. You know, I do not know what I want to be when I grow up, but I want to be involved in aviation. I want to teach students, pilots, fellow pilots, and if they ever encounter what I did, how to handle the situation, how to get the airplane on the ground and then ask questions. It is such an honor and thank you all once again.

The crowd began clapping, and Cindy said, "Great job." I spoke for about seven minutes. Miguel Vasquez helped me down the steps and off the stage. Cindy took the microphone and said, "And to think he does not have a purpose."

We had our pictures made in front of the White House, did lots of walking, and Lincoln stole the show wherever we went. We attended a fifties ceremony, and they had two impersonators. One was Elvis, the other one was Marylyn Monroe, and I danced with her. Becky Umbaugh had a memorable event; she had fallen and broken her wrist.

In addition, Jeffrey Sutton turned over my resume to the AMES Research Center and the Human Resource Center at NASA. Cindy introduced us as she took us around the exhibit hall.

Bishop in Attendance

Sunday morning, November 4, 2007, Lincoln and I had our picture made with the bishop during the adoption of the new church. In addition, the bishop was in attendance because of the foundation of the ministry. Darlene Joy said that picture would be going into the Lutheran magazine. This day, about 170 people and one dog were in church.

Business Class Presentation

In November, I did a presentation for Tamilla Curtis's BA 201 principles of management class. This class included thirty-three undergraduate students. Nance, Lincoln, and I presented to the class the summary of the accident that I lived through.

Sonic Boom

Wednesday, November 7, 2007, I heard the sonic boom from the *Discovery* space shuttle. It occurred before 1:00 p.m. that afternoon, and it landed safely at Cape Canaveral. I thought a tree fell on the town house, and the noise scared me. I called Nance immediately and told her she needed to come home and check things out to see what happened. She told me what it was.

National Federation of the Blind, Daytona Beach Chapter

Thursday, November 8, 2007, Sabrina Deaton emailed me to tell me she sent my story to *Good Morning America*. She received a response from the producer, and that woman wanted some questions answered. Sabrina asked in her email if I had any videos or anything like that. I responded and told her I had the Women in Aviation International video of the taped presentation.

Second GMAA-Batchelor Aviation Scholarship Foundation

Saturday evening, November 10 and 11, 2007, the Greater Miami Aviation Association—Batchelor Aviation Scholarship Foundation awarded me another scholarship at their yearly convention at the Doral Golf Resort and Spa in Miami, Florida. They awarded me a $7,500 scholarship and paid for our hotel room. This room was the nicest room we have stayed in yet. The women were dressed in ballroom gowns and men dressed in tuxedos. I spoke with Mark Henderson along with other people. Steven Dawn explained, "The GMAA Scholarship fund awarded fourteen individuals with a scholarship totaling $80,000. Barry is unique, as he is the first and only blind person in the world to hold aviation licenses by the FAA." The crowd applauded for about seven seconds. Steven explained, "In 1998, Barry was a passenger in an aircraft that was involved in an accident. He sustained serious injuries including the loss of his sight. He had 1,600 hours of flight time and one week away from a job interview with US Airways Express. After two years of rehabilitation, he began studying for the Federal Aviation licenses. The FAA administered the tests to him orally. They had never given a test to a blind person before in their entire history. He passed the written for the advanced and instrument ground instructor's licenses. The FAA has confirmed that he is the first and only blind person in the world to hold these licenses. In 2005, Barry moved from North Carolina to Daytona Beach, Florida, to pursue his master's degree from Embry-Riddle with specializations in aviation safety and aviation operations. He did so with a perfect 4.0 GPA." The crowd applauded for eight seconds. Steven Dawn said, "It gets better! On June 1, 2007, he began working on his doctoral in business administration with an aeronautical safety specialization online program with Northcentral University.

"Barry, on behalf of the GMAA—Batchelor Aviation Scholarship Foundation, I would like to thank you, Nancy, and Lincoln the Navigator for joining us tonight. You represent serving the scholarship fund and why we are here tonight." The crowd applauded for about thirty seconds with some hooting and hollering going on.

Lincoln and I took the podium in front of about 250 people, began by stating, "Wow, good evening, everyone, this is such an honor. Man, this is such a wonderful blessing. Oh, I am just lost for words. However, first off, I would like to thank all of the recipients of the scholarships and congratulations to all of them. Then, I would like to thank the Greater Miami Aviation Association and the Batchelor Aviation Scholarship Fund and all of the other donors here this evening for giving us recognition and the opportunity to carry on our education. Also, of course being able to share my story and unfortunate circumstance with all of the other fellow pilots and future pilots present today. I want to eventually go to work for the FAA, NASA, possibly Embry-Riddle, or a flight school somewhere, and I want to be able to teach what I incurred—what happened to me and prevent all other fellow pilots from encountering what I did. In addition, I would like to share history of Embry-Riddle's first president, Jack Hunt. He stated, 'For most people, the sky is the limit. But for those who love aviation, the sky is home.' I feel everyone here this evening share that wonderful knowledge and experience. It provides me a lot of inspiration and motivation, what I need to carry on to live each day. It inspires me to no end. I am just grateful to be here and alive and doing as well as I am. Thank you everyone, once again. God bless!" The crowd applauded for twenty-five seconds. Mark Henderson said,

"Thank you, Barry, and thank you, Steve. This is why we are here. One more hand!" The crowd applauded for ten seconds.

Kannapolis Citizen

Thursday, December 13, 2007, Joann Garnerman and the editor Joanie Morris with the *Kannapolis Citizen* interviewed me. During the interview, Joanie made pictures of Lincoln and me. On Sunday, December 16, Joann contacted me to answer a few questions she had and clarify a few things. The issue came out on Wednesday, December 19, 2007. The newspaper had a picture of me in a Cessna on the cover and included nine different pictures of me. Lincoln was in a few, and the article was a good one.

Blindness doesn't keep Hyde from aviation career

Barry Hulon Hyde loves aviation. He has since the age of 12 when he worked for Ferrell James, Sr., a pilot for U.S. Airways and the husband of Barry's second cousin. James owned rental properties and paid Barry to help him remodel and renovate the properties. Barry was around airplanes all of the time and took his first airplane ride with Ferrell James, Jr., and discovered his passion...Aviation.

In 1991, at the age of 19, Barry began taking flying lessons. He earned his private pilot's license on June 26, 1992, and was well on his way to securing a lifelong dream of becoming a commercial pilot. In 1994, Hyde graduated from Rowan-Cabarrus Community College with an associate degree in business administration and a certificate in accounting and purchased his first rental property. In 1995, desiring to begin flight school, Hyde sold his rental property to have funds for

tuition and enrolled in flight school at American
Flyers in Addison, Texas. He completed flight
school in January 1996 just a few weeks short of
his 24th birthday. In October that year, Barry was
hired as a flight instructor for Lancaster Aviation
located at Concord Regional Airport. Barry's
career in aviation had begun. However, an unfortunate and unnecessary aviation accident interrupted that career on June 1, 1998.

On the first day of June 1998, Barry had
agreed to ride as a safety pilot for Robert E.
Anderson, a licensed pilot who was working
on getting his instrument ratings current. (The
responsibility of a safety pilot is to look out the
windows while the main pilot flies the aircraft by
instruments.) Anderson had rented a twin-engine
Comanche from the flight school to fly to his
home in West Virginia. The safety pilot for that
flight was twenty-six year old, Barry Hulon Hyde.

Approximately twenty-seven minutes after
takeoff, the right fuel tank ran dry and the
right engine stopped. Ten minutes later, the left
main fuel tank also ran dry and the left engine
stopped. Hyde recalls his last words to air traffic control personnel as "Niner-four Yankee is
going in". (Niner-four Yankee was the identification tail number of the airplane: N7794Y.) The
Comanche crashed near Floyd, Virginia, approximately ninety-two nautical miles from Concord
and approximately fifty-eight nautical miles from
Lewisburg County, West Virginia.

Many articles about Barry have been published since that crash … his broken facial bones
and reconstructive surgeries, the loss of taste
and smell, physical and cognitive rehabilitation,

blindness. They retell his tragedy. This article tells his triumph.

Barry has achieved notoriety in many areas since tragedy stole his ability to fly. Since his airplane accident, Hyde has become the Federal Aviation Administration's first and only blind certified advanced ground instructor and instrument ground instructor. He has earned a Bachelor of Arts degree in History from the University of North Carolina - Charlotte, and in May 2007, graduated with a 4.0 GPA from Embry-Riddle Aeronautical University, the largest flight school in the world, which is located in Daytona Beach, Florida. Hyde achieved his Master of Science degree in Aeronautics with a specialization in Aviation Safety and Aviation Operations. Hyde is the first blind graduate in the school's eighty-one year history. He is currently working on his doctoral degree via online from Northcentral University in Prescott, Arizona, in business administration with an aeronautical safety specialization. On October 31, 2007, Barry spoke in Washington, DC, to members of the Air Traffic Control Association, and on January 4 - 9, 2008, Barry will attend the American Institute of Aeronautics and Astronautics convention in Reno, Nevada, to present his graduate research project entitled "An Examination of the Importance of Properly Executed Preflight Checklists to Ensure Flight Safety".

Mr. Hyde states, "I love aviation. I want to be a part of it some way, in some shape or form. Through my research and through my personal experience, I can share with other pilots what I've lived through and perhaps help them avoid disaster. Pilot error, or pilot negligence, both so closely related, are avoidable with the proper checklists. It is my belief that my personal experience along with thorough research, can provide pilots with information and data that might prevent them from experiencing what I've lived through."

Why has Barry succeeded when others faced with life-altering circumstances stop pursuing their passion? Perhaps it is his positive attitude, his determination, or his resourcefulness as attested to by Dr. Marvin Smith, Hyde's advisor and professor of Applied Aviation Sciences at Embry-Riddle Aeronautical University. Perhaps it is his calling, something so innate it happens naturally. More than likely, Barry Hulon Hyde's success is simply because he loves aviation.

Mighty Eight Air Force Museum

December 30, 2007, driving from Johnson City, Tennessee en route to Daytona Beach, Nance, Jackson, Lincoln, and I stopped in Pooler, Georgia at the Mighty Eight Air Force Museum. Nance made pictures of Lincoln and me standing beside some airplanes. We listened and watched videos from World War II. We met two volunteers that served in the military and they gave us firsthand experience.

American Institute of Aeronautics & Astronautics Inc.
William T. Piper Sr. General Aviation Systems Graduate Award

Funding for this award is provided by endowment gifts from the Piper Aircraft Corporation and the WT Piper Sr. Foundation, in the name of William T. Piper Sr. combined with support from the General Aviation Systems Technical Committee and the AIAA Foundation. Eligible applicants will be actively participating in research endeavors in general aviation as part of their graduate studies. Official recognition will be made in conjunction with the awards presentations ceremony at the AIAA Aerospace Sciences Meeting. In addition, the AIAA Foundation will present the recipient with a special recognition plaque in honor of this award.

January 7, 2008, the flight consisted of flying out of Orlando on a trip for little over four hours to Denver, Colorado, then close to two hours to Reno, Nevada. We stayed at the Grand Sierra Resort. One of the restaurants we ate at was named Johnnie Rockets, and it was a diner. Unfortunately, the United Airbus A321 had an altimeter stuck on nine thousand MSL feet. That delayed the departure; therefore, we did not reach Reno until 2:00 a.m. Pacific Coast time that next morning. During this trip, we were passengers on four Airbus's A321's on United. On January 8, 2008, I received a scholarship from the American Institute of Aeronautics and Astronautics (AIAA). AIAA provided a round-trip travel to Reno, Nevada, to receive the scholarship valued at $5,000 in person, and I presented my graduate research project at their international convention.

I began by saying,

> Good morning to all. First off, I want to begin by thanking (AIAA) for awarding me the William T. Piper Sr. General Aviation Systems Graduate Award. That is a huge honor for me to receive that award considering I lost my sight in a Piper plane crash. I will expand further on that in a few minutes. In addition, I would like to congratulate everyone here this morning that has received a scholarship, as well I feel special like you guys too. Therefore, I would like to begin first by introducing the team here. My name is Barry Hulon Hyde; we have Lincoln the Aviator,

and then my fiancée, Nancy Riedel. Wow, as I said, it is such an honor to be here.

Currently, I am attending Northcentral University, working on my DBA on-line. I graduated May 7, 2007, from Embry-Riddle with a Master's of Science in Aeronautics with specializations in Aviation Safety and Aviation Operations. Currently, I am going to present to you all "The importance of the Properly Executed Preflight Checklists to Ensure Flight Safety". The cause of the plane crash I lived through was due to the pilot in command not following the preflight checklist and I was a passenger on that plane that day. I will talk about six plane crashes altogether. They could have all been prevented. Either the preflight checklist flunked by the pilot or negligence played part if you will. That is checks not properly administered. The six plane crashes I will talk about consist of four commercial and two of which were international, and two were General Aviation, and one of these is the one that I was involved in that crashed.

I want to begin with a research analysis. I looked over the National Transportation Board data, as well as the FAA, the DOT data, and the cockpit, crew resource analysis I pulled together that information and came up with the six plane crashes that I will now discuss. The first one was Virgin Air, Flight 301 that occurred in Porta Plata, Dominican Republic. It took off and crashed into the Pacific Ocean due to the administering of the preflight checklist to the Pitot tube being full of insects. Therefore, as they were climbing out after liftoff and during the climb out the airspeed indicator was above normal.

Therefore, they started to slow the climb down by powering back and increasing the pitch up attitude. The airplane stalled and spun into the ocean killing 189 people on board. That accident should have never happened. I think the date was February 6, 1996.

The next plane crash was Aero Peru, and that was Flight 603. There were 70 people on board and no survivors. Everyone killed on that accident and this one should have never happened as well. The airplane went down for maintenance and they took the airplane to wash it and polish it. They covered the static ports with masking tape and as the airplane was down maintenance did not remove the tape. When the pilots came out to preflight the airplane, they never noticed the clear masking tape over the static ports. Therefore, as you can imagine another plane crash occurred because five minutes after takeoff the pilots were receiving erroneous readings on the airspeed as well as the altimeter. Therefore, once again, I guess they tried to slow the airplane down thinking it was over speeding possibly overcorrecting. Once again, the airplane crashed into the Pacific Ocean close to Lima, Peru where it departed from.

The next plane crash I will talk about, probably, the most recent one that occurred on August 27, 2006. I am sure everyone here has heard about it. It was the Comair flight 5191, out of Kentucky. Does anyone recognize that plane crash? Out of 50 people on board, 49 killed with the co-pilot surviving. How that happened is beyond me, but I am glad someone survived. Now, they took off on the wrong runway and when they taxied out that morning about 6:00 a.m. and ATC cleared them for takeoff. They did not follow the Q & A's to get them to the correct runway. They taxied out and took off from a non-lit and dark runway. The Commercial lit runway was ignored. They went and took off from a non-lit General Aviation runway. Therefore, as they slowly lifted off, the airplane did not have enough airspeed for the climb out and it crashed back onto the ground and engulfed in a ball of fire. I am sure ejection of the co-pilot occurred.

One more plane crash I investigated was US Airways Flight 405, occurred in 1992 out of Flushing Bay, New York. This plane crash killed 27 people and 24 survived. Now, everybody is familiar with holdover time and what I am leading to is when the airplane was deiced, the crew had an 11-minute holdover time. That means, the time the airplane was deiced it had 11 minutes to go and takeoff. Therefore, the first time this happened, 20 to 25 minutes lapsed, and they decided to go back and get deiced. They were deiced a second time and this time held for 35 minutes. This time is 24 minutes after the 11-minute holdover time they had to take-off. This was one problem and the second problem was they did not verify that the airplane was ready to fly. This means that they had all of this ice built up on the wings and they went to do the takeoff roll. Instead of having a normal takeoff, they had an accelerated stall. The airplane took off briefly, then stalled back onto the runway and burst into flames. This accident is one more that should have never happened. Those pilots should have made sure that airplane was ready to fly.

Now, the next airplane crash that I will talk about indicates how hard it is to takeoff with a control lock still in place. Now, come on folks, don't you think even the passengers could see that control lock in place and would say, hey man, what is that saying remove before flight, don't we need to remove that. This plane crash occurred in 2000, it was a Be-95, and there were six people on board the airplane. When you go and do a preflight checklist folks, we always go inside and begin there first. One of the first steps is to remove the control lock because when you go outside and check the control surfaces and check for freedom of movement and check to make sure screws and pins are in place. You have to be able to move the control surfaces like the ailerons and elevator. This pilot could not do a proper preflight checklist because the control lock was still in place, right. Well, when they went to take-off, guess what, they could not move the elevator. The airplane lifted off, stalled back onto the runway, and crashed. It erupted into a big ball of fire and killed everyone on the airplane. Another failed preflight checklist that leads to the airplane crash. That checklist is of prime importance for us to carry on in safety for Aviation.

I lived through the sixth airplane crash. There were two of us on board, the pilot and myself. I was a pilot with one, 600 flight hours and one week away from a job interview with US Airways Express, the commuter airline. I boarded a running airplane folks; I boarded and asked the pilot did you check the fuel? He said oh yes, we are full of fuel. I asked how about the oil. He said oh shoot, I forgot to check the oil. I said taxi us up to the terminal and I will go inside and get two quarts of oil to take with us. I went inside, charged two quarts of oil, came back out, and boarded the airplane. We went and took off from runway 02 and crashed 37 minutes later. The main tanks were out of fuel. First off, the engines would have never quit if there had been fuel in the main tanks. Second, off, if we had been full of fuel, after crashing, we would have burned to death. I can stand up here and talk about that accident a long time because it is very frustrating to know that I had to experience that and live thru that traumatic experience and that negligence. The ground crew members did not do their daily or nightly checklist to fuel all thirteen of the flight school's airplanes that were on the flight line in our flight school that I worked at. I was a flight instructor for the flight school at the airport. Four days in a row, the Airport Service workers did not fuel the airplane. The fuel in the airplane came from another airport 50 nautical miles away. The airplane flew back to the airport, which flew out roughly 30 minutes of fuel out of the main tanks. The pilot I crashed with flew it on Sunday May 31, 2.4 hours, which is two hours and twenty-four minutes. The main tanks had three and a half hours of fuel in it when they are full. We crashed 37 minutes after takeoff on that Monday, June 1. What happened to the fuel in the auxiliary tanks? When the main tanks went dry, we thought we had a mechanical problem. The pilot kept telling me we were full of fuel and I had no reason to doubt him, I had never flown with a lying pilot before. I am sure no one here has flown with a lying pilot either. When the right engine quit the pilot said we are full of fuel what is going on. Well, we did a couple restarts in the main position. Guess what, the fuel lines suck air out of the empty fuel tanks into the lines. Now, we go to the auxiliary position and we get a bunch of blue smoke. We then think we have possibly an engine fire so, we go back to the main position and crank and all the blue smoke goes away. I wonder why, no fuel to burn there, right. We go back to the auxiliary position and we cannot get a restart. We continue to go thru the emergency restart procedures and we cannot get a restart. Therefore, we go back to the main fuel selector. We are doing restarts after restarts and more restarts, with no luck. Guess what, all the fuel in the main on the left engine is exhausted and finally quits. As all the restarts are going on, we are continuing to lose altitude. When the engine eventually quits, we then have to pick out a field to land. We did not make it to the field we hit the trees. The doctors at the hospital pronounced me dead on arrival folks. Miraculously, the paramedics saved my life because they were holding a weekly meeting close by at a local fire department. Fortunately, the house we crashed next to, the woman of the house was home and she thought the noise was the garage door opening. Does anyone wonder why when we crashed; those auxiliary tanks did not catch on fire? The reason why they did not burn was that during the crash, the impact with the trees knocked the auxiliary tanks off, the main tanks were empty, therefore, there was not anything left to burn.

The preflight checklist is of prime importance folks. I have been trying to get everyone to understand and to see how important it is. Now, in summary, the preflight checklist occurs at the beginning of every flight. Nance explained, "On our flight from Orlando, on Saturday, the preflight checklist failed. The Altimeter stuck at 9,000 feet delayed our departure by three hours in Orlando. As Barry stated, that is the reason the preflight checklist takes place. so, as everyone around us was complaining about being delayed three hours because the crew was waiting on a new part to be flown in on another flight to replace the problem real quickly. I was grateful because of everything he has gone through, I would rather them find something on the ground in that preflight checklist, that is the mechanism put into place before you get airborne". For us that survive in Aviation, we have to administer things like the preflight checklist to make sure negligence was not performed and people are doing their job as well as pilots are doing their job and not taking things for granite. Previously, I said I had never flown with a lying pilot and that pilot was the first lying pilot that I had flown with in the airplane. I was a 1,600-hour pilot, I was that close to entering my coffin and miraculously, they saved my life. I am very blessed to be here standing in front of you folks today. I would certainly, like to answer anyone's questions. Please feel free to ask me anything and thank you all for allowing me to share my story.

The crowd clapped for four seconds. The crowd asked several questions. The first question had to do with the regulation of the preflight checklist, and was it mandatory for someone to do the preflight? I answered, "Yes, it is a Federal Aviation regulation." The next question was about if the pilot lost his license. I answered, "The pilot is still grounded today, and the FAA revoked his medical as well, as I am told the FAA took his license." Someone began talking about why my injuries were so bad and the pilot's were not. I asked,

Does anyone want to guess what is missing in a 1965 model airplane. It is missing the shoulder harness and the lap belt was the only protection on that airplane. Therefore, I had that lap belt as tight as I could get it before we hit the trees. Upon impact the seat broke, the control yoke turned completely to the left into the good engine, and it went right into my chest. This impact collapsed both lungs, you can see the scar in my throat, and the paramedics intubated me at the crash site, open the airway to my lungs, and saved my life. I am also getting at; I was wearing a headset and a pair of sunglasses. When my head continually hit the dash, I do not know if the sunglasses cut my eye out or what happened. The doctors found my eye behind my cheekbone. The crash tore my face up and the swelling was so severe, the chaplain at the Roanoke regional Hospital called my family and told my dad that you need to come and identify the body. He came into the hospital room to identify me and he passed out because I was in such bad shape. You folks can just imagine how bad the situation was. My head was swollen the size of a basketball because I had nine broken bones in my face. I was in a coma for 20 days and in the hospital for almost three months. I have been very blessed to rebound and come back as far as I have.

Another person asked a question about different preflight procedures. I explained about a crop duster pilot that flies that same airplane eight hours a day does not even do a preflight.

> Certain pilots feel after they have performed the same checklist procedures 20 times, then they do not even carry the checklist around with them. I disagree with this because after 30 steps on the checklist the pilot will overlook certain items. For electronic checklists, on the survey for my graduate research project showed only three of 34 pilots would prefer an electronic checklist verses a laminated or paper checklist. I used an electronic checklist and I carried it around in my shirt pocket. I used the electronic checklist verses carrying the laminated card or carrying a paper checklist. I would put it in my pocket when I had to check the oil or stand up on the wing strut and unscrew the lid to check the fuel.

One of our participants answered that the best checklist is only as good as the person using it. Someone else spoke about the color of the tape used in one of the international flights. Instead of using clear, could the regulation only allow red, brown, or gray tape instead of clear?

> Something that is very noticeable, like the control lock that is red and says remove before flight. In addition, when administering a preflight on an airplane if you do not look closely at the Pitot tube or put your mouth on it and blow through it then you will not know if it is blocked or air is flowing through it freely.
> The Graduate Research Project I did for my Master's Degree, I identified not only the check-

lists for Aviation. I identified checklist for maritime and the nuclear plants. The checklist for maritime took place in Belgium and my advisor at Embry-Riddle was there when this ferry, the Herald of Free Enterprise sank. It departed the port loaded with cars, the captain did not make sure the entry way for the cars was closed and the ferry capsized and close to 200 people were killed, and many survivors were injured.

We concluded by discussing in more detail holdover time, proper preflight procedures, and people talking about real life-like examples. We thanked them all one more time and received a round of applause.

Lutheran Magazine

Thursday, January 24, 2008, I learned about the Lutheran magazine coming out and it had an article about Lincoln and me in it. Pastor Jack Ottoson emailed Nance to tell her about it. At church, the next Sunday, Pastor Jack told the congregation before service about me being in it and some of the members congratulated me.

Airbus Interview

Tuesday, January 22, 2008, I received an email from Airbus and the Women in Aviation International. They shared with me that I was a finalist for a $5,000 grant, and it is an Airbus Leadership Award. They told me when to expect the interview. Therefore, Thursday, February 7, 2008, at 11:00 a.m., Renee Martin Nagle, who is the vice president and general counsel of Airbus America Inc. interviewed me for the Airbus Leadership grant. This grant's application was through the Women in Aviation International, and this scholarship was valued at $5,000. Renee stated that they received thirty-eight applications. "After going through these applications, four or five finalists were chosen, then we interview them. Two finalists are then picked, and we used to do the interviews at the conference. This year we decided to do it a little differently and conducted all of the interviews by phone. The determination comes from the interviews. We will let the winners know and the official awards will be given out at lunch on a Friday at the conference." She did ask me some questions like, Were you going to attend the conference in San Diego? She asked when I joined and why I joined. I explained that we were a new chapter and I knew several of the women, since we attended school together. I wanted to be a part of the organization, since they were all women, and I felt that was where I wanted to be.

She stated, "Your story is very compelling."

"I was hoping to impress you with my uniqueness."

"You have reversed course and gone about your career in a different manner now."

"Aviation was the love of my life before the accident and continues to be so afterwards. I am continuing to work on my education, and by December of 2010, I would like to be Dr. Hyde versus Dr. Jekyll."

This statement really made her laugh, and she said, "You're funny, and I bet you had jokes about that before. Since receiving your master's degree, what made you decide to keep going?"

I told her that I figured it would open doors for me and allow me to go to work somewhere teaching ground school for students, private pilot licenses, instrument ratings, commercial licenses, flight instructors, and airline transport pilots. "Also, I would like to be in management possibly working for the FAA. I do not know what the future holds, and I never dreamed I would live through a plane crash, but here I am. Somehow, I want to be involved in aviation where I can teach and prevent what happened to me from occurring to other pilots—to teach other pilots if they encounter what I did, how to handle it, what steps are taken, what they should do, and to remember to land the airplane, then ask questions."

Renee asked, "Were you the pilot flying at the time?"

I answered, "No, ma'am, I was a passenger."

"How large was the aircraft?"

"It was a small four-seater Piper Twin Comanche."

"Was it bad weather?"

"No, ma'am, the main tanks were empty."

"It ran out of fuel!"

"The main tanks were empty, and that is the reason we did not burn to death."

"Oh my gosh! I guess since you were out of fuel, you just glided in?"

"Yes, ma'am, you talk about human factors that accident should have never happened. So many negligent parties just did not do their job. For aviation to continue each day, jobs have to be done, whether it is through maintenance, the ground operators, the owners—everybody at the airport has to do their job as well. As a passenger, I had no right to do anything, and I got out of the airplane and got him two quarts of oil. He continued to lie to me even after the first engine quit. He said we were full of fuel. Well, months later, we come to find out no that was the problem—the main tanks were empty."

"Oh my gosh!"

"We crashed thirty-seven minutes after takeoff."

"What? That is true negligence!"

Renee asked, "And?"

"And unfortunately, my income ever since I went on disability is a whopping $554 a month. In January, I received a whopping $13 raise this year, so I am actually up to $567 a month. I was so close to a career as a pilot somewhere, whether it was for a race team for NASCAR or a corporate pilot. My mother was a flight attendant for US Airways Express, the commuter airline. I had a job interview lined up one week after the accident. My mother's last flight was the same day that mine was. I was crashing as she was taking off from Greenville, North Carolina, coming back to Charlotte. She was lining up the interview with the chief pilot, and he was flying the airplane that day. Goodness, I never got to see that interview take place because I was laid up in a coma for the next twenty days after the crash. None of the family thought I would survive, but miraculously, I pulled through, and wow, it is a unique story."

"It really is! What is amazing is your spirit because you were going up in one direction, all of a sudden, you know, fate kind of whopped you and got you off track, and you said, 'You know what, all right.' You were going to try to make lemonade out of this? I can with what I have in the time I have left."

I stated the paperwork shows I became the first blind advanced ground instructor and first blind instrument ground instructor for the FAA. The AGI was two years and five days, and the IGI was two and a half years after the plane crash. I was the first blind person that the FAA had ever tested and read the test to. I made more history, if you will. I told Renee whom I met in Washington, DC, on October 31, 2007, the up-and-coming FAA administrator Bobby Sturgil.

She said, "Oh really, he is a nice guy."

"Lincoln and I had our picture taken with him. That took place at the Air Traffic Control Association Convention. In addition, we had our picture made in front of the White House, the Pentagon, and the Washington Monument. I am happy to be where I am at even though I have to do it in the condition that I am doing it. I am very blessed to be alive and doing as well as I am. It is also such a high honor to graduate from the largest flight school in the world with a master's degree and to be their first blind graduate to do so in their eighty-one year history."

"Wow, you are opening up paths for other people, for them to say, 'If he can do it, so can I.'"

"The blind community and the aviation community are noticing me. I do want to be an inspiration to everyone because like I said, the negligence performed shows that the accident should have never happened. I want to prevent what happened to me from occurring to other pilots."

"It is such a high honor to be where I am at, and I never dreamed that I would live through a plane crash, much less be where I am at today. To be a finalist by Airbus is such a high honor for me."

"How are you paying for your studies? With you only making $564, are you receiving scholarships?"

"The scholarships have been how I have made it as far as I have, ma'am. One example would be, when I was attending Embry-Riddle, it cost me around $43,000 for the master's degree."

"Oh gosh!"

"Therefore, I do not owe a dime to this day, and I was able to pay for that master's degree since Embry-Riddle gave me a $12,000 scholarship. Division of Blind Services here in Daytona Beach paid the rest of the tuition. The GMAA gave me a $6,000 scholarship, and ATCA gave me a $2,500 scholarship, the National Federation of the Blind awarded me a scholarship before beginning the master's degree, the American Council of the Blind gave me one for $1,200. I would not be able to continue my education if it were not for these scholarships. The disability check is not enough to pay my rent. I receive food stamps, and Nancy helps me as well."

"How do you do it? How do you type and study?"

"I use a screen reader called JAWS (Job Application with Speech). It reads letters, numbers, words, sentences, paragraphs, or the entire page. I cannot use a mouse like the one sighted people use. Therefore, I manually type key combinations for what I need the computer to do." I also explained how I would send her an email.

"Do you have a Braille keyboard?"

"No, ma'am, I have Velcro on the important keys like the F7 to use as the spell checker and on the F12 to serve as the Save As. Also, Velcro is on the Tab, Enter, Backspace key, the Delete key, the F key, the J key, and on the five on the numeric keypad."

"Can you see anything? Some people increase the font size. Do you have any sight at all?"

"No, ma'am, I have a 100 percent fully matured cataract covering the lens on the right eye, and the left eye is a glass eye. Occasionally, at night, I may see some dim light on the far right, like behind the cataract."

"Is there hope to have the cataract removed to give you sight in the right eye?"

"There is always hope, but no one will touch it yet. All the doctors say the eye could still be healing. I am very hopeful, and it is in God's hand—he will let me see when it is time. The technology is improving each day, and I am a young man. And if it takes twenty-five years for me to see again, then I will only be sixty-one. If I live to be eighty or ninety, then I will still be able to see again for another twenty or thirty years."

"If you were given $5,000, what would you use it for? But I think I know with you. "Do you have any questions for me?"

I stated, "If I receive this scholarship, would I know before the convention in San Diego?"

"Absolutely, we decided this year, and frankly, it is because of you! We decided to do everything by phone and let people know ahead of time because it did not seem fair to ask you in your condition to go out to San Diego just for an interview and not know. Therefore, you have made a difference here already. That is the reason we decided to do interviews by phone and let people know a month in advance so they could arrange their lives."

"That is wonderful. I am glad I was able to help influence you all! For me to receive the recognition from Airbus is just a dream for me!"

Friday, February 15, 2008, Airbus contacted me to let me know that they awarded me the Airbus Leadership Award valued at $5,000. Monday, February 18, Renee Martin Nagle contacted me to tell me FedEx awarded me a scholarship as well. She thought someone else would be in contact with me. February 19, I found out Airbus wanted to pay for my ticket along with Nance's ticket on Delta totaling $1,870 to fly us to San Diego to the convention. In addition, we received word that the *Daytona Beach News Journal* and the *Kannapolis Citizen* wanted to do news stories on this release.

F-15 Thunderbirds

Saturday, February 16, 2008, Nance, Jackson, Lincoln, and I drove down Clyde Morris Boulevard, Daytona Beach, en route to

Ormond Beach. As we drove past the end of the airport, four F-15 Thunderbirds took off and flew over us. This sound was like no other, and they were taking off to buzz the Daytona International Speedway.

Iwana's Presentation

Friday, February 22, 2008, Nance, Lincoln, and I went to the Iwana's church in Dialand. The presentation was in front of about fifty children and parents. I shared the accident, rehabilitation, achievements, education, and support of my family and friends.

Women in Aviation International

Friday, March 13, 2008, Nance, Lincoln, and I attended the Women in Aviation International conference in San Diego, California, which took place at the Town & Country Resort and Spa. Saturday, March 14, the general Chuck Yeager was the keynote speaker, and this day was in celebration of his 84th birthday. He spoke during lunch for about thirty minutes, and then the women served him a piece of birthday cake with a candle in it. The crowd of over 3,400 women and men sang "Happy Birthday" to him. I felt honored to meet him on that day and spend a few minutes in his company. I asked him how many airplanes he flew. He said 241 airplanes in every country throughout the world, and 208 were military airplanes during his sixty years as a pilot. He went into the military as a mechanic underage. That is when the age limit went from age twenty to eighteen, which allowed him to apply to become a pilot, and he did not have a college education. Yeager broke the sound barrier in an X-15 airplane in 1947.

We met women present that were in the WASP, Women of the Air Service Program. In addition, awarded to me was the Airbus

Leadership Award for $5,000 and the Federal Express Technical Systems Operations Award valued at $2,500.

We met twin sisters Dr. Shirley Phillips and Dr. Sherry Parshley. Dr. Phillips presented to about fifty people on ergonomics in the cockpit and the fitness of the body in the cockpit. Dr. Shirley Phillips, the presenter, shared about the Health Maintenance for Aviation Professionals for Women in Aviation International Conference, March 13–15, 2008. Meeting Dr. Shirley opened the door for later employment online at Daniel Webster College, and assisted me in completing my doctoral degree. Dr. Parshley gave a financial presentation to about fifty people. Dr. Sherry was a professor on several classes from Northcentral University, and she helped and taught me more information than the other professors. This evening we shared dinner with these women previously mentioned, Pam Peer, and her mom, Lillian Peer.

Sonic Boom

Wednesday afternoon, the twenty-sixth of March, the *Endeavour* space shuttle arrived back home safely to the Kennedy Space Center. This was so memorable because I heard the sonic boom from it. It literally scared me; I thought something fell on the town house. This landing was the shuttle's sixty-eighth successful landing. On this flight, it spent sixteen days attached to the International Space Station (ISS).

Patty Wagstaff

April 2, 2008, Patty Wagstaff gave a presentation in the Willie Miller Auditorium at Embry-Riddle's campus, and Nance, Lincoln, and I met her in person. In addition, we took pictures with her and visited her briefly. She signed some photos of her standing by her aerobatic airplane, the Extra 300. She gave Lincoln treats as well, and Nance took those pictures of her doing so as well. She had her dog along. she let her dog check out Lincoln, and their tails were just wagging. I gave her a business card as well.

Jeff Gordon, the president of the Sport Aviation Club at Embry-Riddle, introduced the three-time national aerobatic champion and professional air-show pilot. The crowd of about two hundred people clapped for seven seconds, and Nance and I sat beside Leticia Kolb and her husband, Mike, whom we had dinner with that evening at the student activity center on campus. Jeff stated,

> Patty Wagstaff has been flying air shows internationally, for over 20 years. Her flying displays can only be described as some of the meanest, hardcore rock n' roll of performing snap rolls, tumbles, and I cannot begin to count them. She slices through the air only expanding 15 feet above the ground inverted at over 150 miles per hour with a prop. Additionally, she is one of Raytheon's factory demonstration pilots and she inspects them too and displays a high performance turbo prop, military trainer, air national and trade shows across the book. Patty has also flown many different airplanes, to the P-51 to the F-16. She flies seaplanes, helicopters, and warbirds, and she even has a carrier landing under her belt. Before we continue, I would like to take a brief moment to thank the Women in Aviation club, the 99's, Embry-Riddle Flight Department, thank you so much for coming tonight, and I would like to welcome Air Show Star, Patty Wagstaff.

The crowd clapped for six seconds. Patty began by stating,

> Thanks for having me; it is really great to be here. I have only been here a couple of times and

I have met a number of you. My pilot, my dog, and I flew up from St. Augustine and we would have been here a little sooner but ATC vectored us. I flew my station wagon, my Cirrus SR-22 up here, I brought my ferry pilot, and he flies the Extra this year. Anyway, what I try to do is I am not a lecturer, I love to have conversation and I like to know what you want to know about what I do. I have a short film that Cirrus put together for me to help me to use their video and to help with the talk and their airplanes. Then I want to answer any questions you may have on what I do.

In the video, she explained how she performed the maneuvers and got ready for the air show. She stated that her solo was one of the most high confidence builders that she had ever done. The video played "Rock 'n' Roll," and it showed her doing air shows in her Extra 300, performing aerobatics. Patty explained,

I have been an Air Show pilot for 24 years now. I began Air Shows in Alaska and flew competitions and I did that for 12 years full time. I did Air Shows to balance the two. Everything is graded and it is very hard to get a ten and in Air Shows where you cannot do anything wrong. She says, people always ask me what it takes to be an Air show Pilot or Competition Pilot. I tell them it takes a few things. It takes discipline, focus, and you have to give 100%. There is no room for error in what I do. Discipline is something I have to encroach myself on all the time and remind myself but is fairly engrained in all the time spent on competition. I know what it takes and I know how easy it is to make a mistake and to forget that. I have to scare myself and I do not want to forget those experiences. So, I listen to everybody; learn as much as I can from accidents. I read them almost daily on the FAA's website to see what the trends are; unfortunately, they are mostly human error not mechanical. So, discipline is number one for being a commercial pilot. Having a sense of mission in anything we do, I guess is important in the Air Show world. It is not easy, it is hard to make a living, it is hard to stay in shape, and it takes a lot to do, of course. The way I look at it is when you are doing something especially out of the box and unusual as being an Air Show Pilot, something like that, it really takes a sense of mission. That is just something you have, it is not something you necessarily create and sometimes you just have to find out what that is. It does not come to you at a certain age but it will come to you when you find that mission in anything you like and when you have that and that is the kind of thing you have to do with this. It takes money and she laughs. It is expensive and I get letters from people all the time saying I really want to do aerobatics but I do not have the money, so how do I do this. I really don't have any answers for it other than get a job and work hard. Save your money, join a flying club, find a partner in a plane, and build a plane. I started in a Decathlon and flew when I could and kept working my way. By the time, I won the nationals for the first time I think I rented five airplanes. Each one was a little better and a little more sophisticated. At the time I did not start with the Extra 300, I was flying in 1991, which cost $80,000, which now does not seem like a lot for a top of the line aerobatic plane, but back then it was huge. So, my husband and I could not afford that airplane, but we took it step by step until we could afford that airplane. It is the same for today, everyone has their own circumstances to deal with, but it is available for anyone who wants it. Some of the things it takes to be an Air Show Pilot. I do between 13 and 20 Air Shows a year; I try to keep it around 16 or 17, so I can have some time off. One thing I tried hard is to balance the activities. I try to balance what I do so I am not just about Aviation. I found at one point I was focusing on competition, all my friends were in Aviation, and I had no friends outside Aviation. I had no other parties to mingle with, and one of the reasons I retired from competitions, therefore, I could have a life outside of Aviation. I did not want to be one-dimensional and I think that is very important. I read more as well as other things, I traveled, and I do not try to do too many shows, so I do not get burned out and hate it. I try to do enough to pay the bills, keep my sponsors happy, and still enjoy it. I don't try to take too much time off; I don't want to lag time between shows because it is hard to get back into the swing of things, too. So, every year, at the end of November I put the airplane away and I don't look at it for two or three months. Three months is a little bit too long, I just got the airplane back with a new engine, and Lycoming built it for me. At the end of November, I put the airplane away, do not go to the hangar, stay away from the airport, and that way when February or March comes around I am excited and ready to go and I am ready to get back into the airplane. I realized I am starting to drive too fast. Then,

I wake up in the morning and say that is what was missing, I needed that. So, people say you have been doing this a really long time, when are you going to retire or quit. I don't feel like I am that old and I don't feel like I am ready to sit in a rocking chair yet. So, I am going to do this as long as I need it, as long as I have a need for speed and fly low and things like that. She asked if anyone wanted to hear about Air Shows or what you want to know.

Leticia asked, "How do you make that airplane dance so beautifully to other pilots?"

Patty answered,

How do I make the airplane dance? Practice, practice, practice! Really, the style of aerobatics in the last 20 years, part of it came from bi-planes. Things have really changed since I started and things we are able to do now we could not do 20 years ago. Some of the first model planes I saw were wood wings and it had chains holding the engine to the firewall instead of an engine mount. The airplanes were under built and they did not have the technology they have today. Along with that came flying that is much more aggressive. For example my 300 Extra S and L are certified to plus or minus 10 G's. We have very strong equipment and this allows us to make our corners much sharper.

Someone else asked, "How do you develop a relationship with Cirrus?"

Patty answered,

> That is a really good question. I am a
> Beechcraft person and my husband and I own
> a Baron. I love them and the local rep from
> Orlando called me a couple of times and said
> Patty, when I am in St. Augustine I would love to
> show a Cirrus to you. Oh yes, I am not interested
> she said. I am a little difficult about new things,
> I also want to see improvement and I had to go
> see growth in that market. So, he called a couple
> of times and it took about a year. He came down
> one day and said okay, I am here, I looked at the
> airplane and I thought everything was beautiful.
> It was brand new and it felt like a Lexus. It was all
> I could bear, it is all glass and had the throw over
> yoke, and it felt like something new. The repre-
> sentative and her went out and flew it and came
> in and landed and she said I want one of these.

Patty talked about her aircraft experiences. She made three catapult launches in an F-18 off an aircraft carrier with a highly recognized fighter pilot. She said,

> I did not actually do the landings on the
> aircraft carriers but it was unbelievable though,
> I did do three (CATCC's) Carrier Air Traffic
> Control Centers approaches and three catapults
> with a pilot in an F-18. It was a training flight
> with the head of the Fighter Wing in the Atlantic
> of the F-18 and he was about to retire.

The pilot asked her, "Have you ever been out to a carrier?" and
she answered no. He said, "Would you like to go?" and she answered
yes. Then she went through water training, and that was hard.

We had to tread water in flight school, with all of our flight gear on. They told her she had to pass or she was not going. She learned tricks about trapping air in the helmets to help you float. It was difficult and then we had to swim into like a cage underwater and it had a 90-degree turn in it with goggles that would black out with another person coming the other way. You had to go through it and get out. We went out to the carrier and I have been out in military airplanes before such as the F-15, F-16, and the F-18 before on a number of rides. We were on top of overcast and descended, we were getting low and all of the sudden there is this little boat. Oh yes, they look tiny but they are big, but when you get down to it they are really small. I felt really comfortable with the pilot; he is the highest carrier time American pilot and the second highest in the world ever. So, we came down to the carrier, he was talking to them on the radio, I blacked out, and I don't remember anything. The speed at which we hit the deck was so intense, it was the most intense thing I have ever done and all I remember seeing is the water. I remember thinking everything is quiet and wondering if we were going into the water. Is this right and this is very bizarre, I thought, and then we started being pulled back by the wire. When we landed, we were full throttle. When you go to turn around the nose goes over the water. It was fantastic and the catapult launches are unbelievable. The third landing I was more aware of what was going on. I admire those guys and to land at night now that would be hard.

Someone asked, "How do you stay fit for the extreme lifestyle and environment you work in?"

She answered, "You really have to make it your lifestyle. I do not want to be overweight and come out in a flight suit that is too tight. I want to look okay first." The crowd snickered.

> I have my picture made a lot. Most of the professional pilots stay in shape and it is just the nature of whom we are. It is a challenge sometimes when you are on the road. I like to go to the gym several times a week. I love to ride my horse to stay in shape and work out at home. I do everything like rock climbing, riding my horse, I like to work out, walk, hike, do yoga, and every day I try to do something. I try to eat right and don't drink too much the night before an Air Show.

Someone asked about the G force and how many she pulls when she is performing. She explains,

> I pull about 10 G positive and 7 negative. It takes me about all year to get to that point. Positive G's are not that big of a problem but the negative G's are because of the blood rushing to your head. These can be dangerous because they can break capillaries, you can get vertigo, and affect your inner ear. A real trap is going from negative to positive and I think a lot of people have gotten into trouble there. When you go from negative to positive G's the blood takes a while to stabilize back to normalcy.

A woman asked Patty about safety, education, and how safety most enhances education and what instructors can do to teach safety to their students. Patty stated,

> What I do as an instructor I encourage a student to read everything they can and learn everything they can from incidents and other accidents. Sometimes a tragedy can be turned around to save your life in the future, then something good has come of that. Again, in 100 years Aviation has come a long ways. I really encourage reading flying magazines, books, and anything you can get your hands on. Some magazines I get, I cannot read every article, but I will skip through the pages until I find something including general information that I can get from that. That is part of what I believe, you can teach a really good attitude from human behavior. I feel everything I do is being watched, so I want to set a good example as an instructor not just as an Air Show Pilot. If I do not drain the sumps before I go flying, then what is my student going to do. Do little things like that, talk about it, and set a good example. There is a wealth of information out there, it is just a matter of accessing it. I save articles about flying twins that I will pass on to somebody someday. I take it really seriously and I am sure everybody in here does to.

Another student asked Patty, "What is the biggest scare that you had while flying?"
She answered,

> Probably, the most scared, however when you get to low, things happen so quick you do

not have time to be afraid. That has happened to me. You get scared afterwards thinking how dumb you are but thinking you could be that stupid or you just learn from it. I think when you are planning a trip and bad weather plays part. Most of the smaller airplanes are VFR only especially in the older days and we just have to get to an Air Show; I have missed a lot of shows and days here and there because of weather. I got to low going to an Air Show once and really came close to the ground. It was a human factors thing, I was going through a divorce and I was very distraught, I was distracted, and I was talking to a friend about his divorce before I got into the airplane. It was a huge Air Show and it had about 2 million people there, so it was the largest Air Show in the world. I had been flying low for a while so I was used to the environment. So, before I went up to fly, we were talking and did not walk through my routine, I did not think about it, I was distracted and I jumped in the plane. I was doing this rolling thing and I realized as I was spinning around I did not realize how high I was and totally lost awareness, situational awareness. Therefore, I went waist level and I was close and it was difficult, it was either move on and find a way to deal with it, departmentalize it or you are going to die or you are going to have to quit. That was a big human factor lesson learned about what kind of focus did it take, how to departmentalize, and things I could do when I was under other stresses.

Someone asked about her mission. She explained,

> To me my mission was pretty defined when
> I was competing and I wanted to be the first
> woman to win the nationals. I was lucky that I
> had that goal and I had a very clear goal and a
> very defined objective. Until I discovered flying
> and especially aerobatics I did not have a clear
> goal, I knew I wanted to accomplish something
> in life but I did not know what. So, I was very
> lucky to have a specific goal someone had never
> done and I had a sense of mission about that.
> My mission was I wanted to do it three times
> and I did it. Once you get that mission, any
> athlete will tell you that you have to have a mis-
> sion. Whether you are going to the Olympics or
> whatever you do, nothing stands in your way.
> You are so focused and goal oriented. It was just
> like when I retired from competition in 1996,
> it was hard the first couple of years and I talked
> with folks who retired after winning. I talked to
> people who said it was very hard for them after
> they had won whatever they were trying to win.
> They quit or retired after that and went through
> long periods of depression or a sense of loss, kind
> of like losing someone important. I read books
> about it, I had been so intense for so long, and
> the only way to counteract this is to have another
> goal in its place or the next thing in mind. If you
> do not then you are asking for trouble. Whatever
> you do, you have to retire from an age limit or
> the age plays part.

Another student asked, "Can you share your P-51 experience
with us?"

Patty answered,

> Yes, I have been really fortunate to fly Air
> Shows in a P-51. The plane was a "D" model,
> which is the most common model. I think there
> is 160 that fly in the world. The "D" model
> was first and then gathering the "Mustangs" in
> September of last year, I flew the "C" model,
> which is rare, and there are two or three in exis-
> tence. The "C" model came first and it has the
> greenhouse canopy that opens to the side. The
> one that slides back is the "D" model and it is
> the "D" model that has the kind of bubble can-
> opy that comes back. I really love the "C" model
> and it is a better fit, the cockpit is a little smaller
> and tighter. It has a thinner wing and it does not
> have that dorsal fin on top and feels like the real
> airplane. When you go up you push right rudder
> and when coming down you push the left. I was
> very fortunate to fly the airplane and I felt com-
> fortable in it. The first time I took it off, I thought
> okay, I like this. I had never flown with anybody
> in it so I checked out myself, but I did talk with
> the owner of the airplane and he gave me pic-
> tures of the cockpit. I read the manual, which
> was a 1945 manual. The airplane systems were
> basic but they were really critical. If the airplane
> starts running hot, you have 30 seconds and you
> have to get it on the ground or shut it down or
> else the engine is going to seize. You always had
> to make sure the landing gear is locked in place.
> You don't want to have landing gear problems
> on someone's 2 million dollar airplane. I sat in
> the cockpit, studied the pictures, and memorized
> where everything was located, I understood how

everything worked, and people want to know how you got checked out in that airplane. I took off and then I thought, ho man I have to land this thing. I cannot screw it up and the owner is standing there watching. I am very methodical about every airplane I fly. I go up and get a feel of what the ailerons are like; I slow it down and get the feel of slow flight. I do straight ahead stalls, accelerated stalls, stalls while making turns, spins like at 10,000 feet, and I did some aerobatics in it, then I came in and landed with no problems. It is a neat airplane and when you are in it, you are just like, oh wow! It is so powerful, has such a beautiful sound and there is nothing like it.

Someone asked Patty what her favorite airplane was. She answered,

I asked Scott Crossfield that once, and he said the one I am currently flying. I have to say the Mustang and the Extra. I do get to fly different airplanes and I love flying them all. I love the Cirrus, I love my Baron, I love all of them but when I get back into the Extra, there is nothing like it. There is no other plane in the world, connected to your brain than that airplane is. I read an article once that said it is the controller connected to your brain. There is nothing that I have ever seen comparing to that. There is nothing that compares to the harmony of the controls than the Extra.

A female student stated, "You talked about your favorite airplanes. What are your least favorite airplanes?" Patty stated,

> My least favorite airplane was the TBM Avenger, the torpedo bomber. I am not really into the old antique thing as much as being spoiled because of flying in so many great performing machines. The older airplanes require you to work hard at flying them and I think the TBM, Avenger is one of the least favorite to fly even though it is cool to fly it, you get a type rating. There are only a few homebuilt airplanes that I would not sit in yet.
>
> It is really a pleasure to be back and I appreciate you having us. I appreciate you having Cassidy; she has been a good girl has she not. These days you need to be careful and think about things every time before you get into the cockpit, whether it is unforgiving or not. Thank you for having me.

The crowd clapped for Patty for eleven seconds.

Embry-Riddle Women Student Event

Tuesday, April 15, 2008, Lincoln and I attended the Women in Aviation event at Embry-Riddle. Four hundred and fifty female junior high school students attended the event. We sat between the Wright Flyer simulator and the Cessna 172 simulator, and while sitting there, we met Marsha Pellon, who is the aeronautical science lavatory manager. We answered questions from the girls passing by and visited Letty Kolb, received a hug, and met her daughter Audrey. In addition, we visited with Pam Peer and received a hug from her as well.

Tamilla Curtis's Business Class Presentation

Tuesday morning, April 22, 2008, Lincoln and I gave a presentation to Tamilla Curtis's BA 436 strategic management class with twenty-eight enrolled students at Embry-Riddle. Tamilla said this class was the last capstone course for the graduate business seniors. Her students said they really enjoyed the presentation, and the class interacted with me and asked questions.

American Council of the Blind Interview

Sunday evening, May 11, Mother's Day, the American Council of the Blind interviewed me. This interview was the third interview, and I applied four times. Patty Slaby, Michael Garret, and a couple others interviewed me.

Women in Aviation

Tuesday evening, May 13, Nance, Lincoln, and I went to Dr. John and Maury Johnson's house. Dr. Johnson is the president of Embry-Riddle. The Women in Aviation International and First Coast Chapter met there trying to attract more members. Maury treated us very kindly and was a great host. We visited Pam Peer as well as Letty; her husband, Mike Kolb; and Letty's son Dennis and his girlfriend Dessie. Dr. Johnson asked me to say a few words. Therefore, I stood up and shared about the trip to Washington, DC, the FAA inviting us as well as possibly going on a White House tour.

The Third GMAA-Batchelor Scholarship

Tuesday, May 1, Steven Daun emailed me to let me know they awarded me another scholarship. He congratulated me and invited me to the luncheon at Miami Springs Country Club. On May 14, the Greater Miami Aviation Association—Batchelor Aviation Foundation awarded me the third scholarship. We had a very good lunch, and I spent a few minutes thanking them for another scholarship. We visited with Dan Sullivan, Bill Rivenbark, Mark Henderson, Steven Daun, and only four of us recipients were present and awarded from Embry-Riddle to receive this scholarship. The drive to Miami and the trip back to Daytona consisted of lots of smoke and many fires burning.

Back Problems

Occasionally, my back will give me trouble, and I have to do back exercises to get relief. Dr. Thurman Gillespie, located in Daytona Beach, saw me, and he put me doing therapy. This therapy helped for a certain amount of time.

American Council of the Blind

On May 21, Patty Slaby contacted me to tell me the American Council of the Blind awarded me a scholarship. Patty told me the scholarship award would take place in Louisville, Kentucky. They paid for my half of the hotel room, food, all dinner engagements, and my transportation to Louisville during July 5 through 9.

FAA Conference

Tuesday, May 28, through Saturday, May 31, we attended the Federal Aviation Administration Conference in Washington, DC, that Wednesday and Thursday of that week. We met Joyce Bender, who runs Bender Consulting as well as some DOT employees and FAA managers. On Wednesday, Nance took the microphone and shared with the attendees about some of the complications we were having on the application. One complaint she mentioned, "I did not have a valid driver's license for identification." Thursday evening, we met Miguel Vasquez and his wife, Megan, for dinner. Friday evening we met Bill and Becky Umbaugh for dinner. They picked us up, took us to the Capital Grill, and fed us a fine steak dinner.

Summer Academy Presentation

Friday morning, June 27, 2008, the director of the Summer Academy Pam Peer asked me to give a presentation to the Summer Academy. Nance, Lincoln, and I gave the presentation that morning about the plane crash I survived and related it to safety. Some of the students made Pam feel that they were the only ones in the air and she did not feel some of them were safe. We gave the students real-life scenarios, and I relayed to them to make sure they do not trust anyone, but their mother and to keep an eye on her. The aviation preflight of the presentation covered what can happen when someone does not do his or her job correctly.

Air Traffic Control Association Scholarship

One more scholarship I received in 2008 was from the Air Traffic Control Association (ATCA) for the third year in a row. I accepted the scholarship and thanked the association in front of 1,900 fellow aviators. This scholarship luncheon is where I met the FAA administrator and Ruth Leverance, the deputy administrator.

F-16 Flyover

On July 4, 2008, Lincoln, Nance, and I witnessed the flyover of the F-16 when it flew over the racetrack for the Daytona 400 while enjoying the evening, and we were at the Kolbs', in their condominium at Daytona Beach. I was also listening to the radio communications with the Daytona International Airport tower.

American Council of the Blind

During July 5 to July 8, 2008, we went to Louisville, Kentucky. This trip was on a Canadair Regional Jet through Jacksonville, Florida, then to Cincinnati, Ohio, then on an Embraer Regional Jet to Louisville, Kentucky, on US Airways. As we came home, we came through Charlotte, North Carolina, on a Canadair Regional Jet in US Airways. This delayed flight was due to a thunderstorm in Charlotte. One of the flight attendants on the flight from Louisville to Charlotte gave Lincoln her scarf. Then we boarded a Boeing 737-400, and we were to Jacksonville in fifty-four minutes.

The event was the American Council of the Blind scholarship convention. The scholarship was the Ross N. and the Patricia Pandre Foundation for the Visually Impaired Scholarship valued at $2,500. I was one out of nineteen individuals present out of twenty-one people selected nationwide to receive this scholarship. Nance said the banquet had possibly a thousand people present. We spent $600 on this trip to make $1,900. We paid half of Nance's room, which totaled $150, and parking in Jacksonville. We had 250 miles to Jacksonville and Nance's flight.

A woman came to where Lincoln and I were sitting on the stage and walked us to the podium. I began my presentation by giving thanks to the American Council of the Blind, Cambion or Kerzwell, God, family and friends, Nance, and Lincoln the Aviator. I told everyone that I lost my smell, taste, and sight on June 1, 1998, in a plane crash.

I was a 1600-hour pilot, a Certified Flight Instructor, Commercial Pilot, 1 week away from an interview with U.S. Airways Express, to become a commercial pilot with the commuter airline. I boarded a running airplane that day and we crashed 37 minutes after takeoff. The doctors pronounced me dead on arrival. I was in a coma for 20 days and in the hospital for 3 months. Miraculously, here I am receiving this wonderful scholarship. I received an ovation for 10 seconds. I thanked them all and said it gets a little better. The crowd chuckled and I carried on by stating, I wanted to continue my role in aviation so I began studying with the FAA to become the first blind and only blind Advanced Ground Instructor as well as the first and only blind Instrument Ground Instructor in the world for the Federal Aviation Administration. I received an ovation for a few more seconds. As I was continuing my rehabilitation, I moved to Charlotte, North Carolina to begin my Bachelor of Arts degree in History and did so miraculously in 3 and a half years. In addition, in 2005 Lincoln and I moved to Daytona Beach, Florida to attend the world's largest flight school. I became the first and only blind graduate in their 82-year history to attend. I did so graduating with a master's of Science in Aeronautics with specializations in Aviation Safety and Aviation Operations. Today, I am continuing my education at Northcentral University, that is what the scholarship money pays for, and I am eleven classes away from becoming Dr. Hyde. Thank you all once again.

In addition, I received another ten-second ovation for the presentation. The presentation lasted just over three minutes.

On July 8, 2008, we flew from Louisville, Kentucky into Charlotte, North Carolina, on US Airways. Mom, Terri Leigh, Lauren, and Austin were at the gate and surprised us.

Summer Program Presentation

Friday morning, July 25, 2008, Nance, Lincoln, and I went to Embry-Riddle and gave a presentation to the summer program. Briefly, I visited Pam Peer and received a hug. The topic of the presentation was aviation safety and the accident I lived through because of the preflight checklists not administered properly. There were nine students that soloed, their flight instructors, and six students that had not soloed.

Thanks

Thursday, July 30, 2008, Nance mailed the flight attendant for US Airways that was on the flight with us from Louisville to Charlotte. We thanked her for the scarf by mailing her a thank-you card and a picture of Lincoln wearing the scarf standing with me.

Glass Eye

August 1, 2008, Nance, Jackson, Lincoln, and I went to Lakeland, Florida, to see the ocularist Dr. Johnston. Dr. Johnston was an ocularist from North Carolina. He is the doctor that made all my glass eyes. As we were in his company in Lakeland, he sized and fitted me for a new glass eye. As we came home, we saw John McCain's motorcade where the security blocked Highway Four for them. The Secret Service, motorcycle police, state troopers, two tour buses, and a trail way bus surrounded the motorcade. John McCain spoke at an Urban League Convention in Orlando.

Lincoln's Puppy Raiser

Sunday morning, August 3, 2008, Nance, Lincoln, Jackson, Carole Blake, Lincoln's puppy raiser, and I attended service at Hope Lutheran Church. That morning, eighty-three people and one guide dog attended, and Nance did the children's sermon. We ate brunch. I visited Tony and Kathy Minner, and Tony offered to take me flying in his A36 Bonanza. Tony and Kathy offered for me to give presentations at the Experimental Aviation Association out of Spruce Creek Airport and to the Women of Wings there as well. This day, I received several hugs from Terra Jean Brock, and we came home and visited Carol Blake for several hours.

Spruce Creek Airport

Wednesday, August 13, 2008, Tony Minner came and picked me up, and we went to his house at the Spruce Creek Airport. Tony and I visited with Kathy as well as their friends Bob and his wife, Lois. Bob was ex–Air Force, and he flew with the general Chuck Yeager in the 1950s. We ate lunch at the country club and drove there on their golf cart. Tony introduced me to the president of the EAA Spruce Creek chapter, Keith Phillips, who was ex–Air Force as well. In addition, I met Jimmy, an avionics technician.

Carol Ann Garrett

Wednesday evening, September 3, 2008, Nance, Lincoln, and I went to Embry-Riddle to the Women in Aviation International event to hear Carol Ann Garrett speak about her trip around the world. She gave a great presentation with slides and real-life events. She explained how she completed the trip in seven months in a Mooney, and she is raising money for Lou Gehrig's disease. We met her, we had our picture taken with her, and we purchased her book, which she autographed.

Mom's Husband's Funeral

On the evening of September 7, 2008, TC, Mom's husband, was burning some things out back close to brother's barn. Mom was keeping an eye on him, and she went inside to do something. When she looked outside to check on him, he was fine. Shortly thereafter, she came outside, and he was not there. He had a heart attack and was lying on the ground. He yelled at her to call 911, and Mom rushed to him and began CPR. The paramedics arrived and rushed him to the hospital, and they pronounced him dead at 9:43 p.m. that evening.

In Terry Hugh Carpenter's memory, Nance donated to Daymark, Concordia Lutheran Church, and Guide Dog Foundation. She sent flowers to Mom. I flew home Tuesday, September 9, and Todd and Terri picked Lincoln and me up at the Charlotte Douglas Airport. During the return at the airport, we crossed paths with Buddy Counts and his son Zachary. Zachary is an F-16 pilot, and they had returned from the Reno air races. Buddy Counts is a member of Embry-Riddle's faculty senate, and he flew with Ferrell James. He saw us in the terminal and stopped to say hello. In addition, cousin Dayton Maclean saw us at the TSA area. He had a golf cart waiting for us, and it took us to the gate.

ICASF and GAMA Scholarship

September 18, 2008, Nance checked her email and saw that the International Council of Air Shows Foundation and the General Aviation Manufacturer Association awarded me their scholarship. Wednesday, October 8, 2008, the International Council of Air Shows Foundation and the General Aviation Manufacturer Association scholarship arrived along with a nice certificate and letter. The value of the scholarship was $2,000. The International Council of Air Shows Foundation's part valued at $1,000. The General Aviation Manufacturer Association sponsored the other half.

Electronic Version of Daytona Beach News Journal
Barry Hulon Hyde: Blind but still reaching for
the sky By phyllissalmons |

Note: A Feb. 21, 2007, story by News-
Journal staff writer Mark Harper told about
the saga of Barry Hulon Hyde ("Crash survivor
eager to teach at ERAU - Blind aviation student's
dream in sight"). Barry recently wrote this update
and about his guide dog, Lincoln.

In 1998, while flying as a passenger, I survived a plane crash with traumatic injuries—
including losing my sight and being pronounced
DOA when airlifted from the crash site. Prior
to the accident, I had accomplished over 1,600
flight hours and was one week away from interviewing with US Airways in Charlotte, N.C., to
become an airline pilot.

After two years of recovery and rehabilitation, I began studying for several aviation licenses. In 2000, I passed the Advanced
Ground Instructor (AGI) and Instrument
Ground Instructor (IGI) test. The FAA has
confirmed that I am the first and only blind
person to hold these certifications. The FAA
had never administered these tests to a blind
person before.

My leadership skills have served me well as
both a sighted and blind person. While sighted,
in addition to my flight hours, I provided ground
and flight instruction to numerous individuals to
achieve their licenses and ratings.

After losing my sight, I attended the
Carolina Rehabilitation Center to re-learn mobility and orientation skills, learned Braille, learned
independent living skills for a blind individual,

and learned my audible screen-reader, so that I can use my computer.

In the summer of 2000, I attended Southeastern Guide Dogs and received my guide dog, Lincoln. I began an undergraduate degree in 2001 and received my Bachelor of Arts degree in History from the University of North Carolina in December 2004. I graduated from Embry-Riddle Aeronautical University in May 2007 and, in June 2007, I began (to pursue) my Ph.D.

My goal is to obtain a professional position in aeronautical education, management, research, or development that will utilize my education, certifications and experiences in flight instruction, aviation safety, aviation operations, and human factors.

I want to share my life experiences with other pilots to prevent an accident like I was involved in from ever happening again. My dream was to become an airline pilot and enjoy the lifestyle that comes with that privilege.

But now, I have the opportunity to once again be an instructor to future pilots and have them gain insight into my knowledge and experience. I want to be a role model that disabled people can look up to and know there are no limits to what a disabled person can achieve. I also want to be a role model in the aviation industry of the heights a disabled person can obtain to accomplish their goals. I want to inspire people to keep reaching for the sky.

I am currently studying for my Ph.D. degree with Northcentral University, Prescott Valley, Ariz. (online). My major is Business Administration with Aeronautical Specializations. I was recently awarded the ICAS Foundation (International Council of Air Shows Foundation)—GAMA (General Aviation Manufacturers Association) Scholarship to aid in pursuit of the degree.

Air Traffic Control Association

Friday, September 26, 2008, Cindy Castillo contacted me through email to let me know that ATCA awarded me another scholarship. She relayed a message to me that someone else would be contacting me as well, and she congratulated me on my third scholarship from ATCA. Carrie from ATCA contacted me on Tuesday, September 30. She enlightened me that I would be receiving a $5,000 scholarship.

Experimental Aircraft Association

Thursday evening, October 16, 2008, Nance, Lincoln, and I gave a presentation to the Experimental Aircraft Association (EAA), chapter 288, at the Spruce Creek Airport, in Daytona Beach, Florida. We had dinner with Tony and Kathy Minner, and they rode with us to the hangar where the meeting took place. Keith Phillips, the president of the EAA Spruce Creek Chapter, introduced me, and he began by stating,

"I found out he was blind, and when I first met him, I was impressed. He is the first FAA certified blind ground instructor. So he is going to tell you how he arrived at this stage in his life and how he has done since then, which is pretty inspiring. So, Barry, you are on."

The crowd applauded for seven seconds. Nance showed me where the microphone and podium were located. I said, "Good evening, everyone." I began by introducing myself, "My name is Barry Hulon Hyde, and this is my guide dog Lincoln the Aviator, and this is my fiancée Nancy Riedel." We received applause for five seconds.

Nancy began by stating that we received a little flack tonight because Lincoln was wearing a US Airways bandana.

I began by stating,

> I want to give a brief history of myself. Back in 1995, I went to American Flyers in Addison, Texas. Let me go back to 1991, on December 21, 1991, I soloed. June 26, 1992, I received my Private Pilot License in Statesville, North Carolina at the Statesville Municipal Airport. I decided I wanted to continue my aviation career so, then in 1995 I went to American Flyers in Addison, Texas where I received my instrument rating, commercial license, flight instructor license, and my multi engine rating which came at the Redbird Airport. I came home and worked for a while with the James remodeling houses and performing the upkeep on rental property, then went to work as a Flight Instructor at the Concord Regional Airport and worked there for 20 months up to the day my life, so dramatically changed. June 1, 1998, I was riding as a safety pilot on board a Piper twin Comanche. The 1965-model airplane lacked something and does anybody want to guess what was missing on it to cause such bad injuries to me. Someone in the crowd answered shoulder harness and I said there you go, a shoulder harness, I heard that. Therefore, the seat had broken and forced me forward into the control yoke and that collapsed both of my lungs as well as my head hit the dashboard while wearing a headset along with my sunglasses because the airplane lacked a shoulder harness. I had nine broken bones in my face, my left eye knocked completely out, lost four teeth, jaw bro-

ken four times, the roof of my mouth knocked completely off my face, sinus cavity destroyed, three cracks in my cranium, nose torn completely off, and right leg broken four times. Pronounced dead on arrival, left side of my body paralyzed, in a coma for 20 days at the Roanoke Regional Hospital, and I do not see how I lived through that, but obviously it was not my time. The pilot in command might I add, only had both broken legs and he was still conscious at the crash site. Therefore, I guess we all have rode as a passenger in an airplane and I never served as a safety pilot because the pilot in command never put the hood on. We took off from the Concord Regional airport at five minutes to four that afternoon; we went off Roanoke's radar that afternoon. Therefore, 37 minutes into that flight we crashed and hit the trees. We were at 9,700 msl, I was trying to file a flight plan with the Flight Service station, and the right engine started missing, spitting, and sputtering. Let me go back before boarding the airplane and I was out flying with another person in a Cessna 172 doing takeoffs and landings with this pilot and I got out of that airplane, went, and boarded the twin Comanche. The pilot already had the airplane running, so I boarded and I asked the pilot, did you check the fuel and he said oh yes, they topped us off. I said what about the oil and he said oh shoot; I forgot to check the oil. So, I said let me get out and run inside and I will get two quarts of oil to take with us. He said all right, I got out of the airplane and ran inside, picked up two quarts of oil, came back out, and we took off on runway 02. We took off northbound and about twenty, some minutes after takeoff as we were trying to file a flight plan. We were going to Livingstone, West Virginia and that was our destination. We got about 30 miles south of Roanoke when the airplane actually crashed in Floyd, Virginia. Oh man, it was bad, it started as if I said at 9,700 feet and we could not get the right engine started back. We continued to start and switched fuel selectors from main to auxiliary position and kept cranking, kept cranking, and could not get a restart, then back to the mains, kept cranking and cranking and back to the auxiliaries and we could not get a restart. I asked does anybody want to guess what could have happened. Someone said you were out of fuel. I said, very good, the main tanks were empty. Therefore, 60 gallons of fuel that the pilot said was there, was not there. As you can imagine, each time we switched back over to the main tanks, we were sucking air back into those lines and we could not get a restart for the right engine to stay running. It was shortly thereafter all the fuel ran out of the left side and the left engine quit. If anyone has ever flown in a twin Comanche, they know it glides like a rock and we came down in a hurry. We picked out a softball field to land on but unfortunately, we hit a stand of pine trees and they did not give a bit. The impact tore the airplane all to pieces and almost killed me. I stated, let us go through these slides very quickly. Nance spoke up and said do you want to tell them about your AGI and IGI. I said, let me brag very quickly. I had 1,600 hours, I was one week away from a job interview with US Airways Express, and my mom was a flight attendant for the commuter airline out of Charlotte. I really wanted to fly for race teams out of Concord, but at the time, I was unaware that they had an interview lined up already. Therefore, after the accident occurred and my rehabilitation began, I had to learn to walk again since paralysis went throughout the entire left side of my body. If you can imagine, when you hit hard enough to knock an eye out and knock your nose off along with knocking four teeth out, that is a pretty hard impact. Therefore, I had to have major rehabilitation, the good Lord watched after me and blessed me up to this point in my life, and he is still doing so at this time. June 6, 2000, two years and five days after that plane crash, I became the first blind and only blind Advanced Ground Instructor in the world for the FAA. Several months later in October of 2000, I became the first and only blind Instrument Ground Instructor in the world for the FAA. Someone told me that I am still the only blind person in the world to hold those certifications. That is awesome, I do not see how I passed those written tests, but I did. The guy that gave me the Multi-Engine Instructor check ride back in February of 1998, in the same airplane I crashed in, an examiner for the FAA. He still works for the FAA and is getting close to retirement. He is the man that gave me the oral test for both of those licenses. He did not know how to administer the test to me, so he contacted the FAA up in Washington. They told him that they did not know, they had never had to do this for anyone before, so they contacted Oklahoma City. Oklahoma contacted Washington, they were going back and forth, and they did not know how to administer the test to me. They said all we can do is read him the test and get you to type the answers on the computer and let him answer you, orally. That is what they did and I surprised myself when I passed the test. The FAA wanted to give him a certificate of achievement and I said, hey do I not get one of those. The crowd laughed. All I received was my license and they flew him to Washington to award him the certificate of achievement. The crowd laughed once again. Nance reminded me that I scored higher than Rich did. I said hey I scored higher than he did on the written, what about me I want one of those. I do have to brag one more time, last night I found out about another scholarship that I received. I have not received it yet, but they said they would send me the money in a couple of weeks. The International Council of Air Show Foundation and the General Aviation Manufacturer Association gave me their award this year. They only award one person a year and I surprised myself if I did get that one. I am very blessed to receive that one as well. The crowd clapped for seven seconds. Next, I spoke of having family there in Kannapolis, North Carolina where I am originally from, the home of Dale Earnhardt if there are any NASCAR race fans out there. On the screen is a picture of my cousin's 1930 model WACO. I flew in this airplane as a passenger when I could see and after losing my sight. My cousin has a grass strip there in Kannapolis, he is a retired US Airways Captain on the Boeing 767, and his son was a Captain on the Fokker F-28.

Nance began explaining,

> This is his cousin Ferrell, the Fokker pilot, standing in front of their hangar that is full of Piper J-3 Cubs. This picture is actually one of the pictures taken of Barry two weeks before the accident and this photograph is one the surgeons used to rebuild his face. This is actually the presentation we are going to go thru quickly that is, a presentation for a class at Embry-Riddle. Barry graduated from Embry-Riddle in May of 2007, and he was their first blind graduate in their 82-year history. They have never had a blind student at Embry-Riddle because aviation is sight dominated. Barry graduated with a Master's of Science in Aeronautics with two specializations or two majors, Aviation Safety and Aviation Operations and did so with a perfect 4.0 GPA.

The crowd applauded for six seconds. Nance said,

> He is not one to sit still very long, even though he graduated in May of 2007, in June of 2007, he began his PhD degree. Embry-Riddle does not quite have their PhD degree in an aviation program, yet he was not willing to wait for it. Therefore, he started his PhD program about a year and a half ago with Northcentral University who has a partnership with Riddle. The degree will be a PhD in business Administration with his aeronautical specialization. He currently has a 3.92 GPA and after two more classes he will begin the dissertation.

The crowd applauded for five seconds. Nance continued,

We will go thru these slides quickly. The
tail number was N7794Y. We will talk about the
history, what happened, why did it crash, and
recommendations that Barry has offered in his
Master's thesis and will continue in his Doctoral
dissertation. We will describe information on
the airplane. It was a 1965 PA-30 Piper twin
Comanche. All maintenance records were current and up to date. The airplane had four seats,
it had two 160-horsepower Lycoming engines,
and a total fuel capacity and as you heard this
is very crucial in this accident. The fuel tanks
held 90 gallons total and 84.5 useable. Barry
was the safety pilot on board and the pilot in
command had his commercial pilot certificate,
single-engine land and multi-engine land instrument airplane. He had a total of 801 hours and
168 of that was multi-engine time. He actually
had more multi-engine time than Barry did at
the time of the crash. Next, I will talk about
Barry as the safety pilot. Barry was listed on the
NTSB accident report as a passenger and it was
just he and the pilot on board that afternoon. As
he talked about, he worked as a Certified Flight
Instructor for 20 months and four months as a
Multi-Engine Instructor. He worked seven days
a week and accumulated over 1,200 hours of
flight time to get a total of 1,560 hours. He was
on his way with an interview with the chief pilot
of US Airways Express out of Charlotte, North
Carolina. So, what happened, on Monday afternoon, June 1, 1998? At 1632, the PA-30 went
off Roanoke's radar in Virginia and crashed 37

minutes after takeoff. Serious injuries occurred to the pilot and the passenger on board. Visual meteorological conditions prevailed on a beautiful, clear spring day in Floyd, Virginia at the site of the crash. The aircraft crashed due to engine failure. The right engine failed first at 9,700 feet and the pilots agreed it was due to mechanical failure. The pilot conducted emergency restart procedures and approximately ten minutes later, the left engine quit. The aircraft crashed into a stand of trees next to a home and the auxiliary fuel tanks were knocked off during the impact. Nance shared about the crash photos shown and as Barry said earlier, those pine trees did not give.

Nance explained about the pilot freaking out from all the commotion and me taking over control of the aircraft. She also explained that I was keeping the airplane from rolling into the dead engine. She asked me, "What was the last thing you remember?"

I explained, "Standing on the left rudder and turning the control yoke almost all the way to the left, banking into the good engine."

Nance said, "They were aiming for a softball field and the picture shows how close they were to two houses." She asked about another picture, "What is missing from the airplane?

Someone said, "The tail." That person was correct. One more picture was of me in the hospital on life support. Next were details why the airplane crashed. Multiple errors played part, beginning with the pilot not doing a proper preflight. She showed a diagram of the fuel tanks in the Piper Twin Comanche.

The two main tanks were the inside tanks, inboard the engines. The two auxiliary tanks were the two tanks outboard the engines or on the wingtips. Factor number two, the pilots were full of fuel but the PIC forgot to check the oil. Barry got out

DR. BARRY HULON HYDE

of the aircraft, entered the terminal and charged two quarts of oil for the amount to the aircraft. The important facts, the fuelers on the ground did not do their job. At the time of the accident, Barry was a CFI working for a flight school at the Concord Regional Airport. The boss owned 13 aircraft in the flight school and during the evening, the fuelers were to check all but two aircraft when the airport was least busy and top off all fuel tanks. Documentation proves after the accident, the last known fuel came from Greensboro, NC. This last known fuel came four days prior to the accident from Greensboro on Friday. The aircraft flew home on Friday, where a half hour was flown out, the aircraft was not flown on Saturday due to rain, the pilot and Barry flew it on Sunday 2.4 hours, and they crashed 37 minutes after takeoff on Monday. Barry's boss, told him Sunday evening to go on home and he would have the airplane topped off and put back online. Nance shows a memo to the crowd that had a date of June 23, 2008 on it. Twenty-two days after the crash, Misty Smith gave this document to Barry's family. At the bottom of this memorandum, it states and the sentences highlighted, the airport's service workers are not topping off Lanny's planes at night. This is a nightly check to see if the airplanes need fuel.

Twenty-two days after the accident, ASW's were still not topping off the flight school's aircraft. Factor 4, the employee behind the service desk asked by Barry that morning to make sure that the aircraft was topped off. This became more personal because this person was the girl I was dating at the time of the accident. Therefore, as we said before the first engine began failing 25 minutes after takeoff and the pilot to this day still claims the aircraft was full of fuel. After the crash, both engines were removed and sent to Textron Lycoming for tests and they ran perfectly. One more factor, the pilot chose not to land at a closer airport when the first engine failure occurred. We have a copy of the ATC tape and you can hear Barry's voice on the tape. The trip was to take them to Livingston, West Virginia to see his mother. Robert Anderson rented the airplane to receive his instrument currency and Barry was his safety pilot. When the engine first quit and made the mayday call, which we have a copy of, ATC told Anderson about three closer and smaller airports rather than Roanoke and they had clearance to land at one of those airports. The pilot wanted to go to Roanoke to rent a car and he truly thought it was mechanical and he could get the airplane worked on there and he could leave Barry with it. He was unsure if he could get a car at one of the smaller airports. Therefore, in teaching safety, the first thing to learn is anytime something happens, get the aircraft on the ground then ask questions later. One of the critical factors is not to continue the flight, immediately get it on the ground. Next, she shows another diagram of the fuel selectors out of the Pilot's Operating Handbook. The pilot alternated switching the fuel selector back and forth from the main position to the auxiliary position. Now if the pilot's knew the airplane was low on fuel, then fueling the aircraft would have occurred before the flight. If the main tanks were full, then the engines stopping would never occurred. As all restarts failed, the right engine failed, and the left engine lost power ten minutes later. The aircraft was already getting low on altitude. Best glide was 110 knots and the aircraft glided like a rock practically 128 miles per hour. The pilot and passenger impacted the aircraft into a group of trees next to a house trying to land on a softball field.

Barry devoted his Master's thesis and the doctorate dissertation on the preflight checklist. The title is "The Proper Execution of the Preflight Checklist to ensure Flight Safety." If you do not do good preflight checklists or skip items then you are taking a chance of something bad happening because you did not check it. The first recommendation that Barry is teaching fellow aviators is that one negligent act may turn into multiple negligent acts if the incorrect performance of a job occurs.

In addition, have three checklists to follow for airport chores, morning, afternoon, and night. Have an airport employee to review the checklist periodically to make sure employees are following it. One more recommendation is to reinforce proper procedures to the pilot during his Biennial Flight Review and if a pilot cannot follow, the preflight procedures, then revoke his currency until that person can follow the preflight procedures in the airplane. The next recommendation is for the NTSB and the FAA to interview passengers involved in accidents. Now, Barry was in a coma for three weeks and his accident was June 1, 1998, but the FAA or NTSB did speak to him, but he does not remember the conversation.

Next, bring the pilot up to speed and increase training on the proper preflight training on airplanes in the Biennial Flight Review. This is taken directly out of the accident report;

the NTSB determined the following cause of the accident, as the pilot's improper selection of the fuel tank selection of the fuel tank position resulting from fuel starvation to both engines.

Barry has a favorite saying, life goes on and so do we! He and Lincoln have been up to quite a bit. These pictures taken in the last 18 months, in the upper left was when we were in San Diego. He received the Airbus Leadership Award and the FedEx Technical Systems Operations Award. The woman holding his certificate is the general council and the vice president of Airbus America in Herndon, Virginia. In addition, he spent about ten minutes with the general, chuck Yeager. General Yeager approached them and the first thing he said to Barry that animal is a good-looking dog!

The crowd snickered, and Nance said we enjoyed his company.

The next picture came from when we were in Washington last fall at the Air Traffic Control Association convention, where awarded to Barry was his second scholarship. We spent just a few minutes with the acting FAA administrator, Bobby Sturgil. One more picture from February of 2007, Barry rode a bomber at the Flagler County Airport and it was the B-24 Liberator. I stayed on the ground with Lincoln, the people had no problem with Lincoln riding however, they were concerned with the amount of noise, and they said it was as loud as 110 decibels. Barry was so elated about the flight. The next picture shared came from when we visited Boston, Massachusetts at the Collings Foundation. They opened their estate, hangars full of airplanes and antique cars for a fund raising event, and Barry was the keynote speaker. They actually owned the airplane, the B-24 he rode on. The Collings Foundation supported the Harvard Eye Research Institute and previously called this Gala the eyeball. Bob Collings offered to auction off rides on his vintage aircraft and gave tours of his hangars.

Barry with B-24 bomber

Nance gave me the podium, and I answered a few questions. The first question was, How much fuel was in the auxiliary tanks? I answered,

> Yes sir, the auxiliary tanks had an undetermined amount of fuel in them and if topped off that meant a total of 30 gallons or 15 per side.

The report stated an undetermined amount, so when the trees knocked them off, then, I feel sure some leaked out. The reason there was not a fire was because the main tanks were empty, and the trees knocked off the auxiliary tanks and there was not anything left to burn. That was a blessing in a way that there was not any fuel to catch on fire.

Nance asked, "Do you want to share about the blue smoke and air in the lines?"

I stated,

I am sure everyone is familiar with starting an engine once you feed fuel to the cylinders and it burns sending blue smoke out of the exhaust. We encountered that on those restarts, going from the main selectors to the auxiliary selector and we thought we were having an engine fire. Therefore, we went back to the main tanks a few times and once the blue smoke went away, then we assumed something mechanical was going on. We just thought it was not receiving fuel from the main tanks. In addition, we think the reason we could not get a restart was so much air went into the fuel lines. I had never flown with a lying pilot, that is just one thing pilot's do not do is lie about the preflight on an airplane. The accident should have never happened. The FAA grounded the pilot in command because they took his medical. Six months after the crash, the flight school closed its doors in December of 1998. Of course, I am grounded for the rest of my life until I get sight back in my left eye, then I will be the first blind man to fly legally.

The crowd chuckled. Someone asked, "Were the fuel gauges operational before the accident?"

I said,

> I do not remember, even if they were or were not, I do not know if I would have trusted the gauges when the pilot did the preflight. Hindsight is 20/20, but I had to believe him. Here again, It was a learning process for us all and I hope everyone in here believes that accidents can happen to the best of us. Things we need to do to prevent them from happening is doing simple things like the proper preflight of the airplane and doing it properly. I am very blessed to be alive and doing as well as I am, succeeding, and continuing to persevere no matter what obstacles I incur each day. I want to thank everyone for listening and I do not want to tie anymore time up. Is there any more questions?

Someone in the crowd asked, "Did the injuries occur more from the impact of the airplane hitting the trees or more so from the seat breaking?" I explained,

> It was a combination of both, sir. The last thing I remember was pulling down on that lap belt and tightening it as tight as I could get it. When we hit the trees, the seat knocked me forward, and it was as if someone hit me from behind and knocked me forward into the control yoke and the dashboard. The lungs collapsed due to hitting the control yoke and the head injuries from my head hitting the instrument panel. Another blessing was the paramedics intubated me at the crash site. If they had not opened my airway at the

crash site, I would be either dead or a vegetable in a bed somewhere. The woman that intubated me never got it to work the first try, it always took her two or three tries, she dropped to her knees and prayed to God and she hit my airway first try. Miraculously, here I am standing to tell about it. Let me share one more story with you. The paramedics and fire department were holding their weekly meeting just right up the road. The call came across the radio and they responded and were at the crash site in minutes. They got me out of the airplane, intubated me in minutes, and saved my life. They left the pilot in the airplane and they were working on me while he was hollering and yelling at them. We filed a lawsuit against the City, the pilot in command, the owner of the flight school, and it went in front of three judges in Raleigh, North Carolina in the state court of appeals. The judges ruled that because I did not have a contract with the City, therefore, I could not sue the city. Therefore, they threw it out of court.

The crowd said "wow" and "no way!" I said, "Thank you all." The crowd clapped for eight seconds.

Keith asked me to tell the crowd about what the doctorate degree is in, what it will be in, and what I want to do when I graduate. I told the crowd that I was working on a PhD in business administration with a specialization in aeronautical safety. I was finishing a forty-two-page paper in the business and technology class.

On October 1, I will begin a Homeland Security class, beginning in January I will begin a statistics class and the dissertation process will begin April 1, and that will be an expansion of the proper execution of the preflight checklist to ensure flight safety. I would then like to go to work for the FAA, NASA, DOT, AOPA, or a flight school. I am going to make it in this world, I might be the only blind man to do it but I am going to make it one way or the other. I am very fortunate and 2008 has been the best year yet. I received the news of another scholarship I learned of yesterday. I met Chuck Yeager March 14 in San Diego and I met Patty Wagstaff April 1 at Embry-Riddle. I went to Reno on January 7, 2008, to receive the American Institute of Aeronautics and Astronautics scholarship. This is rather amazing, since I crashed in a Piper which was the William T. Piper Senior General Aviation Systems Graduate Award and I thought that was awesome as well. The American Council of the Blind gave me their top award over July 4 and we flew up to Louisville, Kentucky to receive that one in person with 19 other scholarship winners.

Nance and I shared about the survey I needed for the dissertation, and I hoped to get their input on it as well. I thanked them once again, and they clapped for eight seconds.

Display at ERAU

Friday afternoon, October 17, 2008, Embry-Riddle had a display on campus of the Wright Flyer. It sounded like a two-piston engine. It was only a twelve-horsepower engine, and it was very loud. Nance took Lincoln's and my picture beside the two-place jet airplane that John Travolta learned to fly a jet in, which he donated to Embry-Riddle Daytona beach campus, Florida, on November 14, 2001. Award-winning actor, international superstar, and jet pilot

John Travolta had donated one of his personal airplanes, a Canadair CL41 Tutor, to Embry-Riddle Aeronautical University. The gift, which includes spare parts, is valued at more than $700,000. The Canadair CL41 Tutor is a turbine-powered two-seat aircraft designed originally by Canadair as a training aircraft for the Royal Canadian Air Force (RCAF). In addition, the Snowbirds flew it by the RCAF demonstration squadron. It flies at a maximum speed of 480 knots (552 miles per hour), a maximum altitude of 40,000 feet, and a maximum distance of 593 nautical miles. Manufactured in 1967, the plane donated by Travolta was used initially for more than two decades as a trainer by the Royal Malaysian Air Force, which renamed it the Tebuan ("wasp"). After Travolta acquired the jet, he had to receive special authorization from the Federal Aviation Administration to fly it because, as a military aircraft, it was classified as an experimental aircraft for civilian pilots.

During this particular afternoon, we went by Pam Peer's office, visited briefly with her, and received an awesome hug. In addition, we visited with Dr. Marv and some other faculty and staff. Dr. Marv told us that he and Sid McGuirk would be in Washington at the ATCA convention and they would see us there.

Greater Miami Aviation Association

The Greater Miami Aviation Association awarded me a third scholarship on Saturday evening, October 18, 2008. This event took place in Miami at the Intercontinental Hotel. The award ceremony was over dinner with several hundred people in attendance. Four scholarships were awarded at $8,000 apiece and all attended Embry-Riddle. Steven Dawn presented the award to me, and I was the only one in person to receive it. The crowd applauded for eight seconds for Lincoln and me. This hotel was very close to where the carnival ships dock on the Biscayne Bay. This was valued at $8,000 and was the largest scholarship I had received yet.

Lift Magazine

Tuesday afternoon, October 28, I spoke with Rebecca Douglas, who is the author of the article written about Lincoln and me in the *Lift* magazine at ERAU. She is from Illinois, and she interviewed me for about an hour. Rebecca said my story would be either the cover story or the centerfold article. In addition, more interviewing took place on Thursday, November 6.

RFB&D

Thursday, October 30, 2008, Julie Hagathe contacted me. This woman shared with me that the Recording for the Blind and Dyslexic wanted to do an article on me, and they wanted to publish it in their electronic magazine in the December or January issue.

Glass Eye

On Friday, October 31, Nance, Lincoln, and I went to Lakeland, Florida, to receive a new glass eye. Dr. Edwin Johnston is an ocularist, and he made all my glass eyes going back to the originals in North Carolina. He and his daughter, Lisa, are the only people I have seen in reference to the glass eyes.

Air Traffic Control Scholarship

Sunday morning at 7:30 a.m., our flight departed out of Daytona Beach going through Charlotte, and we arrived in Washington around 10:45 a.m into Reagan National. Sunday evening, November 2, 2008, after arriving in Washington, Nance, Lincoln, and I had dinner with Renee Martin Nagle, the vice president and general counsel of Airbus America Incorporated. We had dinner at the Wardmon

Park Marriot and had a great visit. In addition, we visited with Pete Dumont and Dr. Marv several times.

On November 3, 2008, the Air Traffic Control Association awarded me a third scholarship, and we went to the Wardman Park Marriot to receive the honors in person. We flew out of Daytona Beach, Florida, into Charlotte, North Carolina, on a Canadair Regional Jet 700. Then we were on a Boeing 757from Charlotte into Reagan National Airport.

The convention was fun, and the exhibit hall was an awesome experience. We met many people, and everyone loved Lincoln. In addition, the entertainment was fun as well. The twenties event we attended agreed with us. The luncheon was great, and several hundred people attended. I was the only scholarship recipient in attendance, and they asked me to say a few words. Ruth Leverance, the deputy administrator for the FAA, and CFO budget director, ran nine regions within the FAA and spent thirty-three years employed by the FAA serving under many administrators. Ruth knew how to manage programs and money, and she announced that she was retiring at the end of the year. Ruth spoke highly of Bobby Sturgil and spoke briefly on the order and transition of Next Gen. She said, "Next Gen is vitally important and essential to the world, transportation, environment, infrastructure, and commerce." She applauded ATCA, a wonderful industry day forum last September. The FAA heard all she said, she told. Next, she said,

> Let's turn to why we are all here today, the scholarship program. I want every one of you, the contributors and the companies that gives to a wonderful legacy; it is for you all to contribute to the scholarship program. It is hard work to organize fundraisers and special events to raise money. However, what a difference it makes, leveraged for years and years and years to come. Therefore, I applaud all of you for that. Another spirit, of presidential matters I been reminded

that George Washington since his first term of office, there is nothing better deserved for people than the promotion of science and literature and the continuing study. Knowledge is in every country that shares pages of public happiness. Therefore, here at ATCA, we are walking the walk and talking the talk. Barry Hulon Hyde who is here with us today, I want to share with him and all of you, some words of an email that I received from Cindy Castillo. She regrets she is not here today. It is through inspiration and motivation, my life has been touched and is better today. I am very passionate about education and to all of the applicants, families, educators, friends, and we salute you all because it is all of you that play a part in this banquet. I hope a few things for this scholarship, the opportunities, and your freedom to encourage more people to go and be contributors in the future.

Ruth closes by saying, "Thank you very much!" The crowd applauds for seven seconds. Becky Umbah is an aviation associate and has been involved with ATCA since 1986. Becky Umbah was the presenter of the awards, and the crowd applauded for her for five seconds. She has supported the ATCA scholarship program for fifteen years. She said,

Years ago, we were thrilled when we were able to give away a $500 scholarship and today, we have set a record for giving away our first $5,000 scholarship. Scholarship funds are set up to help support the financial need of those who have chosen to seek a higher education in air Traffic Control. We also support the children of Air Traffic Controllers of the Buckingham Award.

She also thanked those who helped in the selection process like Cindy Castillo and Larry Fortiea. Becky Umbah filled in for Cindy Castillo since she missed the event because of surgery. She explained the scholarship awards were in four different categories. The first was awarded to students enrolled in a two- to four-year program. The next category award went to students; this scholarship was awarded to students enrolled half- or full-time for a bachelor's or a higher degree in an aviation-related course. There were four recipients in this category.

Becky stated,

> About the next presentation and this one is a unique written letter as well. Dr. Marv Smith, who is out there somewhere, we have a letter from Dr. Marv about Barry Hulon Hyde. Dr. Marv says he has enough character to fill a barge. So let me tell you a little about Barry. He is working on a PhD in Business Administration with an Aeronautical Safety specialization. He received a BA in History from University of North Carolina. He received a MS in Aeronautics with specializations in Aviation Safety and Operations from Embry-Riddle in 2007 with a 4.0 grade point average. He is in his first year at Northcentral University with a grade point average of 3.89. His FAA certifications include Commercial Instrument Airplane, Certified Flight Instructor, Multi-Engine Instructor, Advanced Ground Instructor, and Instrument Ground Instructor. In March of 2008, he received an Airbus Leadership Award. In March of 2008, he was also the recipient of the FedEx Technical Systems Operations Award. The thing I did not tell you, is that in June of 1998, Barry was in a plane crash and lost his sight. Can you imagine overcoming all that Barry has overcome? We are so glad to give him a $5,000 award today for his scholarship.

The crowd clapped for six seconds. Becky said,

> Barry is here and I am going to ask him to say a few words when we are finished with all the presentations. Barry, you are amazing, congratulations and thank you for being our friend. The next category is a full time employee scholarship category. This means you are working full time and you are going to school either at night, morning, or on-line, and it is not convenient but you are still doing it. The last category is the Buckingham Memorial Scholarship. The scholarship is an award to children of Air Traffic Controllers. There is a pattern of growth that we have in our scholarship fund. Now, our goal is to have $500,000 in the fund. However, what we do is award anything over and above $500,000 and what we earn by donations or receiving from numerous events. So, as you can see in 2004, we had seven awards for $13,500 and this year we had 14 awards, $48,500. We have come a long ways and thank everyone for your continued support. At this point, what I would like to do is introduce Barry Hulon Hyde. Barry is the largest award winner of any of the scholarships presented. Barry if you can stand up and say a few words, he is here with Lincoln the Aviator, his guide dog which will be reaching retirement real soon, and Nancy, his fiancée.

I stood up, took the microphone, and said,

> Good morning everyone. It is very awesome to be a part of this program. First off, I would like to thank God. I thank God for allowing me to be

here and I never dreamed I would live through a plane crash but God obviously has something left for me to do in this world. I do not know what that is but that is alright. I would like to thank the Air Traffic Control Association for awarding me a scholarship for the past couple of years. I would like to thank Becky for giving me a few minutes and I wish Cindy were here to share in this experience. I would like to thank Lincoln the Aviator, I would not be where I am at today without him. Lincoln will be retiring but he will be with me for the rest of his life. I also want to thank Nancy for helping me as well through all of my difficulties. Education wise, Becky was right, I had a 3.9 GPA and my last grade increased up to a 3.93 GPA.

The crowd applauded for four seconds. I said thank you. I have said this before, but I have to say it one more time. Jack Hunt, who was the first president of Embry-Riddle, said, "For most people the sky is the limit, but for those who love aviation, the sky is home." I want to continue to help fellow aviators to reach for the sky. Thank you once again I said, and the crowd clapped for seven seconds. Becky said, "Thank you so much for being here. You are a wonderful, amazing man, and we are so privileged to have you in our program."

ICASF and GAMA Magazine

Monday, November 10, the International Council of Air Shows Foundation and the General Aviation Manufacturer Association sent me their magazine. This magazine had a picture of me in it as well as a brief write-up about me being a scholarship recipient. I was one of eight given out and the only one for the ICASF and GAMA.

Endeavour

Friday night at 7:55 p.m., November 14, 2008, Nance, Lincoln, Jackson, and I went to Cape Canaveral in Titusville to witness the liftoff of the space shuttle *Endeavour*. Nance described how much the sky lit up to me, and the sound of everyone yelling and hollering made it memorable. The intense sound of the liftoff sounded like nothing else I have ever heard, and that sound lasted for forty-five seconds where we stood.

Barry & Jet at Endeavour launch

Recordings For the Blind and Dyslexic

RFB&D* E-NEWS
Issue #17, December 8, 2008

Our two profiles this month are written by members themselves—Barry Hulon Hyde and William Trudell—and provide inspiration for all of us on reaching for the sky and never giving up. Thank you to Barry and William for sharing your stories.

In his own words, Barry Hulon Hyde's story from losing his sight in a horrific plane crash to graduating with a master's of science in aeronautics:

Inspiration to Reach for the Sky

Without RFB&D*, I could not have become the first student who is blind to graduate from the world's largest flight school!

In 1998, while flying as a passenger in a small plane, I survived a crash with traumatic injuries. I lost my sight, sense of smell and taste, and was pronounced dead on arrival after being airlifted from the crash site. Prior to this accident, I was a pilot with over 1,600 flight hours. In fact, I was just one week away from interviewing with US Airways to become an airline pilot.

I have loved flying and aviation all my life, and the 1998 plane crash did not diminish my love of flight. RFB&D's audiobooks allowed me to pursue my education after becoming blind and inspired me to continue my love of aviation.

Following two years of recovery and rehabilitation, I earned licenses as an Advanced Ground Instructor (AGI) and Instrument Ground Instructor (IGI). The Federal Aviation Administration (FAA) has confirmed that I am the first and only person who is blind to hold these certificates.

In 2007 with RFB&D's help, I graduated from Embry-Riddle Aeronautical University (ERAU) with a master's of science in aeronautics and a 4.0 GPA. I am the first student who is blind to attend ERAU in its 82-year history. I am now pursuing my PhD in business administration with a specialization in aeronautical safety at Northcentral University, where my current GPA is 3.93.

My favorite place to listen to RFB&D's audiobooks is while I'm flying—which I do as often as I can!

Living on $567 per month Social Security Disability income, I could not continue my education without the assistance of scholarships. Over the years, the confidence in me has shown through these awards, which has been unbelievable. It has been a huge privilege to be recognized in this way.

Having survived a plane crash in a Piper aircraft, it was ironic that in January 2008, I received the William T. Piper, Sr. General Aviation System Graduate Award. Later, in May, the Greater Miami Aviation Association (GMAA) granted me a scholarship for the third year in a row.

Also, for the third year in a row, I received a scholarship from The Air Traffic Control Association (ATCA) and, on November 4, my guide dog, Lincoln, and I traveled to Washington, DC, to receive the award in person.

These scholarships, and others support my education to date. In November 2008, I was extremely happy to accept an offer from Daniel Webster College (an aviation college in Nashua, NH) to be an adjunct professor teaching an online aviation safety and security class. Shirley Phillips was the lead instructor for these classes. I will begin teaching in the summer of 2009 as I continue studying for my doctorate degree.

In the first week of January 2009, Lincoln, my guide dog will be retiring and his replacement, another black Labrador, like Lincoln, will be arriving. Lincoln and I have spent over eight years together and have flown together about 40 times!

As I continue my studies, RFB&D will remain an important part of my life. Together, we will achieve great things!

Barry Hulon Hyde

On Monday morning, December 15, 2008, Jensen Larson Photography for Embry-Riddle took our pictures for the *Lift* magazine article. Nance took us to a maintenance hangar on campus. They took pictures of me leaning on the tail of a Cessna 172. In addition, they took pictures of me sitting on a stool with Lincoln's head on my lap. We also went to the beach, and they photographed Nance, Lincoln, and me walking up and down the beach.

AIAA Video

Wednesday, January 7, 2009, I received a video from the American Institute of Aeronautics and Astronautics (AIAA). This video was the interview I did last year when I attended the scholarship convention in Reno, Nevada. The three-and-a-half-minute video they put together for people involved in Aviation tells about how I fell in love with aviation and why I wanted to be an aviator.

Women of Wings

On Sunday evening, January 19, 2009, I did a presentation for the Women of Wings at the Spruce Creek Airport. Nance, Lincoln, and I were present, and Nance and I spoke about how we met. Nance told about the pictures on the PowerPoint slides given to the facial surgeon as well as the injuries I suffered along with the amount of broken bones. The next discussion was about the history of the aircraft, what caused the crash, why it crashed, recommendations, and analysis. Nance told about my education at Embry-Riddle and becoming the first blind graduate in their eighty-one year history. She told about me graduating with a perfect 4.0 GPA. She shared about the master's graduate research project titled "The Proper Execution of the Preflight Checklist to Ensure Flight Safety." In addition, the education I sought after is the PhD in business administration with a specialization in aeronautical safety at Northcentral University. Currently, the GPA is a 3.95. We also talked about becoming the first AGI and IGI in the world confirmed by the FAA. I received several ovations for the success. There was a nice turnout of women and a few men in a hangar that evening. At the end of the presentation, the women asked questions, and I answered them.

Jet

On January 20, 2009, introduced to me was Jet, my new guide dog. He was only twenty-two months old and weighed sixty-six pounds. He is an English Labrador Retriever, whereas Lincoln was an American Labrador Retriever. Mike Gallagher delivered him to me, and he flew him from New York to Tampa. Jet's original name is

Eric. We did not like this name, so Ginny Tate, an academic advisor at ERAU, recommended we call him Jet, and that name fits.

Daniel Webster College

January 24, 2009, Dr. Shirley Phillips contacted me and asked me if I would be interested in teaching online for Daniel Webster College. Dr. Phillips explained that they fired a professor, and they needed someone to fill in to help in teaching an aviation safety and security class online as an associate professor. She knew I just finished a Homeland Security class because she and her sister Dr. Sherry Parshley helped in proofreading some of my writings. I accepted the proposal. That pay of $1,500 was the second pay since the accident, and it was the easiest money I ever made. The class was an AM 635 class, and she asked if I could help over the summer school beginning July 12. We talked frequently, and we participated together on a chat line Wednesday evening, February 11, with her sister and a few others from Daniel Webster College.

Joyful Time

The week of February 23, 2009, was a real rewarding week. I received a grade of 95 on my most recent assignment for the strategic leadership class I took. In addition, I received my first paycheck valued at $750 from Daniel Webster College, and this was my first real paycheck in ten and a half years. In addition to these previous mentioned highlights of my life at this time, the *Lift* Magazine came out on the twenty-fifth of February. Lincoln and I were the centerfold in the magazine. We were in there, in four different places. One was me leaning on the tail of a Piper Arrow, and another was a picture with Lincoln and his head on my leg as I was sitting on a stool with the College of Aviation building in the background. This was the building I spent all our time working on the master's degree.

The two other pictures consisted of Lincoln and me standing with Renee Martin Nagle of Airbus and with the Federal Aviation administrator Bobby Sturgil. In addition to the four-page article, my name was included in what the president of Embry-Riddle Aeronautical University said in his letter he shared.

Doctor's Results

March 6, 2009, Nance, Jet, and I went to Dr. Waykins office for him to write my prescriptions and review the results of the CT scan I had done on my heart. I have a blocked coronary artery, and the heart was only pushing out 45 percent of the amount of blood that it should be pushing. Dr. Waykin's physician assistant Jamie lined up the cardiologist appointment. This person will schedule the next tests.

Recordings for the Blind and Dyslexic

The RFB&D wanted to do a follow-up article on me. Since I received Jet and was continuing my education, they wanted to share my success.

RFB&D* E-NEWS Issue #18, March 2009

Update on RFB&D Member Barry Hulon Hyde

Barry Hulon Hyde, who was featured in our December Listen Up! newsletter wrote to tell us that his new guide dog has finished training in Smithtown, NY, and is now at home with him and his longtime canine companion, Lincoln the Aviator. Barry, an airplane aficionado, has already changed his new guide dog's name from Erik to Jet. To view a video about Barry posted on the website of the American Institute of Aeronautics and Astronautics (AIAA), visit the AIAA website and then click on "watch videos" and "Dr. Barry Hulon Hyde." Barry was also recently featured in Lift Magazine, the alumni magazine of his alma mater Embry-Riddle Aeronautical University.

Lift Magazine

Enclosed you will find LIFT Magazine, the official alumni magazine of Embry-Riddle Aeronautical University.

Hulon is featured in this edition. You will find him in several places:

- Cover—listed on the right hand side, second bullet

- Page 1—Table of Contents—photo with Lincoln as well as full story listed on page 12

- Page 2—Letter from the President—next to last paragraph Dr. John Johnson shares his feelings about Hulon

- Page 12—Centerfold article—Hulon is the feature story for the next 4 pages. On the main photo spread on pages 12-13, the College of Aviation building is seen in the background. This is where Hulon & Lincoln took all their classes while at Embry-Riddle for their Master's degree.

Enjoy this wonderfully-written article about our favorite pilot!!

Keynote Speaker

Tuesday, March 10, 2009, Andrea Aiello contacted me and told me about seeing Lincoln and me in the *Lift* magazine. Andrea is the academic adviser for the worldwide campus in Albuquerque, New Mexico, for Embry-Riddle Aeronautical University. She asked me to be the distinguished guest keynote speaker for commencement on May 9. I accepted, and this event was awesome.

Jet's Second Birthday

March 14, 2009, is Jet's second birthday. How ironic—he shares a birthday with the general Chuck Yeager. He is a fine animal, and I am happy to say God brought another guide dog into my life to help me.

Discovery Launch

Sunday, March 15, 2009, Jet, Lincoln, Jackson, Nance, and I went to Titusville or Cape Canaveral to watch the space shuttle *Discovery* lift off successfully. Departure time was 7:43 p.m., and it was an awesome event to witness! This liftoff was the fifth one I witnessed. The sound was an experience like no other. Nance complimented how beautiful the glow was, and the rumbling sound was an experience. The crowd yelled and screamed during the liftoff. That intense sound lasted for forty seconds. Nance said when the solid rocket boosters fell off, they glowed as the contrail disappeared.

Heart Procedure

Wednesday, March 18, Dr. Henderson did a cardiac catheter on me at Halifax Hospital. The most painful issue was the IV in the right arm. I never felt the doctor enter the femoral artery, and I never knew when he was finished. It took him about five minutes to see that I had a perfect working heart and I had no problems, blockages, or defects. However, the procedure did make me a little sore. This appointment made our day as well as our year.

National Aviation Training Symposium

Monday, March 16, Tuesday, March 17, and Thursday, March 19, Jet and I attended the National Aviation Training Symposium at Embry-Riddle. There were many presentations on aircraft manufacturing businesses to safety issues implemented. Monday evening, Nance, Jet, and I went to dinner at the maintenance hangar, and I met the grandson of John Frasca. The grandson told about some history of the Frasca simulators and that they began building them in 1958. I had a total of 46.1 hours in a Frasca simulator.

Cessna 172 Flight

Saturday, March 21, was Pam Peer's birthday, and at her birthday party was where I met the pilot Ashley, who took me flying. Sunday, March 22, I went flying with Ashley Vliet in a Cessna 172. Ashley, a friend, a pilot, and an employee of Pam Peer's, flew to the practice area with her giving directions for me to try to hold a heading. We practiced a few steep turns, and during one of the steep turns, we flew back into our own wake turbulence. We also did a few takeoffs and landings; we did one at Dylan and one back into Daytona. The flight was very windy and bumpy, but Ashley did a fine job flying us.

Discovery Return

The *Discovery* space shuttle came in and landed at 3:14 p.m. on March 28. The astronauts worked on the *Hubble* satellite and installed new cameras. They had some real problems loosening a few screws for the removal of the old cameras.

GMAA Interview

Monday morning, March 30, 2009, Ed Cook from the Greater Miami Aviation Association and Batchelor Aviation Scholarship Fund interviewed me for another scholarship. He asked many questions—where I was attending school to my studies. He said he was filling in for Steven Daun, who was over the scholarship program.

Palm Sunday

Sunday, April 5, Carole Blake, who was Lincoln's puppy raiser, came and attended church with Nance, Jet, Lincoln, and me. We had a good service and brunch with everyone that morning.

GMAA Scholarship

Tuesday, May 5, Steven Daun called me and said they awarded me another scholarship valued at $7,500.00. In addition, he said they wanted to invite me to the luncheon on Wednesday, May 13, to receive it in person.

Presentation at Seabreeze High School

Friday, April 17, 2009, Nance, Jet, and I did a presentation at Seabreeze High School. This presentation was for Janet Marnane's private pilot's operations class. Janet began by stating,

> I want to give a warm welcome to Barry Hulon Hyde, Nancy Riedel, and Jet. Nancy works with me in the AI program. She is the person I give all of your grades to, that I give all of your extraction forms to, so she knows everything about all of you. Barry Hulon Hyde, the distinction of an Embry-Riddle graduate and got his Master's degree from there in Aeronautics. He is actually working on his PhD right now and he has the distinction of being the first and only blind Advanced Ground Instructor and Instrument Ground Instructor. Now, he was not always blind and he is going to tell you how he got to this state, he is going to talk about aeronautical decision making, the accident chain, and has a good way to wrap this class up by graphically showing what he has been through.

Nance said, "Why don't you tell them about the airplane you and Lincoln are standing in front of?"

I began by saying,

> Good morning. That airplane is a 1930 model Waco, and does anyone have any clue what the acronym Waco stands for? There has to be some communication going on here. I cannot see you, so you guys will have to speak up.
>
> The acronym stands for Weaver Aircraft Company. I had flown in the front cockpit before

the accident and the first airplane ride after the accident. This airplane is priceless and I am told that there are only six-left flying in the world today.

Janet spoke about AOPA giving a Waco away valued at $700,000 and the guy they gave it to could not afford to keep it because he could not afford the income tax on it. Nance shared about me being from North Carolina and my cousins were both US Airway captains.

My cousin owned this particular airplane as well as hangars, a grass airstrip, and 90 acres. The airplane is not insured and rarely flown. The airplane flies occasionally to fly-ins and is test run several times a year. My cousins took me for my first airplane ride, I also work for them, and they were the ones who developed my love for aviation. That is being around them and seeing how they lived and what they brought home as a paycheck every month. In fact, I remember one month what the older cousin brought home as a paycheck for $24,000. I thought to myself, I want one of those for myself. I will continue to share with you why I never have to see that. They build Piper J-3 Cubs, sell them, and this is like a side job for them.

Nance said, "Moving on and here are some pictures and they are not too bad. Barry was in a bad plane accident on June 1, 1998. This picture was with Ferrell wearing his coveralls, and they were standing in front of a table full of catfish. Ferrell Jr. is the man who was the son of the owner of the Waco and the J-3 cubs. Ferrell Jr. was a Captain on Fokker's F-28s with US Airways."

She said a lake full of catfish touched their ninety acres and that my family lived five minutes away. She said we went fishing quite frequently at night. She told about the number on the airplane I crashed in was N7794Y. She explained that we would go through the history, what happened, why it crashed, and what we found out since then. The maintenance records were current and up to date.

Nance asked me if I wanted to tell them what I was onboard to do because the slide that was up now was the pilot-in-command information.

Well, I was a passenger on board shown by investigations by the FAA, NTSB, and the insurance company. However, I was a Certified Flight Instructor but not that day, I was serving the purpose of a safety pilot. Now, I do not know if anybody knows the definition of a safety pilot. That definition is when the pilot in command goes under the hood, therefore, puts foggles on, that is puts something on that he can no longer see over the dash and cannot see through the windows. All he can see is the instrument panel and that is flying under the hood. Therefore, for the FAA to allow him to do that, you have to have a safety pilot on board, who is someone sighted looking out the windows to make sure you do not run into another airplane. Therefore, that was my purpose that day. First off while we are discussing this accident, I want to share with the class today, can anyone guess what was missing on a 1965 model airplane that caused the horrendous injuries that I lived through. I volunteered, let me give you more detail, how about what is connected to the seats.

Someone said, "A seatbelt?" and I said, "I had a lap belt on, but I was missing what?"

A student said, "A shoulder harness," and I said, "Yes, a shoulder harness. Therefore, when we hit the trees the seat broke, which forced me into the control yoke and allowed my head to hit the dash.

If there had been a shoulder harness, my head injuries would not have happened. Okay, carrying on."

Nance said, "All right. Therefore, as we said Barry was not the pilot in command." A student asked about the harness.

> The shoulder harness was not a required piece of equipment on that model aircraft. It is a requirement today. The PIC was a man named Robert Anderson and he rented the airplane from the flight school. He was a commercial pilot; he had single engine land, multi engine land, and was instrument rated. He had a total of 801 hours of flight time and of those 801 hours 158 hours were in multi engine airplanes.

Nance continued reading the slide, now about me. She said they listed me as a safety pilot in the accident report. "He worked as a certified flight instructor (CFI) for twenty months for Lancaster Aviation at the Concord Regional Airport."

I said, "I helped eight private pilots receive their license, helped two add on an instrument rating.

"He helped a few get their commercial license, and he also assisted in training two commercial pilots for their certified flight instructor license. This gave him a total of 1,560 hours."

Janet asked if that included any simulator time, and I said, "I had 46 hours of simulator time, but that was not included in the total time."

Nance continued reading the slides,

> Monday afternoon, June 1, 1998, at 1632 they went off Roanoke's radar and crashed 30 miles south of Roanoke. The passenger had serious injuries and was pronounced dead on arrival, and the pilot broke both legs, a concussion, and was conscious. Visual meteorological conditions pre-

vailed, a beautiful spring day in Floyd, Virginia. The crash occurred due to engine failure.

Nance asked me to talk about what happened when the first engine quit and what was going through my mind.

Before I boarded that airplane, I was out flying a Cessna 172 with another Private pilot practicing takeoffs and landings with him. As we stayed in the traffic pattern, I could see Anderson pre-flighting the Piper Twin Comanche. As we came down and landed and tied the Cessna down, went back into the airplane and filled out his logbook and his bill. Then, he went into the terminal. I walked over to the Comanche, the engines were already turning, and burning so, therefore I could not participate in any portion of the preflight checklist. Now, if you do not take anything away from this presentation, take away, do not trust anyone but your mother, and keep an eye on her.

The students laughed, and I said,

As I say that you will be able to take more away about what I am talking of in more detail. When I boarded the airplane I asked Anderson, did you check the fuel, he said we were full of fuel. I then asked what about the oil and he said oh shoot; I forgot to check the oil. I said no problem, taxi us up to the terminal and I will go in and get two quarts of oil. Because I know this airplane, it burns oil and I know the airport in West Virginia may not have the correct type of oil. We will take two quarts of oil and we will not have to pay for it. Therefore, we did, he taxied us to the terminal; and I went in and charged two quarts of oil to the flight school. Then we went out and took off from runway 02 and we crashed 37 minutes after takeoff. As we were climbing out to 10,000 feet, I was filing a flight plan with Raleigh Flight Service Station. Shortly thereafter, the right engine started spitting, sputtering, and then finally quit. Then, as we were going through the restart procedures and could not get a restart. The reason why, folks, was because the main tanks where 60 gallons of fuel that was supposed to be there was missing. We did not know that until months later after the crash. Now, going back a little further, the airplane did not burn because why, there was not anything there to burn. So, as we were alternating from the main tanks selector, let me give you a picture of what I am talking about here, on each side of the fuselage are the main tanks, 30 gallons per side. Then you have the engines then the tip tanks, the auxiliary tanks that held 15 gallons per side. Therefore, we have 90 gallons and 84.5 gallons useable. The main tanks were supposed to be full and they were not. That is the reason the engines quit that quickly after takeoff. We can back up even further, we crashed on Monday and Sunday we flew that airplane 2.4 hours or two hours and twenty-four minutes and the ground fuelers that night did not do their job. Hey, there are two people we do not trust, the pilots and the ground fuelers on the ground. It gets deeper, Saturday it rained and none of us had to fly that day. Friday, the airplane flew back from Greensboro, North Carolina to Concord and 30 minutes of fuel was flown out of those main tanks. Okay, let us do the math again. 2.4 hours, which is two hours and twenty-four minutes and 30 minutes on Friday, and this shows roughly two hours and fifty minutes flown out of those main tanks. Previously, we crashed 37 minutes after takeoff almost 40 minutes after takeoff folks. Now, all we have is three and a half hours of fuel in the main tanks, gone. We cannot get a restart because we have already sucked air into the fuel lines and then we go to where the fuel is at and we cannot get a restart on the dead engine. The good engine is still turning and burning. It would not have quit if we would have placed the selector on the auxiliary position and never touched it again. It did not happen that way because the pilot is saying we are full of fuel, he said, I did the preflight and I know this sucker is full of fuel, what is going on. I said, no obviously, we were not. Originally, the engines would not have quit if we had been full of fuel.

I asked the class if things made sense and if everyone was following me. Nance spoke up and said, "Explain how the aircraft banked."

I explained what was stated in the pilot's operating handbook (POH), which is a part of AROW.

What is AROW? It is the Airworthiness Certificate, the Registration, the Operating Handbook, and the Weight and Balance. It is a requirement therefore; it has to be on board the airplane. It states in the operating handbook, the airplane cannot fly with the fuel selector in the auxiliary position except during straight and level flight. Now, as we are trying to do a restart, the airplane is flying through the air at an angle. The reason why is because the airplane is trying to roll or turn into the dead engine. Therefore, the left engine is producing all this power, the right engine is dead, and the airplane is trying to roll to the dead engine. We are standing on the left rudder and we have a bank into the good engine.

I asked if everyone was following me thus far or if I was confusing everyone.

So, instead of allowing the airplane to roll, we are turned into the good engine and standing on the good rudder also trying to maintain a heading as well. If we would have automatically landed the airplane as soon as that right engine quit we would have been fine. The pilot did not want to land at the closest airport; he wanted to press on to Roanoke so he could get the airplane mechanically worked on because we thought we were having mechanical problems. Here we have a lying pilot telling me we were full of fuel and I had no reason not to believe him because he did the preflight. I said, okay, are you wondering what the fuel tanks said? Has anyone thought of that? Let's think about that now, you have the pilot telling you that you are full of fuel, are you going to believe what those fuel tanks are telling you?

Nance reminded the class that it was a forty-four-year-old aircraft. I said, "He is the one that did the preflight and he saw how much fuel was out there in the tanks."

I asked if we care what those fuel tank gauges said. A student spoke up and said, "You just said never trust anyone."

Nance said "That is what he learned," and I said, "I learned that the hard way."

She said, "He learned that afterwards."

Janet Marnane said, "Remember what we learned about fuel gauges in airplanes."

A student answered that they only have to be accurate with a fool in it.

Janet Marnane said, "Are you counting the number of links in this accident chain in all the different places that something could have happened to avoid this?"

> Now, I have not said anything about the owner of the airplane. That Sunday evening after we flew those 2.4 hours, Robert Anderson and I came into the office in the airport and we spoke to the guy that owned the airplane and ran the flight school. He told me to go on home that way I will be ready to go to West Virginia tomorrow. He told me to take the rest of the evening off, which it was already 5 o'clock that evening. He said he would put the airplane back on tie down and have it topped off. The top off and tie down was not done and I know because when I came to work that next morning the airplane was in the same position.

A student said, "Now you have three people responsible."

> That Monday morning when I got to work, I asked the girl I was dating to make sure N7794Y received a top off. I worked at this airport for 20 months and I knew all the ground crew members, all the employees at the airport, and everyone knew that I was there very frequently; they knew that I was a safe pilot, and here all parties

were lying to me. I trusted them because I had been around all of them and we all knew each other's jobs and personalities. We had caught them many times not fueling airplanes because we did proper preflights. Twenty-two days after the accident they were still not fueling airplanes and Nance will show you a slide that proves that.

Nance said,

One thing that Barry has not mentioned is the Concord Regional Airport is the only airport in the state of North Carolina owned and ran by a City. At night when the airport is less busy, the airport service workers fueled the 13 airplanes in the flight school. The ASW's have a checklist and it is their job to check these fuel tanks in these airplanes every night. What Barry is saying is for four days in a row they never fueled N7794Y. The investigations show that the last known fuel in that particular airplane came four days earlier in Greensboro, North Carolina. Four days in a row, the ground fuelers never checked that airplane.

She spoke briefly of Lincoln's picture and then the pictures of the crashed airplane. Nance explained the picture that portrayed the right seat leaning forward and how it was not sitting straight up. "He has memory up to the point of impact. Now what have you guys learned?"

When you are up in an airplane, you should always be looking around because if something happens and you have to put it down quickly, you have to know where to put it down. What they were aiming for was a softball field. They did not make the softball field they picked out and how close they were to hitting a house. There were two houses and a stand of pine trees and they were very fortunate to miss the houses.

She asked, "In the picture, what is missing?" A student answered, "The tail and the wingtips."

I stated,

> The NTSB diagnosed an undetermined amount of fuel in the auxiliary tanks; however, the main tanks were empty. Therefore, after all investigations were completed, they said the fuel selectors were in the wrong position. I suffered many injuries. The emergency team airlifted me to Roanoke regional Hospital and was in a coma for 20 days. The right side of the airplane took the brunt of the impact. I had my headset on along with my sunglasses and I feel the sunglasses cut out the left eye.

Nance told about what happened, "Factor number one was the pilot did not do a proper preflight. If he had, then he would have noticed that the main tanks needed fuel."

I stated, "The attorney and I concluded that the pilot only looked in the auxiliary tanks. We feel if he had checked the main tanks, he would have seen they were not completely full. It is not hard to take a lid off a tank and look down into it."

Nance continued with the slide by saying, "Pilot question. The reason there is a question is the pilot is not being truthful."

I stated, "To this day, he is still saying we were full of fuel. What happened to it? Did it evaporate? After thirty-seven minutes of flight, it evaporated."

Nance read on, "As Barry stated earlier, explaining the diagram of a Piper Twin Comanche. The two main tanks were in the middle, auxiliary tanks were on the wingtips. It was a good thing that the auxiliary tanks were sheared off because they would have possibly caught fire."

She explained the accident was June 1, 1998, and about the memorandum that Misty Smith, the girl Hyde dated that worked behind the desk, gave his family twenty-two days after the crash. The last line highlighted that ASWs are not topping off Lancaster Aviation airplanes at night. This checklist needs to be performed every night or at least someone should check to see if the airplanes need fuel. Nance said,

> Another factor was the pilot not wanting to land at the closest airport. He wanted to land at Roanoke so he could get a rental car. He had rented the airplane to go and visit his mom up in West Virginia. He knew he could get a rental car in Roanoke but was unsure about the other airports. The Air Traffic Controllers he was talking with at the time, once they had reported engine trouble, then, they told them you have three closer airports rather than Roanoke. The pilot decided not to land and continued on to Roanoke. His idea was to leave Barry and the airplane in Roanoke and that was a huge mistake. Like Barry said, at the first sign of trouble, get the airplane on the ground and ask questions later. The pivotal mistake was they did not land that airplane sooner.

Janet Marnane asked, "Barry, did you try to convince him to land it sooner? I know a lot of human factors play part. For example, when the Korean Airliner went down in Guam, right seat pilot is just that, but the captain is the captain."

Nance said, "The PIC was fifty-five, and Barry was twenty-six. Robert Anderson had twice as much twin engine time than Barry."

I spoke up and said, "If the left engine quits, I am kicking your ass!"

Janet Marnane stated, "Talking about pattern matching, characteristics of when we see things, when we have a preconceived notion of what is going on, it is easy to continue to try to fit the pattern that is in your mind to what is really going on. It delays taking appropriate action because the pilot was so convinced that there was fuel in there he never even thought about what if I am wrong. This happens a lot in aviation."

Nance spoke about the glide in.

> The best glide speed was 128 mph when they impacted the trees. Next, we went over some recommendations. Barry is a firm believer in a proper checklist. The airport workers should have checklists as well. The proper preflight procedures for the pilot and go thru those during the Biennial Flight Review. The FAA took all of the pilot's licenses. In addition, by the end of 1998, Lancaster Aviation closed the flight school.

I explained that the FAA found Lanny Lancaster was signing people's logbooks with an expired expiration date with his endorsement. Some other false information located in the accident report stated that I watched the preflight from inside the airport.

Nance explained,

> He was a graduate from Embry-Riddle with a perfect 4.0 GPA and did so in a year and nine months. At the end of January, he began teaching an on-line Aviation Safety and Security class for Daniel Webster College. He had to meet some special people like the FAA administrator, General Chuck Yeager, the curator of the

National Air and Space Museum. He rode the B24 Liberator about two years ago out of Flagler County Airport.

Nance asked if anybody had any questions. Janet asked, "When you met Bobby Sturgil, did you not mention to him that you would like the accident investigation reopened?"

I answered, "No, ma'am, I was just glad to be in his company."

Janet Marnane said, "One of the things I always tell my students, no matter what goes mechanically wrong with the airplane, almost always there will be some element of pilot error found."

I stated, "About 75 percent of human factors play part in accidents." I explained how important June 1 was to me and how certain things shared on that day. June 1, 1990, I graduated high school. June 1 of each year was the beginning of hurricane season. June 1, 2007, I began the doctorate degree. June 1, 1968, Helen Keller died, and that was ironic because the accident occurred thirty years to the date of the plane crash, June 1, 1998. I concluded by stating, "Flying is the most fun you can have with your clothes on."

Keynote Speaker in Albuquerque

On May 8, 2009, Nance, Jet, and I flew out of Orlando on a Southwest B-737-300 direct to Albuquerque, New Mexico. Andrea Aiello Howald invited us on this all-expense-paid trip, and they gave us a rental car as well as hotel reservations at the Albuquerque Marriot Pyramid North. Andrea Aiello Howald asked me previously to be the keynote speaker at the Worldwide Campus commencement for Embry-Riddle Aeronautical University on Saturday, May 9, 2009. The commencement took place at the Anderson-Abruzzo Albuquerque International Balloon Museum in New Mexico.

The commencement consisted of the graduating class, faculty, staff, and dignitaries, all marched into the venue while listening to the "Pomp of Circumstance" played by Troy Brown. Next, the

University of New Mexico Air Force ROTC honor guard marched in and presented the colors. The singing of the national anthem was by Carol Curry. The chaplain Robert Mueller shared the benediction with the attendees. The introduction was by Andrea Aiello Howald.

> It is now my pleasure and great honor to introduce our commencement speaker, Mr. Barry Hulon Hyde, Distinguished Alumnus, DB class of 2007. Every year when we consider who to invite to be our graduation speaker, we take into account a number of factors. We look for someone who has achieved a level of respect in his or her chosen field, someone who will be inspirational. Who can speak to the value of perseverance, who perhaps has overcome some sort of adversity to attain his or her goals? Of course, if this person has a background in aviation on top of it all, we try to close the deal. In addition, we look for someone who will accept the gig—that is a big plus. Fortunately, for us, Barry Hulon Hyde fulfilled all of those criteria. Barry had 1600 flight hours and planned to be a commercial pilot, but things did not work out that way. However, Barry has made and continues to make a significant contribution to the invaluable discipline of Aviation Safety. He is a much sought-after speaker in the aviation industry and we are very privileged to have him as our graduation speaker today. The Albuquerque campus extends a warm welcome to Mr. Barry Hulon Hyde.

The crowd applauded for nine seconds. Nance helped Jet and me to the podium. I stated, "Good morning, everyone. Wow, what an honor it is to be here with everyone. First off, I would like to thank Andrea Aiello, wherever she went."

The crowd laughed, and she said, "I am behind you."

I said, "Yes, ya can see her. Ya will know where she went." The crowd laughed, and I thanked Andrea once again and thanked the worldwide campus here at Embry-Riddle.

Certainly, thank God, for allowing me to attend this wonderful event. I certainly, want to congratulate all of the graduates here today that will be excepting their honor and it is very awesome to be a part of this and to be a part of the world's largest flight school folks. I mean, when you graduate from Embry-Riddle the name says it all. They are the largest flight school in the world and they have been for the last 83 years. I am so honored to say that when I graduated there, two years and two days ago, what a honorable day this is for you all because this is your day in the spotlight. May 9 of 2009, is a day that will go down in infamy for all of you graduates. Just like May 7, 2007 was for me. Just like June 1, 1998, when my life so dramatically changed. I thought I was to be a Certified Flight Instructor as a Commercial pilot and a week from a job interview with US Airways Express. Unfortunately, that day changed my life forever and I had to get a different game plan together if you will. I said that my life changed since the doctors pronounced me dead on arrival at the crash site, 30 miles south of Roanoke, Virginia. I had 14 broken bones, both collapsed lungs, nine broken bones in my face, and a head injury like no other. I am still on one, 500 milligrams of anti-seizure medicine today. I am very grateful that God spared me and gave me a second chance to share my story with everyone and possibly inspire a few along the way. Dates as you can tell are very important to me. Just like December 17, 1903, does anyone have any meaning on what that date is about? Did I hear anyone say First Flight, Kitty Hawk, North Carolina? The crowd laughed. Kitty Hawk, North Carolina is very important to me because June 6, 2000, two years and five days after my life changing experience and that plane crash, I became the first and only blind Advanced Ground Instructor in the world for the Federal Aviation Administration and did so in North Carolina. Now, that date is very memorable and I will remember that date for the rest of my life. Of course, many things happened for me in June. June 1, 1998, the plane crash occurred. June 1, 1990, I graduated high school. So, you had better believe June 1 is important to me, but it gets better. June 1, 2007, I began my doctorate degree at Northcentral University. How ironic, who would have ever thought I would live through a plane crash much less be working with my second guide dog. I never dreamed I would live through a plane crash much less be where I am at today. However, like I said, God spared me for a reason and I do not know what that reason is yet, I do not know if I will ever know, but when I meet God, I am going to ask him a few questions.

The crowd laughed. I continued,

When I get in front of God and I will say, hey, what was June 1, 1998, about? What was I supposed to learn from that? That is all right, I am going to live each day as if it is the last day,

because, hey folks we are not promised tomorrow. We have to live each day to the best we possibly can. I will continue about a few more dates.
June 12, 2000, six days after becoming the first
blind AGI, I received my first guide dog, Lincoln.
We originally called him Lincoln the Navigator,
but after graduating May 7, 2007, from Embry-
Riddle, we promoted him to Lincoln the Aviator.

The crowd laughed. I thought that was sensational as well.

After I received Lincoln in Palmetto, Florida
from Southeastern Guide Dog Incorporated and
that was mid-July and I came home and said,
what in the world am I supposed to do now?
Therefore, I had to figure out what I wanted to
be when I grew up. I wanted to do something
involved in Aviation, so I said let me check
and see if I can become the first and only blind
Instrument Ground Instructor in the world. I
would be darn, I began studying and I was prepared in mid October to take that written. The
Federal Aviation Examiner asked me the questions orally and typed the answers on the computer. After we received the results back that day,
he said, darn Barry, you made a higher score than
I did.

The crowd snickered. I thought that was sensational as well to
achieve that.

Let me see, some other dates that I remember and of course folks, what we do in this world
all makes a difference for each individual one
of us. It may be today or it may be tomorrow.

The education you folks received, today, when you walk across here and receive that diploma in person will help prepare you for your future. Whether you apply for a job in the Aerospace industry, the Aeronautical industry, the Aviation industry, even management, business, accounting, or whatever it may be in, it is like I said a while ago, there is nothing more valuable than the name Embry-Riddle in the Aviation field. The name Embry-Riddle sells people with just the name. When you receive that education here in a few moments and folks, you talk about a party, man, it is going to be a party man, and it is going to be a party here in a little bit. That is an awesome accomplishment and I am so proud of you all and please know this is a very meaningful time for all of you, as well as for all of the families. Let's talk about some more factors that have influenced me and have made a difference in my life. When that plane crash occurred folks, my disability check, right now is only $599.00 a month. Well, some people ask how in the world can you afford to go to school with that whopping income. I said that education came from scholarships after scholarships after scholarships after scholarships. When I say that, here is an example, this past Thursday, the Greater Miami Aviation Association/Batchelor Aviation Scholarship Fund, of course out of Miami, contacted me. They said Barry, we would like to award you another scholarship and I said, really, you have to be kidding me! Folks, that made the number four, for the fourth year in a row, and that totaled 18 since I have been in school going back to 2005. The Bachelor's degree goes back to

2001 but the scholarships came when I began the Master's degree at Embry-Riddle in 2005. My Bachelor of Art's degree came with Lincoln. This guide dog is Jet, in case I forgot to mention him. Lincoln, my first guide dog and I walked 1,800 steps one way back and forth to the University of North Carolina at Charlotte and we lived there for three and a half years in Mallard Creek apartments by ourselves. I graduated with a Bachelor of Arts degree in History.

The crowd laughed.

So, I said, I want to do something involved in Aviation. I know I am blind, hey; it is a sight-dominated industry. I do not care; I want to share my love and continue to be involved in Aviation. What happened to me, I want to be able to prevent that from ever occurring to other pilots. So, I stated I have to move to Daytona Beach, Florida and begin the Master's degree. So, May 7, 2007, was a wonderful day for Lincoln and me at the time, of course, Nance helped me pull it off too. She helped me thru all the difficulties, you can imagine, and when I said the 83-year history of Embry-Riddle, hey, I was their first blind graduate. Hey, you had better believe I am proud of that, I did so with a perfect 4.0 grade point average, and that average brings a lot of accomplishment to me and my heart to receive that. I have to brag very quickly, at Northcentral University, where I am working on my degree at and I am seven classes away from becoming Dr. Hyde. I currently have a 3.95 GPA and I am proud of that as well.

Now, some important people that have come into my life since the plane crash, for example Renee Martin Nagle with Airbus. The Airbus Leadership Award was from the General Council and Vice President of Airbus America Incorporated. She granted that award to me in person at the Women in Aviation, International Conference in San Diego, California. The next award was the Fed-X Technical Systems Operations Award. At this Convention, General Chuck Yeager spoke and this day was his 84th birthday. We all sang happy birthday to him and he spoke for 30 minutes. After his speech, they awarded me the scholarships in front of everybody. I received a standing ovation from everyone. I said that was awesome to be a part of that as well. In addition, we crashed in a Piper twin-engine Comanche on June 1, 1998. Some of you may or may not know what kind of airplane that is. However, that airplane would not hold altitude on one engine, and as we were going thru the restart procedures, the other engine quit, and we crashed into a group of trees in Floyd, Virginia. January 7, 2008, the award from the American Institute of Aeronautics and Astronautics gave me the William T. Piper Senior, General Aviation Systems Graduate Award. I thought, how ironic is that, I lived through crashing in a Piper Twin-engine Comanche and here AIAA is going to give me a Piper scholarship. The statements made the crowd laugh. I thought that was fascinating, here again, making a difference in people's lives, the scholarships are allowing me to continue my education, persevering, and getting me where I am at, eight classes away from becoming Dr. Hyde, once again. Several other scholarships I received came from other blind organizations. I do not know if anybody has ever heard of the International Council of Air Shows Foundation and the General Aviation Manufacturer Association. I have never been in an air show before, but they are going to give a blind man a scholarship. I said, hey, you talked me into receiving that one. It was awesome to receive that one. These scholarships have brought awesome people I have encountered and been able to meet. One more is the female aerobatic champion, Patty Wagstaff. We were in her company at her presentation at Embry-Riddle last year, April 1, 2008. We met with her and had some pictures made with her, and met her dog that she brought with her. Lincoln really enjoyed her and that was awesome to be in her company. We also met the curator of the Air & Space Museum in Washington D.C. when we were there to attend the ATC convention. The Air Traffic Control Association awarded me three scholarships, for three years in a row. As we were up there, receiving them in person, we met the FAA Administrator, Bobby Sturgil, Lincoln received some treats from him and that was neat being in his company as well. In addition, we met the Deputy Administrator, Ruth Leverance and we thought that was awesome accepting an award in front of them as well. Let's see, my goodness, I could talk forever, but I will try to keep it quick. Just remember folks, everything we do does make a difference. Just like the negligence performed June 1, 1998, and had it not been for that negligence, that accident would have never occurred. The things that could have prevented that would have made a difference and prevented that plane crash. The graduates located here today, know whatever you do in society, will affect you, will affect your family, and will affect other people like me, and other fellow aviators, possibly. Now, one thing in closing I want to tell everyone. Jack Hunt, who was Embry-Riddle's first president, had a famous saying. For most people, the sky is the limit, but for those who love aviation, the sky is home. For us fellow aviators, I want to continue to keep helping people reach for the skies and continue their love for aviation. Therefore, to prevent what I lived through from occurring to other fellow pilots, and to other individuals that are involved in what I lived through. When I say things like that, living through and having the head injury I had, I am very blessed to be allowed to go as far as I am and being here to share my story with you all. I am very blessed once again for Andrea and the World Wide Campus for inviting me here to share what I have with you all. Thank you all, once again. God bless.

The crowd clapped for thirteen seconds. Andrea asked me to stay there for a minute. Andrea also said, "I think that is excellent, and I did not bring a treat for Jet. I noticed that everyone else Barry talks to, always speaks to Jet."

The crowd laughed. She continued,

Embry-Riddle, an aeronautical university, recognizes individuals that distinguish themselves through professional accomplishments, public services, or special contributions to the aviation and aerospace industries. We are very pleased to honor Barry Hulon Hyde. We have a distinguished speaker award with this as you honor such speakers as Barry, as special insight in the university, especially, students and faculty. We at Embry-Riddle proudly, present to you Barry Hulon Hyde, this distinguished speaker award.

I said thank you, and the crowd applauded for ten seconds. Andrea explains, "It is a Navajo peace pipe, and it is made by a Navajo artist here in the Southwest."

I said, "Wow!"

"You can display it prominently in your office, and I think your students will want to know what you are doing with that, and it is a good conversation piece."

"Thank you, Andrea. Oh my gosh, that is awesome. Ma'am, thank you." Nance walked Jet and me back to our seat and Andrea continued with the commencement. Eight bachelor students received their diploma, five master students received theirs, and the program coordinator hooded the graduates.

That evening, Andrea invited the graduates, staff, and us to the Santiago Mexican Grill for dinner. This location is where the Sandia Peak Aerial Tramway is located for a ride to the top of the Sandia Mountain. ERAU's program stated,

> Meet the Guest of Honor, Barry Hulon Hyde (07, DB), the first blind FAA advanced ground instructor and instrument ground instructor. Barry is also the first blind student to earn a Master's of Science degree in Aeronautics from Embry-Riddle. Read more about Barry in LIFT magazine.

A spectacular stargazing program near the tram with the physics and astronomy instructor took place, who was also president of the local astronomy club. Telescopes were set up for viewing.

The Fourth Greater Miami Aviation Association Scholarship

Wednesday, May 13, 2009, Nance, Jet, and I went to the Wyndham hotel by the Miami International Airport to receive the fourth scholarship during the luncheon from the GMAA and the Batchelor Aviation Scholarship Fund.

Mark Henderson, the previous past president of GMAA, introduced himself. He explained,

> Dan Sullivan who is currently the president eating some exotic food in China, right now where several of our Board of Directors are at this particular moment. So, Dan asked me kinda pinch hit in and bring welcome. We have a very good program today, we have three scholarship winners, and we have a presentation of a flag that is very emotional and very nice. Tee Garth Bishop who is sitting in the back, who is a former scholarship winner, twice if I remember correctly. He will come up in a few minutes to make a presentation. But first if everyone will stand we will do the pledge of allegiance to the flag.

We all said the Pledge of Allegiance together. Mark Henderson asked Tee Haydoo to lead us in prayer. Tee Haydoo said a nice prayer. Mark Henderson said,

> What I would like to do now is if we do have folks here for the first time, we would like you to say your name and who you are with and give your introduction. We always do the beauty before the beast, so if you will raise your hand and let me know that you have never been here before.

Three people introduced themselves, and Mark thanked them all for coming. He asked, "Is there anybody else who has not been here before?"

Nance said it was Jet's first.

"Does he want to pant or anything?"

Mark said,

> Do you want to woof, no you just want to lick my hand! Not a problem, Barry Hulon Hyde who is one of our winners and this is his second guide dog. His first dog was Lincoln and I forgot his name. Lincoln has retired but he is still with Barry and Jet is the new replacement. Jet is a little friskier than Lincoln was. He is much younger, how old is he?"

I said two. Mark said, "He is two years old? That explains it as well. He is still basically a puppy."

Mark Henderson begins by stating,

> Okay, before we get into eating and after you have eaten and partaken, then we are going to get up, do the presentations and the awards. Most of you know what is going on in Iraq. I am one of those people who wish this war were over. I wish this current president did not have to deal with this and obviously the shift is going over to Afghanistan and it is already going on at this particular moment and hopefully that will not take as long as the current war in Iraq has taken. We have lost a lot of good men, a lot of good women, a whole lot of good people that have made a tremendous sacrifice for this country to keep everybody in this room free. Now, I ask Tegarth Bishop who served over there to come

up and make a presentation of a flag. Where is the rest of the Board of Directors, if they would come up please? As they are coming up, we have a couple of new board of Directors that have just joined on the board under the immediate past president. Tegarth, I am going to ask you Stewart to do this as I talk. If you would give us some information about the flag, where it was, who had it, the significance of it, and then, I want you to make the presentation."

Tegarth explained,

The flag was driven by deployment from January up until the end of March in Iraq. This flag flew in an actual mission over in Iraq, which we took out a bunker that had a terrorist in it. As I mentioned before, it flew on an actual mission. The certificate is Operation Iraqi Freedom, a pilot fighter aircraft, the F-16 fighter on a combat mission on the first greatest medal of honor of the United States Armed forces engaged in Operation Iraqi Freedom. Armed with the most advanced weapons members of the three-thirty second expedition of fighter squadron delivered in justice 246. The vice president of those attempted to honor members of the coalition who bravely fought for freedom. Flown on February 6, 2009 in honor of the Greater Miami Aviation Association a Major Thorp flew the mission over Iraq. I would like to present this award and this flag to the Greater Miami Aviation Association for all they have done for me as I mentioned earlier. I am a prior scholarship winner, I believe I was actually a first to receive two scholarships from GMAA to pay for my Associates of Aviation Management and Professional Pilot Technology degree and this is my way of saying thank you very much for all the good that GMAA has done for me while pursuing my passion for Aviation.

The crowd applauded for six seconds. Pictures taken were of the flag and of the board of directors. Mark said,

Thank you Board of Directors we appreciate that. Thank you so much Tegarth, we deeply appreciate that and thank you for your service to this country that is deeply appreciated by all of us in the room. We want to take a minute and recognize our sponsor who is Embry-Riddle and we always thank them for all that they do. I am going to ask and I know he does not want to come up but I am going to ask him to stand, but I am not going to let him off the hook, Michael stand up please. Michael van Husen is the director.

The crowd applauded him. He congratulated all the recipients. Mark said,

Ladies and gentlemen, thank you very much. Okay, Jet is over here panting and looking at me like when am I going to get my bowl of food, okay it is coming. Please enjoy your lunch and we will be back in ten or fifteen minutes to the program, because we know some of us have to get back to work. Jet over here will have to get back to work helping Barry in a few minutes come up.

They served us a soup, salad, rolls, pork loin with sweet potatoes. Mark continued,

> So, we do want to move this along. The
> George Batchelor Foundation is the actual pre-
> mier of this organization and since Bill was a pre-
> vious president, I asked Bill how long, bill stated
> I would say at least 20 years. Many students have
> come through here and many students have been
> very successful, obviously, we have one in the back
> over there, Tegarth and we appreciate you apply-
> ing and being one of our recipients and giving a
> presentation on the flag. However, we have three
> students that we selected by members of the com-
> mittee other than Nelson and me. In fact, I am
> going to ask the committee members to come
> up here. I am going to ask Nelson Gonzalez who
> is the vice president who will be filling in for
> Steven Dawn of course, who is the president that
> is gone to China, and so, it looks like everybody
> was going to China this week for some particular
> reason. There is something going on, everybody
> is over there, so Nelson has the honor of talking
> about and inviting up our three scholarship win-
> ners. Each one of these scholarship winners are
> truly deserved individuals. One of which, Barry
> Hulon Hyde and I will say this much, Barry this
> is the last time.

The crowd and Mark laughed.

> Barry, I say that truly and this is his fourth
> scholarship and he just keeps on receiving them,
> he truly is a miracle and his story is amazing in
> itself. Everybody should be tenacious as Barry is

and without further ado I am going to ask Nelson to take over.

Nelson Gonzales took the podium and stated,

> I will make this as quick as possible and I want to thank everybody for coming today. Tegarth Bishop, that was an excellent presentation and we are honored that you gave us the flag today and I am sure that everyone alive and the rest of us want to thank you. I want to thank everybody for coming to the luncheon and I was kind of a guest speaker today, not by choice. However, I had the honor of working with George Batchelor for probably; I do not want to date myself, but at least 30 years. I did not receive a scholarship from him but I did receive an honorary scholarship from him because I got to work with him, closely in maintenance and business. While he was a fair and public businessman, he did have a soft side to him. Not everybody saw it, but I did, especially as he got older and one of the things that he always wanted to do was to share a little bit of the Aviation in Miami and some of the things he had done. One of the things he had done and one of the things he did do is the scholarship fund, with that I was always grateful for him, and I am sure everybody here is. This year's recipients were actually selected out of a large group and it is an honor to announce Barry, as everybody knows who has done this and who has had this honor a few times already. Everything he has done in his lifetime I am sure this is a small award. Mr. Barry Hulon Hyde, will you come up?

The crowd clapped for six seconds. Nance helped Jet and me to the podium. Nelson stated, "On behalf of the George Batchelor Scholarship Fund it is our privilege and honor to you, not only for a fourth time but for another time."

The crowd laughed and applauded for eight seconds. The photographer took our pictures with the other scholarship winners, Nelson, and Mark.

I took the podium and stated,

> I would like to thank the Greater Miami Aviation Association and the Batchelor Aviation Scholarship Fund for recognizing me once again. This is such a high honor for me, I am very blessed, and gracious to receive this with the honor I am receiving it. In addition, I would like to thank you and share with everyone, this past weekend, the World Wide Campus of Embry-Riddle invited Nance, Jet, and me to Albuquerque, New Mexico to be a part of commencement there. We did so, I was the guest keynote speaker, and once again, that was a large blessing to be a part of that event. That was taken with such a high honor and once again to represent Embry-Riddle. In addition, I am shooting to graduate with this professional student degree, the doctorate degree, that way I can become Dr. Hyde finally.

I mentioned I was shooting to be finished by December of 2010, that was, if everything goes well. I asked if that was a book yet, and the crowd laughed.

> I currently want to brag briefly, since achieving that 4.0 Grade Point Average at Embry-Riddle, I thought that was good, but now, the 3.95 Grade Point Average at Northcentral is really

good, and that makes me happy as well. I am very blessed and thankful to be alive and doing as well as I am, I never dreamed I would live through a plane crash much less get the recognition from sponsorships that I have attained and I want to thank you all once again and God bless you all!

The crowd applauded for seven seconds. Nelson introduced the second scholarship winner and said, "Mr. Barry, I did not want to embarrass him about my grade point average. It probably was a lot lower than his out of all the people in the room. I don't know, but mine was probably a 2.5 grade point average."

The crowd laughed. Lastly, Nelson introduced the other scholarship winner. Mark took over and said, "Thank you to our committee, Nelson. Thank you very much, ladies and gentlemen. Thank you very much and give them a round of applause again, please."

The crowd clapped for six seconds. Mark said,

Now, actually what we are going to do is ask all of you to come back up once this is over, and we will actually ask Mr. Roberts for a photograph of all three of you together. A couple of things before we close out, and I think they are serving dessert and coffee.

A couple of things before we close out, we do have a little token of appreciation to give our sponsor today, that is Embry-Riddle. Michael will you come and pick them up. GMAA, Dan Sullivan, and from myself who is representing Dan Sullivan, want to say thank you as usual for your support. Michael always does a great job in supporting this organization, Embry-riddle is a premier Aviation school, and I say that carefully, because I have one of my other schools that I have to be on the board.

I tread a little lightly but I try not to make it a problem. Thank you Michael, we appreciate that.

The crowd applauded for five seconds. They did a 50/50 drawing and a drawing for a free lunch. Mark said, "Good job, thank you, everybody, and have a great day!" We took pictures with Nelson and Mark as well as visited a few minutes. We also visited Bill Rivenbark, Connie, and Andrew and had lunch beside Kristen, who is a board member.

American Council of the Blind Interview

The interview with the representatives from the American Council of the Blind (ACB) took place at 7:30 p.m., Thursday evening, May 14, 2009, over the telephone. Michael Garret contacted me from Houston, Texas, and then he brought on Moneta Garner from Romney, West Virginia, and Mike Gravid from Pittsburg, Pennsylvania. The interview lasted close to twenty minutes.

Michael asked me to bring them up to date on what I have been doing over the past year. I stated,

> Yes, sir, I am currently working on the doctorate degree, and I have improved the GPA up to a 3.95. I have begun the dissertation process and I am seven classes and four assignments away from becoming Dr. Hyde. I have received my newest guide dog on inauguration day, January 20, and his name is Jet, like a Jet airplane.

Mike said, "How about that? And was that planned?" I stated,

> Yes, his original name was Eric and we just did not think a guide dog's name should be Eric. I wanted an aviator's name, someone suggested Jet,

and we had to make sure he walked like a Jet instead of a slow poke, so we call him Jet now. I thought about calling him Jekyll since I am going to be Dr. Hyde and my fiancée Nance would not let me.

They laughed. I continued,

Goodness, I have been working and training with him and every couple of days we would get out and walk. Currently, I am working on my book and it is at 102 pages. Publishers want it at 200 pages of text with 20 pages of pictures. We have the pictures of course, we just need another 100 pages of text and I will be able to get that published. Michael asked about the details of the book. I explained the book is an autobiography and how I overcame the obstacles in my life as well as achieving the education processes that I attained. In addition, my success in Aviation and in the sight-dominated industry as a first if you will. In fact, this past weekend, the Embry-Riddle Aeronautical University, World Wide Campus, located in Albuquerque, New Mexico, contacted me at the end of March and asked me if I would be their keynote speaker at commencement. Therefore, I accepted and they flew us out there, and we were able to participate in graduation on Saturday, May 9. You talk about a large event for me, now, that was a huge blessing for me to play part. For me, I am very grateful, to be a leader in Aviation and to be able to let those graduates see me and my perseverance, and I think I inspired a few people while I was there and I was very glad to be a part of that. I think I showed them how the disabled could succeed, and no matter what life presents us with, the obstacles in people's way will make us have to find ways to get around them, and handle them. So, I showed them how to set goals even after what I faced, continued to persevere, and carry on and showed my graciousness to God and how he has helped me, how he has continued to answer my prayers and so forth. Goodness, I have been staying busy with schoolwork because you know the research for this doctorate degree is very intense. The title of the dissertation is "The Proper execution of the Preflight Checklist to Ensure Flight Safety". The flunking of the preflight checklist was the cause of the plane crash I lived through. So, as you can tell, that is what I am striving for is to prove that the pilot's negligence caused that plane crash, and if I prevent other pilots from encountering that situation and that problem, then I feel that is what God left me here to do.

Michael said,

> Speaking of pilot error yesterday on the news, and they have been talking about this for the past couple of days, I just heard they were talking about a regional airline and the lack of training. The Continental Connection, specifically, the crash in Buffalo, New York. Do you think there is some validity to that?

I said,

> Yes sir, I think that comes from lack of experience and lack of proper training. The Captain is the Pilot in Command who may be making actions incorrectly. First off, he should have turned that autopilot off. Secondly, instead

of him pulling back on the yoke to create a stall and then a spin, he should have pushed forward to pick up airspeed. If he would have just pushed forward on the control yoke instead of pulling backwards, to prevent that stall, they could have continued on the approach and recovered. Of course, the right seat or first officer, a female only 24, and at age 24 she did not have enough time and experience to be in that capacity. Of course, pilots that are more senior in making the proper decisions and the proper training is needed, once again. Therefore, that is my take on that issue.

Michael said,

The company paid them improperly and that was only $24,000 a year. They said that was not enough for her to stay in Jersey. She would fly to Washington State to New Jersey, and she had just flown there for her trip.

I stated,

Yes and you have to remember, these flights are an opportunity for pilots to get the experience that they need. To improve their skills and this is the reason for a two pilot operation in the cockpit. Because one of the persons is so much more experienced and that is the one who is the pilot in command, the one who everyone relies on, which is their safety. This accident is one of those accidents that should have never happened. Just like the accident I lived through, it should have never happened.

Michael said,

> They are actually cutting back on training because of the cost of smaller companies, but the larger companies are outsourcing flights to the smaller companies. Are you going to speak out against that?

I answered,

> I think in due time they will come out with more of a consensus of what will be the way to approach this situation. It is like the old saying we live and learn. The NTSB and the FAA will take this situation, they will research the heck out of it, and they will come to the best conclusion to prevent this type of accident from ever occurring again. That may mean more training, more preventative training, and so forth. Therefore, it will take more time for everyone to get a grasp on how to handle this situation. Of course, I think yes, personally, training is the key and the culprit. Once again, training is what prevents accidents, and it is the amount of training that plays part. The report said all the Captain had was training in the classroom. He did not have enough training in simulators to help him in flying this aircraft. That is a lot to take in but it cost 50 people their life because of that negligence and to me that is what that is, someone is making a shortcut instead of fully doing their job, they are cutting costs. Hey, things have to be safe for everyone to fly safely.

Michael said yes, and Mike stated, "On the other hand, you have the accident in the Hudson, and this gives you the good side of the situation."

I said, "Yes, does it not though! Yes, that was just miraculous! That was experience to the tee though because those guys made that decision in minutes—I mean seconds."

Mike asked, "Have you heard those air Traffic Control recordings?"

I answered,

> Yes sir, and Sully made that decision quickly and he barely missed that bridge. When he landed on the water clearing that bridge and the Hudson covered with ice, it is a wonder that things did not get worse instead of the process allowing time for them to unload. I was very pleased to hear of that taking place. I think that was a good, inspiring flight as well as a recovery for that accident.

Michael said, "Last year, you talked a lot about the FAA and potentially becoming more involved with the FAA. Is that still in your plans?"

I answered,

> Yes sir, I would really love to be a part of the Federal Aviation Administration. I would love to go and teach at a flight school. Once again, to teach and to prevent what I lived through that occurred that day, June 1, 1998. June 1 is approaching and that is my 11-year anniversary.
>
> You gentlemen and lady are familiar who Helen Keller was. It is rather ironic that on June 1, was her anniversary of when she died on the same day of the plane crash just different years. The doctors pronounced me dead on arrival that

day. I was in a coma for the next 20 days thereafter. So, many things on June 1 have occurred. For example, June 1, 1990, I graduated high school. June 1, 2007, I began the doctorate degree. Yes, June 1 is a very important day in my life, but it is also a very traumatic day because my life so dramatically changed that day. However, I do want to go to work for a flight school somewhere along the way to teach the ground schools to better pilots. Unfortunately, like I said a while ago, in a site-dominated industry, I am at the bottom of the totem pole, but I am not giving up. I want to be able to teach flight safety. The largest aspect of all is the reason I am receiving the education I am going after is to better myself. I want the doctorate degree to open doors for me that I felt closed, almost 11 years ago when the plane crash occurred. To me, the doctorate degree will be a PhD in Business Administration with a specialization in Aeronautical Safety. Once again, the Aeronautical Safety is my future. I have an Associate Degree in Business Administration but, the doctorate degree; I am hoping the doctorate opens doors wider for me. Of course, I want to be able to help the blind as well because once again, I am doing something for the blind in a site-dominated industry and the Aviation industry does not know what to think about me yet.

Michael chuckled. I continued,

However, I am making a name for all of us that have the disability of being blind. Therefore, that is just what I am trying to do, carry on one day at a time and make the best of my life that

I have left to live. I do believe God left me here for a purpose and I will make the best of that reason. Michael stated, you are a trailblazer, huh. I stated I am trying to be, yes sir. Michael continued to laugh. I stated I am trying to be the pioneer in Aviation like the Wright brothers. Of course, the Wright brothers and I have something in common. They are famous for first flight in Kitty Hawk, North Carolina, December 17, 1903, Mike said yes. I became the first blind Advanced Ground Instructor, June 6, 2000. Two years and five days after I lost my sight in that plane crash. So, both of these accomplishments occurred in North Carolina. Yes, I have something in common with them, and I have to brag about that because I am very proud of that. In addition, becoming the first Instrument Ground Instructor too, but that is another great accomplishment. As well as the first blind graduate of Embry-Riddle in their 83-year history and to me that is rather phenomenal, alone, by itself. I am very blessed and thankful once again.

Moneta stated, "I believe, Barry. You said you had seven more classes?"

I said, "Yes, ma'am, seven classes and four assignments."

She continued, "do you expect to get your doctorate in December 2010?"

I stated, "Yes, ma'am."

She asked, "Did I read you are a part-time student now, instead of full-time?"

I explained about what Patty Slaby and I talked about, and I clarified it with her.

I am in three classes that last for 12 weeks apiece. Then, the five other classes will transfer to 16 weeks in length per class. The research is much more intense and I did not have to do that extra research for the core classes like for the Bachelor and Master degrees. I did not have to do as much research investigating other plane crashes and how they related to that preflight checklist. In addition, the dissertation process, I am interviewing around 400 pilots to get their take on a survey why certain things occur in a preflight checklist that they can forget or they can use the checklist so they do not forget certain items. I thought going to school was in general, difficult, but not until I became involved in this doctorate did I think it was intense. However, like I said a while ago, how blessed I am to improve that GPA to a 3.95 and I only receive three more grades. The last five grades will be a pass, fail, or an incomplete. The 3.95 can only improve a little more; therefore, I will never have a perfect 4.0 on the doctorate because an A- was the first grade received. One A- is from a 93 to a 90 and the rest is from a 94 to a 100. Yes, I find this rather frustrating but at this point in the ball game I cannot complain, as I said a while ago, I have been very blessed. Michael laughed and spoke, striving for perfection, huh? I stated I am trying to, but my goodness it is so intense, though. This research is hard enough in the way we have to do things with JAWS. It is not as if we can read one particular part of a paragraph, we have to read the entire darn thing. It is so much more time consuming.

It is paying off thus far and I have been very fortunate to make it as far as I have. I am ticking away one day at a time and this is where I am. Without the support of you all helping, me last year that is helping with those two classes I would not be able to be where I am at today. The scholarships mean so much and it is so hard to live off my whopping $599.00 a month disability check. I received a large 5% raise this year and that took my income from $567.00 to $599.00 and I am slowly trying to get up to $600.00, but I guess I will wait to next year, however, I am going to make it one way or another. I am very blessed that you guys are talking to me and considering me, and that means the world to me.

Michael said, "Well, you are welcome."

I said, "Yes, sir, thank you all once again."

Michael stated, "Well, you know, your story is touching. It is a good story, and you have hung in there so diligently."

I said, "Thank you, Michael."

"You are an inspiration to many folks, you know."

I answered,

Man, I hope so, I do want to be a leader, Michael, and I do want to persevere, continue, and be a motivational speaker. I would like to go on the motivational speaking tour eventually. However, I want this doctorate before I try to do something like that. I want the doctorate to open more doors for me just as if it continues to do so. For example, just like it did when Andrea asked me to be the commencement speaker at ERAU's campus in Albuquerque. For me, that was huge, I never dreamed of living through a plane crash much less being able to achieve the goals that I am now attaining. I do want to be the pioneer and I do want to be the role model that everyone admires and looks up to. I want to teach people.

Eleven-Year Anniversary

On June 1, 2009, the American Council of the Blind interviewed me for another scholarship. Michael Garret contacted me, asked me how I was doing, and asked me if I was ready for another interview. He brought Patty Slaby on, and she said she wanted to talk with Jet tonight. I said, "He is lying here beside me, and he will hear every word you say." We all laughed. Next, came on was Shelley, and she said she did meet me last year. She was on the scholarship committee and from South Dakota. I asked how she was doing, and she responded she was doing great. Don Courshe said he was from Indianapolis, Indiana. He said he met me last year, and I asked him how he was doing. He said he was fine. Michael Garret said, "Of course that you know me. We have been talking for years." Everyone laughed, and I said, "Yes, sir, Michael."

I said, "Thank you all once again for the consideration and I am very much honored."

Patty began by stating, "You continue with all of your hard work, right?"

"Yes, ma'am, just continuing one day at a time, and today is the eleven-year anniversary of the plane crash. "How ironic is that?"

Shelley said, "Wow!" and Patty said "Really?"

"Yes, ma'am, eleven years ago at 4:32 p.m. that afternoon, I went off Roanoke's radar in the plane. Therefore, today is the eleven-year anniversary that the plane crash occurred in Floyd, Virginia."

Patty said, "Your new birthday!"

"Yes, ma'am, my new venture in life, if you will. A very traumatic story, a life-changing experience, but obviously God has a different purpose for me. Here I am."

Patty and Shelley laughed. Shelley asked me if I could talk about the last year since they saw me at the convention, kind of what I have been up to and how things have gone for me.

I stated, "Certainly. Currently, I am seven classes and two assignments away from becoming Dr. Hyde."

Shelley said, "All right!"

I continued by saying I was very proud of that and I have to brag, currently, that I have a 3.95 grade point average and am chipping away on improving it. I had begun my book, and it was up to 154 pages now, so I was chipping away on it too.

Shelley said, "Wow!"

"In addition, Jet, my new guide dog, came into my life on inauguration day, January 20. He and I have been working together each day, training, and trying to get him to grow up and mature a little bit. He is only two years and two months old so, he versus Lincoln, who is ten and a half, there is a big difference in dogs there."

Patty and Shelley laughed.

"His original name was Eric, but we did not like calling the dog Eric, so I wanted a name in aviation, so I called him Jet."

Shelley laughed.

"He runs me like a jet and he runs to everywhere I want to go."

Patty and Shelley laughed and said, "You are flying?"

I said,

> Yes, we are flying high again, just in a different way, if you will. Goodness, I talked with Michael, a couple of weeks ago about the Embry-Riddle World Wide Campus located in Albuquerque, New Mexico. They contacted me and asked me to come out and be their guest keynote speaker for their commencement. We went out there and participated in the graduation ceremony. Andrea Aiello Howald awarded me a Navajo peace pipe for being the distinguished guest speaker.

Shelley said "Wow!" and everyone laughed. I said,

> Yes, I have not found anything to smoke in it yet, but that is all right. Everyone laughed. They awarded that to me in front of everybody at the commencement ceremony and Andrea told me that I could hang it in my office. I said, shoot, I need an office first. I thanked them in person for that and I thought that was very memorable to receive that and play part in the commencement. The graduation ceremony took place at the Balloon Museum there in Albuquerque and I do not know if anyone is familiar with Steven Vaucet, the guy who was the first person to fly a balloon over the Atlantic Ocean.

Shelley said, "Yes!"
I said, "His balloon is on display there in that museum, and Nance took a picture of Jet and me in front of it."
Shelley said, "Cool!"
I said,

> I thought that was historical as well. Therefore, I am just setting the trend to be this pioneer in the Aviation industry as well as the blind industry. As I said, God is continuing to open doors for me that I felt were closed 11 years ago today. Of course, I still want to be the role model once again, that everybody admires and looks up to. I am continuing to take it one day at a time and wonderful things keep happening for me.

Patty asked me, "Tell us about your studies and how that is going, your online coursework."

I replied,

> Yes, the dissertation topic is "The Proper Execution of the Preflight checklist to Improve Flight Safety". The next class will begin on July 1. This class will be in reference to doing a survey on 200 to 400 pilots and will be a list of about 20 questions that I will have to put together. I will send it out to different Aviation organizations to play part in taking the survey. I then will have to write an analysis and portions of the book will relate to that. Professors tell me the book will have to be around 200 pages long. This work will consist of seven more classes and one of those will be the oral argument. The current class and two more classes will be the only three left to receive a grade. Therefore, I cannot improve the 3.95 up but just a little more. All of the grades are in reference to that dissertation that I am seeking. It is coming right along just one day at a time.

Don asked, "What is your timeframe? When would you like to be finished?"

I replied,

> Yes sir, I am shooting for and the goal is December 2010. I would like to graduate and walk next June 2010, however, the graduation ceremony does not take place at Northcentral University but once a year and that is in June. If I cannot do that next June then I want to do June 2011 but I am still shooting to be done with all the class work December 2010. Therefore, like I said a while ago, I do not know what God has left for me to do in my future, but I know he

has a game plan for me. I will continue to keep after things one day at a time and see what other doors open up for me. However, I would like to go on the professional speaking tour to go out and inspire other people and share my story and let them know that we all deal with obstacles in our lives. Some are just bigger than others are. The people like us that have disabilities, I want to be able to inspire and motivate them. That is to help them follow their dreams and not give up on what they are doing in life whether it be becoming a doctor if I want to accomplish that, which is being a part of the Aeronautical Universities and institutions. I want to be able to share my knowledge and my story, if you will. The story I have to share is miraculous in many ways, and that shows I survived the difficulties in front of me. Once again, I am very thankful for being alive and doing as well as I am.

Patty asks, "What do you do outside your class studies and stuff and involvement?"

Well, that is funny; I am so devoted to my studies I do not take much time personally for myself. However, this past week, Nance, Jet, and I went out to dinner with a couple of friends Nance works with and I believe that was Thursday night. Of course, we attend church on Sundays. We are involved with the American Council of the Blind and their activities frequently. As well as the blind awareness programs that the Daytona Beach chapter holds whether that is for blind walks with guide dogs or white cane users.

Shelley asked, "Barry, I know last year was the first time you came to a national convention, right, for the American Council of the Blind?"

I said, "Yes, ma'am."

"What was your feeling on that, did you feel you got a lot from that or what was your take on spending a few days that you were able to spend there with people in Louisville?"

> Yes ma'am, it was very meaningful and I had a very high honor to receive that scholarship that helped me with several classes. It was very inspirational for me to be a part of that program, to receive that scholarship in front of everyone, and to show my success. To show people once again, it does not matter what we incur or face, we all seek to succeed in what we need to overcome in this world. It was very honorable to be a part of that program, ma'am. In addition, Shelley, that awesome time is one part of my book that is included in my writing. The wonderful things I get to be a part of are included in the book like this interview. The book is an autobiography that is a very important part of me and I feel I want to share it with everyone that will be able to read it. Once again, I am very blessed to be part of wonderful things that I can be a part of in my life.

Michael said, "I look forward to reading your book!"

I said, "Yes, sir!"

Patty asked, "Can I get it in an alternative format?"

I said, "Absolutely, and you will even get a signed copy." Everyone laughed!

Patty said, "You are so busy. Do you actually take time to sleep?"

Patty said, "We will be back in touch one way or the other, Barry."

I said, "Thank you all for considering me once again and taking the time to talk to me, and I hope you all have a terrific evening. This is very awesome to be a part of this interview on my anniversary date for me."

Michael stated, "All right, Barry!"

Everyone said, "Thank you, Barry!"

I said, "I hope everyone has a terrific evening and thanks again."

B-747 Carrying Space Shuttle

Tuesday evening, June 2, 2009, Nance, Jackson, Jet, Lincoln, and I were in Nance's van in Sonic's parking lot. We were having dinner when people sitting outside at the tables began yelling, "There is the shuttle!" It was the Boeing 747 carrying the Atlantis piggyback, and the crowd was excited. The airplane and shuttle were around 1,000 to 1,500 feet above the ground.

ACB Scholarship

Wednesday evening, June 3, 2009, Patty Slaby contacted me to share some fantastic news with me. She said the American Council of the Blind awarded me the Jim Olsen scholarship. Patty shared the details with us of the convention and the days she wanted us to attend.

St. Augustine Yellow Jackets Presentation

Thursday, June 4, 2009, Nance, Jet, and I went to St. Augustine High School. David Thompson's tenth grade class consisted of around thirty-five students. The class was an aeronautical science class for private pilot operations. We gave a presentation on aviation safety and how the preflight checklist played part in the accident I lived through. We drove sixty-eight miles to the school and spent the entire class period, which was for forty-five minutes, speaking about the crash.

American Foundation for the Blind Scholarship

Friday, June 12, 2009, I learned of another scholarship. The American Foundation for the Blind sent me an email to inform me of the award. The scholarship was out of New York, New York, and it will arrive in the mail; therefore, we do not have to go anywhere to receive it. This scholarship is the Karen D. Carsel Memorial Scholarship valued at $500, and this scholarship is number 20.

American Council of the Blind Scholarship

Saturday, July 4, 2009, we attended the American Council of the Blind Convention at the Rosen Center in Orlando, Florida. Nance, Lincoln, Jackson, Jet, and I went to Orlando Saturday afternoon, and Jet and I attended the convention Saturday night for dinner. Patty Slaby, Patricia Castillo, Michael Garret, Don Courshe, Minetta Garner, and two graduate scholarship winners sat with Jet and me. The ACB committee fed us a great meal as we socialized with each other. Sunday morning, we attended the luncheon, and Michael Gravitz and his wife sat with us as well as Ardis Bazyn and her husband along with another man and his guide dog. Early on Tuesday morning, July 7, we attended the scholarship banquet. There were only fourteen scholarship recipients present to receive the award, and we all sat on the stage. Patty Slaby introduced all of us and told a brief story about each one of us before we spoke at the podium in front of around two thousand spectators. Jet and I were the only guide dog team present to receive the awards.

Patty stated,

> Our final winner today is awarded the
> James R. Olsen Memorial Scholarship. Barry
> Hulon Hyde is completing his PhD program
> in the upcoming school year. He is attending
> Northcentral University, which is an on-line col-
> lege. His degree will be in Business Administration
> with an emphasis in Aeronautical Safety special-
> ization. Barry comes with his new guide dog and
> it is a pleasure for him to be here again, so, we
> will give Barry a chance to stand here, and give
> a speech.

The crowd applauded for six seconds. A man walked Jet and me
to the podium. I began by stating, "Good morning, everyone!" and
the crowd responded with a "Good morning!" I said,

> What an honor to be here with you, once
> again. Certainly, I am very blessed to be here
> and I would certainly like to begin by thank-
> ing the American Council of the Blind and all
> of the recipients as well, congratulations to you
> all. Certainly, I would like to thank God, because
> here again, God bless America and God bless us
> all! Certainly, I would like to thank my guide dog,
> Jet, how ironic, my previous dog that was with us
> last year, Lincoln the Aviator, who retired. I would
> like to thank Nance, wherever she is down there
> taking pictures, my fiancée. In addition, I would
> like to thank my family and friends for helping
> me get here, for allowing me to carry on, and live
> my life like I am. I would like to share my educa-
> tion with you all. I have six classes left and an oral
> argument and then I will become Dr. Hyde.

I am looking forward to pulling that off. Currently, my last class helped me improve my grade point average up to a 3.96 and I am proud of that. Wow, I do not know if anyone remembers from last year about how my life so dramatically changed. Actually, today, 11 years, one month, and three days ago, or on June 1, 1998, was when the plane crash occurred and I was pronounced dead on arrival. The impact knocked my left eye completely out and miraculously I survived. I have been able to carry on, persevere, and many good things have occurred. Now, I know each one of us in this room encounter obstacles each day and some worse than others. I do believe that the many blessings God has provided me with has allowed me to carry on. Wow, I am very honored to be here, once again and thank you all and God bless you! Thank you!

The applause lasted for six seconds. In addition, Nance took pictures of the recipients with their certificates with three different cameras.

Association of Blind Citizens

Monday night we went to Cape Canaveral to watch the *Endeavor* space shuttle launch but there was a weather delay. We came home and there was a message on the phone from John out of Northbrook, Massachusetts. He left a message congratulating me on becoming a scholarship recipient.

Transportation Club International

Tuesday, July 14, 2009, Bill Blair sent me an email that stated,

Dear Barry,

The Scholarship Committee has deliberated long and hard and I am delighted to be able to tell you that you have been chosen to receive the TCI Valedictorian award in the amount of $2000.00".

Due to the extremely high quality of the applications this year the Committee, as allowed under the Trustee agreement, decided to tweak the awards and the amounts in order to allow more scholarships to be given out than ever before. In doing so, new scholarships created in some instances. Yours is one such example. We were thoroughly captivated by your drive and desire in overcoming such adversity".

As a winner, you are eligible to attend the TCI Annual Conference in Chattanooga, Tennessee between 17th and 19th September. Scholarship certificates are issued there at a special luncheon. Scholarship payments are made directly to the relevant Institutions of Higher Learning, immediately after the conference".

I hope you will be able to find time to attend for any or the entire event. You will be asked and expected to speak for 3/5 minutes about yourself and your career path".

Please let me know if you will be there and we will work on setting up accommodations and travel arrangements.

Best regards,
Bill Blair

Endeavour

Wednesday evening at 6:30 p.m., the *Endeavour* space shuttle lifted off successfully from Kennedy Space Center. Nance, Jet, and I met Linsley Peitch and her daughter, Heather, and all of us went to Cape Canaveral or Merritt Island to watch it. We watched the *Endeavour* space shuttle lift off across the Banana River while looking at the Kennedy Space Center. The liftoff was tremendously awesome, very intense, and as it climbed out, I could hear it for about five and a half minutes. The crowd of about 150 people around us screamed and yelled during the liftoff. The Space Transportation System (STS) 127 went off successfully to the International Space Station with seven astronauts on board. Previously 498 people have been to space, and now there are seven more, six Americans and one female, who is a Canadian astronaut.

Grade

On Monday, July 20, 2009, I received my first 100 on an assignment. As a student for over eight years, the hard work was continuing to pay off for me. This grade improved my average for the research and data class to a 96. Dr. Bret Gordon gave me this grade on the second assignment, which was out of 12 due over a period of twelve weeks. August 4, I received my second 100 in this class.

ERAU Summer Academy Program

On Friday, July 24, Nance, Jet, and I went to Embry-Riddle to give a presentation to twenty-seven summer school students in ages ranging from thirteen through eighteen. Some flight instructors were present as well as a few other people, like two church members, Walt Riedey and Helen. The students were very interactive and asked lots of questions. The presentation consisted of the plane accident I lived through, the negligent parties involved, recommendations on how it could have been prevented, my education, the people I have met, and my future. Lastly, we did visit briefly with Pam Peer, the summer school coordinator.

Targeted Disability FAA Job Fair

Sunday afternoon, August 9, 2009, Nance, Jet, and I flew to Reagan National out of Orlando on a Boeing 737-400 on US Airways. We stayed at the Capital Holiday Inn, downtown Washington. The disability job fair was on Monday, and it was packed with people in a ballroom. I took thirty-five resume packs and only gave out four. We spoke with a few aviation safety managers and one human factors manager. Most were dressed to impress, and some were in shorts and T-shirts. The room only had room to stand, and the temperature was very hot for the disabled in attendance and managers.

Monday evening, we had dinner with Miguel Vasquez in the hotel restaurant. We had a great visit, and then on Tuesday morning, Becky Umbaugh contacted us. She and her husband, Bill, picked us up, and we went to lunch at one of their favorite diners. As we were going to this diner, they witnessed three of the president's helicopters when they came into land at the White House. After a terrific lunch and great company, they took us to the airport. We flew back to Orlando on another Boeing 737-400. Both flights were really packed, and we had the same crew members.

Air Traffic Control Association Scholarship

Tuesday, August 18, 2009, Brian Fourtier contacted me from the Air Traffic Control Association to let me know about them awarding me a scholarship valued at $5,000. This scholarship totaled my twenty-third one, and it made the sixth one this year. We will attend their fifty-fourth convention at the Gaylord Resort and Hotel on the Potomac River located at the National Harbor, Maryland.

Discovery

Friday night, August 28, at 11:59 p.m., Nance, Jenny Marie Tate, Jackson, Lincoln, Jet, and I went to Cape Canaveral to witness the *Discovery* liftoff. This Discovery liftoff was the twenty-fifth anniversary and was STS 128 with seven astronauts on board en route to the International Space Station. They were to do three space walks, and the one female astronaut, Nicole Stott, a graduate from Embry-Riddle will be left behind for three months.

The *Discovery* liftoff took place without a problem. The glow lit up the sky, and the sound was like nothing else ever heard. This liftoff was the seventh one watched and was just as good as the others. We could hear it for over five minutes as it climbed out!

Experimental Aircraft Association Scholarship

On Wednesday morning, September 2, 2009, I received an email from Jane Smith, scholarship coordinator for the Experimental Aircraft Association. The email said they selected me to receive the EAA HP "Bud" Milligan Scholarship. The scholarship was valued at $500, and the check would require my signature and Northcentral's signature. This makes the seventh scholarship of 2009.

Transportation Club International

Thursday, September 17, 2009, Nance, Jet, and I flew on a fifty-five-minute flight from Daytona Beach International Airport on Delta's Canadair Regional Jet 200 into Atlanta's Hartsfield Airport. We had a layover in Atlanta for a couple of hours then flew on another

CRJ-200 on a twenty-five-minute flight to Chattanooga, Tennessee. In Atlanta, Andrew Coughman met us in the jetway and took us back onto the airplane and into the cockpit of the CRJ. He flipped the master's switch on, which lit up all the buttons and instruments, and I sat in the co-pilot's seat. Nance took our picture. I put my hands on the control yoke and the throttle, and she took a couple more pictures.

The TCI conference was in the Sheraton Read House Hotel in Chattanooga. We attended a luau at the Eagle Bluff Country Club where TCI fed us dinner, held a silent auction, and had a live band.

On Friday, September 18, the scholarship luncheon was in the Chattanooga ChuChu in the Roosevelt ballroom. TCI fed us lunch as we sat with the other scholarship recipients, and the TCI president Dennis and his wife, Lori, sat with us as well. There were around 150 people in attendance, and each one of the scholarship recipients spoke and thanked TCI for the scholarship and gave a brief summary of the degree sought after. Bill Blair, who was over the selection of the scholarship recipients, introduced each one of us. Bill stated, "The last category we did we made this year, the TCI Valedictorian, because we have someone who is special, Barry Hulon Hyde."

Nance walked Jet and me to the front of the room, and Lynn gave me the microphone and said, "Don't forget to introduce Jet."

I said, "Okay, roger that." I began by stating,

> Well, good afternoon TCI and everyone else. Certainly, thank you all once again, for allowing me to be a part of this wonderful organization. Thank God, thank this wonderful Guide dog Jet, thank Nance, my fiancée, thank my family and friends, certainly, once again, thank God! I would not be here without all of these people helping me. The reason why folks, June the first of 1998, I lived through a traumatic plane crash. That plane crash changed my life forever and I want to share it with you, briefly. Eleven years,

three months, and 17 days ago, I lost my smell, taste, and sight, 14 broken bones, both collapsed lungs, left eye knocked out, nose knocked off, and sinus cavity destroyed. Four teeth knocked out, nine broken bones in my face, jawbone broken four times, right leg broken in four places, and I have lots of metal in me, so I set off all the alarms at the TSA gates when going through the airports.

The crowd chuckled. I continued,

I have been very blessed folks, God has continued to bless me and open doors for me that I thought were closed. That plane crash as a passenger, once again, changed my life forever and open doors for me that I thought would close, but have continue to open. Certainly, TCI has allowed that to take place. When I say that the plane crash occurred on June 1, 1998, then on June 6, 2000, I became the first and only blind Advanced Ground Instructor in the world for the Federal Aviation Administration.

The crowd clapped for seven seconds.

June 12, 2000 my first Guide dog, Lincoln came into my life. Then, in October of that year, I became the first and only blind Instrument Ground Instructor in the world for the Federal Aviation Administration. I thought what do I do now? I thought I have to continue my role in Aviation and I have to figure out what I want to do when I grow up. So, I decided I would attend the University of North Carolina at Charlotte. I went to work on my Bachelor's Degree in History.

So, miraculously, Lincoln, my first Guide dog and I walked 1,800 steps every day for three and a half years to receive that degree. We graduated in December of 2004. I got to that point and I thought, what do I do now? I want to continue my role in Aviation. So, I said let me see if we can attend the largest flight school in the world? So, I moved to Daytona Beach, Florida and began attending Embry-Riddle Aeronautical University. Lincoln and I graduated in a year and nine months from the largest flight school in the world and did so with a perfect 4.0 grade point average.

The crowd clapped for five seconds.

So, I thought I felt special then, I said, I am getting really good at this education thing. So, I said once again, what do I do now? Lord, what do you want me to do now, you continue to open doors for me, what is next? The anniversary of the plane crash came around, June 1, 2007. He said, I want to continue, on your doctorate degree. Currently, folks I am six classes and two assignments away from becoming Dr. Hyde. When I pull that off, we are going to have a party. The crowd really laughed. I cannot wait to achieve that goal. For me, the sky is home because I will continue to persevere and carry on. To share my love for Aviation and continue to teach what I lived through, to teach how to prevent it from happening to other pilots, and I will continue to help me reach for the skies. Also, helping me to achieve dreams that I thought I would not be able to achieve and now TCI has allowed me to achieve another dream. I want to thank you all once again, and God bless everyone, Amen and Alleluia.

The crowd stood and applauded for twenty-two seconds for Jet and me. Lynn took the microphone, and she and Anita had their picture taken with us as I held the certificate they gave me.

The Letter of Thanks to TCI

Received: 2009

Dear Bill, the Scholarship Committee, & all our Friends at TCI:

I wanted to send you my sincere thanks for your generosity in awarding me the TCI Valedictorian Scholarship Award at the 87th annual conference in Chattanooga last week. It is through your kindness and selflessness that blind individuals like me can lead productive and happy lives and achieve their dreams.

You heard tidbits of my story and how I lost my eyesight, but allow me to provide a little more information to help you understand who you are helping through your generous scholarship. I was sighted until 1998 when I endured a horrific airplane crash as a passenger that forever changed my life. On June 1, 1998, I was a 26-year-old pilot with 1,600 flight hours—flying every day, living my dream in aviation, was one week away from interviewing with US Airways for a pilot position, with a bright future ahead of me. The pilot of our aircraft that day and the negligence that caused my accident took away my future as a pilot - everything I worked so hard for. I was dead-on-arrival at the hospital when airlifted from the crash site. My life as I knew it was over and I had to make some difficult life decisions.

The biggest decision I made was to go on with life and not give up. I was not going to sit in my parents' home and feel sorry for myself. I began a long road of recovery and rehabilitation. Through love and support of family and friends and an unwavering strong Christian faith, I overcame the worst time in my life.

In 2000, I became the first and only blind Advanced Ground Instructor (AGI), and the first and only blind Instrument Ground Instructor (IGI) for the FAA. I earned my Bachelor of Arts degree in History from the University of North Carolina. I was born in Kannapolis, North Carolina and lived there before moving to Charlotte in 2001 to obtain my undergraduate degree.

In 2005, I moved with my guide dog to Daytona Beach, Florida to pursue my Graduate degree. In 2007, I became the first blind graduate of Embry-Riddle Aeronautical University in their 81-year history. Aviation is a sight-dominated industry and no other blind person ever attended ERAU, the world's largest flight school. I proudly earned my Master of Science in Aeronautics degree with specializations in Aviation Safety and Aviation Operations - and I did so with a perfect 4.0 GPA. I am now half-way complete with my PhD in Business Administration with a specialization in Aeronautical Safety. My current GPA is 3.96. I hope that you can see that I am deeply devoted to my education and I work extremely hard every day in my studies. I hope that you are happy that I was selected to receive this very special scholarship and I want to make you all proud. My goal for the future is to obtain a full time position in the aviation industry. Possibly with the FAA, the NTSB, NASA - somewhere that I can contribute to aviation safety and show people how the blind can do what sighted people can do...just differently!

Thank you again from the bottom of my heart. Without the kindness and generosity of folks like you to help me, I could not continue my education. My sole income until I become employed is $599/month Social Security Disability. Your scholarship will be applied towards my tuition expense in my PhD program.

Thank you for allowing me to pursue my dreams and may God richly bless you as He has blessed me! Nancy, Jet and I thoroughly enjoyed meeting you all in Chattanooga and I hope our paths cross again soon!

Barry Hulon Hyde and Jet
Doctorate Candidate

Aviation Safety Analyst

Wednesday, September 23, 2009, Mary Pat Baxter contacted me from the Federal Aviation Administration. She was a manager in the Commercial Operations Branch (AFS-820) Flight Standards Service. We talked briefly, and after I explained to her that I would be in Maryland to receive the Air Traffic Control Association

Scholarship, she showed an interest in setting up an interview with me. She called back later in the day and scheduled the interview at 10:00 a.m. on Wednesday, October 7, in a conference room in their office. In addition, Mary sent me the knowledge, skills, and abilities (KSA) questions to answer over email and asked me to send it back to her before October 2.

At lunchtime on this date, September 23, Mom had surgery on her rotor cup. The tendon was torn more than originally thought, and some arthritis showed up during surgery. The doctor spent a little more time than anticipated on her shoulder.

Air Traffic Control Association Scholarship

Sunday morning, October 4, 2009, Nance, Jet, and I flew out of Orlando on a US Airways B-737-400 into Reagan National Airport. We rode in a Lincoln town car from the airport to the Gaylord Resort and Convention Center at the National Harbor in Maryland. The rooms were $209 per night. Food was very expensive, but the room was the nicest room we have slept in yet.

Monday morning, we attended the opening session, and the administrator Randy Babbitt spoke. Afterward, a group panel discussed Airspace, NextGen, and Safety.

Tuesday, October 6, 2009, the scholarship luncheon took place in the Gaylord Resort and Convention Center at the National Harbor in Maryland. Peter Challin began the luncheon and said some nice words about Larry Fortier, his commitment to the scholarship program, and his many years of leadership to the scholarship program. In addition, Challin spoke highly of Fortier's commitment to $60,000 to the fifteen scholarship recipients. Challin asked everybody present, around five hundred in the crowd, to give Larry Fortier a hand, and the crowd applauded for eight seconds. Challin introduced the new chair of the scholarship board—previously on the scholarship committee—someone who has a lot of energy, a lot of focus, and a lot of love for the scholarship program, Cindy Castillo. The crowd applauded for four seconds. Cindy thanked the crowd for participating in helping raise money for the scholarship program by contributing a dollar, participating in functions, or as a sponsorship. She thanked everyone for what they have done for the scholarship fund. Cindy shared some history of the scholarship fund from its inception. The first scholarship award was given by Larry Fortier in the amount of $2,000, and it was the next year the scholarship fund was formerly organized. In 2005, the goal was to reach $500,000 of principle, mainly by the effort of Larry Fortier. This allowed the amount of scholarships given out as well as the dollar amount given out each year. The program was a success today due to numerous people promoting the program to give contributions, increasing awareness and participation in the application process, and volunteering, so many hours and time on the scholarship selection committee. Cindy thanked the previous scholarship board members. She believed the past couple of years, the program had achieved a greater level of visibility and participation with sponsorship and donations due largely to efforts of Pete Dumont, Peter Challin, and Neil Planzer. Cindy formerly recognized the founder of the scholarship fund, Larry Fortier, and presented him a plaque for his contributions. The crowd applauded for eight seconds. Larry Fortier spoke about how the scholarship fund began, and he spoke with thanks. Cindy then introduced Gisele Mohler, and then Gisele began speaking about the recipients. She was currently working on the scholarship board and had served the past two years on the scholarship selection committee. She was a pilot, and the FAA currently employs her.

Gisele Mohler explains about the next student scholarship category, which were students that were enrolled in aviation-related programs of study, and there were six winners.

The photo-tron showed me as

> Barry Hulon Hyde, $6,000. Attending Northcentral University and working on his PhD

in Business Administration with a Specialization in Aeronautical Safety, (2nd year). In 2007, Master's in Aeronautics from ERAU. In 2008, Awards include Airbus Leadership Award and FedEx Technical Systems Operations Award. FAA Certifications include Commercial Instrument Airplane, Certified Flight Instructor, and Multi-Engine Instructor. He desires to help keep people reaching for the sky. We have a very special person and Cindy and Jet are going to walk Barry Hulon Hyde up here. I will tell you a little about him. Barry is a four-time winner and currently, he is in a doctorate program. Barry has an impressive story of survival and dedication to his passion in Aviation. You see, Barry logged 1,600 hours total flight hours prior to losing his sight in an aircraft accident on June 1, 1998. He is the first and only FAA certified blind Advanced Ground Instructor and Instrument Ground Instructor in the world. He desires to be a role model that a disabled person can look up to and know there are no limits to what a disabled person can achieve. Barry will be part of this year's Combined Federal Campaign and he will present his amazing story at the kickoff tomorrow at the FAA auditorium. The CFC theme this year is "The Compassion of Individuals the Power of Community." Barry is going to say a few words.

The crowd applauded for seven seconds. I stated,

Good afternoon! What an honor to be here once again. First off, I would like to thank the Air Traffic Control Association and all the sponsors that have awarded us, all of the recipients the scholarships, and being so kind for awarding me the fourth scholarship for the fourth year in a row. That is a very high honor for me. In addition, I would like to thank God, I would like to thank Nance, my fiancee for helping me get to where I am at today. In addition, I would like to thank this wonderful animal up here with me that is bumping me and saying hey dad I am down here. In addition, everyone probably remembers Lincoln, the guide dog that was with me for the past three years. That wonderful animal has been retired officially; we retired him to the couch, so he is now the couch potato.

The crowd snickered, and I said,

And now Jet is filling his shoes. Next, I would like to speak briefly about my Aviation career. As Gisele previously stated, I was a 1,600-hour pilot that fateful day, I boarded the airplane as a passenger, I had never flown with a lying pilot before, and I boarded the running airplane. We took off from the Concord Regional Airport in North Carolina and crashed 37 minutes later. You talk about a life changing experience folks; we went off Roanoke's radar at 4:32, Monday afternoon, June 1, 1998. The doctors at the Roanoke Regional hospital pronounced me dead on arrival with 14 broken bones, both collapsed lungs, nine broken bones in my face, and my left eye knocked completely out. In addition, my sinus cavity was destroyed, four teeth knocked out, left side of my body paralyzed, right leg broken in four places, and I had a broken vertebrae. So wow, that was really exhausting!

The crowd laughed.

I do believe in overcoming that disability, God has a purpose for me. Fortunately, during that recovery and rehabilitation, I had to go thru numerous amounts of rehabilitation from cognitive therapy to speech therapy, physical therapy, mobility training, psychological therapy, and a whole lot of other fun stuff, for example, attending the Rehabilitation Center for the Blind in Raleigh. I spent seven months at the center to learn all of the new living skills as a blind individual. Then, I knew I wanted to continue my role in Aviation and I thought, what do I need to do now?

As Gisele said, I began studying for the Advanced Ground Instructor License. Rich Burns, an examiner at the time out of the Flight Standards District Office in Charlotte, North Carolina. He told me that no one had ever taken the FAA written test orally, so he said I would have to check on that. Therefore, he called Washington and then Washington called Oklahoma City and then Oklahoma City called Washington and they could not figure out how to do it because the test never had been given to a blind person before. So, I said, well just tell me how to do it, I will follow your directions. Sure enough, June 6, 2000, two years and five days later after the plane crash, I became the first and only blind Advanced Ground Instructor in the world and I thought that was really something. Two years and 11 days later, Lincoln came into my life, June 12, 2000. After achieving that awesome goal, the FAA awarded Rich a certificate of achievement.

Next, I wanted to continue my role in Aviation, so I became the first and only blind Instrument Ground Instructor in the world for the FAA in October of 2000. I began thinking about things, so I said; the next step for me to persevere and carry on is for me to seek out the Bachelor of Arts degree in History from the University of North Carolina at Charlotte. That is where Lincoln and I persevered and walked back and forth 1,800 steps, 1 way to class everyday for three and a half years. We pulled that off and graduated in December of 2004 and that opened the door folks, for me to attend the largest flight school in the world, which is Embry-Riddle Aeronautical University.

I moved to Daytona Beach, Florida, in July of 2005 and graduated May 7 of 2007 with my Master of Science Degree in Aeronautics with specializations in Aviation Safety and Aviation Operations. I graduated with distinction or with a perfect 4.0 grade point average.

The crowd applauded for five seconds. I continued,

Thank you, wow! Of course, I have to say I was their first and only blind graduate in their 83-year history. I am very proud of that as well. Now, I am working on the doctorate and I have a 3.96 grade point average and I am six classes and one assignment away from becoming Dr. Hyde.

The crowd clapped for seven seconds.

  I want to share some more good news. Tomorrow, I have a job interview with the FAA for an Aviation Safety Analyst position.

The crowd clapped for four seconds.

That is a huge honor to be recognized in that capacity. Of course, living through a plane crash and then trying to receive a safety job.

The crowd snickered.

  Thursday morning, I was asked to be a keynote speaker for the (CFC) Combined Federal Campaign kickoff, in front of the FAA and I am looking forward to that as well.

The crowd applauded for four seconds.

  Oh my goodness, I could keep talking but I am going to conclude here. I am getting all excited here. In conclusion, I certainly, want everyone to know that I do believe that ATCA has allowed me to carry on and helped me to achieve some dreams that I thought 11 years ago when the plane crash occurred, I thought my future in Aviation would be over with. ATCA is helping me to realize that my dreams are continuing and I am becoming a pioneer in Aviation. Simply, because I continue to open the door for the blind as well as helping sighted pilots in the sight dominated industry. Pilots are continuing to learn from the endeavor that I faced that unfortunate day Once again, if everyone remembers about Jack Hunt, the first

president of Embry-Riddle, who had that famous
saying. For most people, the sky is the limit, but
for those who love Aviation, the sky is home. We
all love home, and the sky continues to be our
blessed home! I thank ATCA and I thank the
sponsors once again. God bless you all!

The crowd applauded for twelve seconds. Gisele thanked me
and continued with the reading of other recipients. Cindy helped
Jet and me off the stage and walked with us back to the ATCA table.

FAA Interview

Wednesday morning at ten o'clock, the manager of Commercial
Operations Mary Pat Baxter, as well as two men, Craig and John,
interviewed me on the eighth floor in the Flight Standards District
Office at the FAA Headquarters. The interview was for an aviation
safety analyst position and lasted for over two hours. Each person
asked me a question for a total of ten. Then, those ten questions
built onto other questions. The questions were very similar to the
five knowledge, skills, and abilities (KSA) questions asked over
email earlier in the week. Jet and I met some nice people, and Mary
showed us around the Flight Standard's office. Mary and the men
involved in the interview answered the questions I had, and they
filled me in on other relevant information. For example, the pay
band, which is an I or J, which pays from $70,000 up to $135,000.
In addition, they explained the drug test and the background check
required as well as the length involved. Mary shared with me about
the next step, which required human resources contacting me with
negotiable offers.

Interview with Jerry Lavey

Wednesday afternoon, October 7, 2009, at three o'clock, Jerry Lavey interviewed me in the FAA's studio in the headquarters. Jerry Lavey is the deputy assistant administrator for Corporate Communications. The interview on the FAA's website began with the sound of an airplane flying by then went into playing music for the introduction.

Jerry Lavey began by stating,

Thank you for joining us. It is a real pleasure and an honor for me and I mean that in a very sincere sense. We have with us a very special guest, Barry Hulon Hyde. Barry, it is so nice to meet you. Barry is going to be our principal speaker, tomorrow at the Combined Federal Campaign. You would have never guessed a few years ago, right Barry, that you would be at the receiving end of some of the CFC's sort of thing and what a blessing. Pleased to have you hear, my friend. Let me start by reading some of this stuff. Here is a person that has tutored students at Embry-Riddle Aeronautical University, a flight-training lab in Daytona Beach. He has prepared them for FAA written, oral, and flight tests. He has done all kinds of amazing things. Now, six courses short, if I am correct at Northcentral University in a PhD program. A Business Administration Degree with a specialty in Aeronautical Safety. Now, I could go on and on about all of this stuff you have done and you have done that despite, and I am going to question you about whether you are handicap. I don't think you are disabled. The blindness, can you tell us how that happened and when it happened, etc.

I replied,

> Yes sir, thank you for having me to be a part
> of this Campaign. I would like to begin by first
> telling you that June 1, 1998, my life dramatically
> changed by boarding the flight as a passenger. We
> crashed 37 minutes after takeoff that fateful day.
> The impact of the 1965 model airplane and at
> that time they did not require shoulder harnesses.
> Therefore, all I had on was a lap belt. I was in
> the right seat and the pilot in command was in
> the left seat. The seat had broken and forced me
> into the control yoke and the dashboard. The
> control yoke collapsed both of my lungs and
> my head hit the control panel numerous times.
> My sunglasses, I feel cut my left eye out and the
> doctors at the hospital found my eye behind the
> left cheekbone. I had nine broken bones in my
> face, nose knocked completely off, and the roof
> of my mouth knocked loose from my face, four
> teeth knocked out, jawbone broken four times,
> and both collapsed lungs once again. My right
> leg was broken in four places, a broken vertebrae,
> the left side of my body was paralyzed due to the
> head injury or the brain injury, and still on 1,500
> milligrams of antiseizure medicine today.

Jerry said, "Yet you are sitting here talking to me lucidly and
you are working on a PhD." We laughed, and he said,

> That is amazing. We were talking off camera
> that I do not think he is disabled. Quite honestly,
> I think you like to refer to yourself as being differ-
> ently abled and I think that is correct. Therefore,
> you were in the hospital for a very long period

and practically every part of your being was damaged in some way, right.

I replied, "Yes, sir."
Jerry asked, "How long were you in the hospital, Barry?"

I answered,

Just shy of three months. Numerous amounts of rehabilitation afterwards, I had gone through cognitive therapy, speech therapy, physical therapy, psychological therapy, as well as mobility training. I had to learn to walk again with a broken right leg, the left side of my body paralyzed, and lots and lots of therapy to go through before rebounding to where I am at today. In addition, I attended the Rehabilitation Center for the Blind in Raleigh for seven months.

Jerry said, "Wow, it must have been devastating because flying was your passion, right?"
I stated, "Yes, sir, that was the love of my life."
Jerry continued, "The love of your life, and all of a sudden, you cannot fly anymore. Therefore, what did you do? What were you thinking as you went through this stuff? 'What am I going to do with the rest of my life?'"
I answered,

Yes, I was considering that as well as I was trying to figure out and put all points together on why the plane crash occurred. I had never been in this situation before because of course; I had never lived through the crashing of an airplane. So, as we were putting the points together, I was still trying to figure out what I wanted to be when I grew up.

Jerry asked, "How old were you at the time of the accident?"

"Twenty-six."

"Twenty-six, wow."

"Yes, sir."

"That is ten or eleven years ago."

"Eleven years, four months, and six days."

Jerry said, "But who is counting, right?"

We laughed, and I said, "A couple of hours."

Jerry asked, "So how did you reach the decision 'I am going to continue in aviation,'?"

I stated,

> Well, like you said, a while ago, Aviation was the love of my life. It was what I wanted to be a part of in my future. I knew if I could not continue to be the pilot in command, I wanted to be the ground instructor. To help prevent fellow pilots from encountering the situation I did and if they did how to handle the situation. By getting the airplane on the ground and then ask questions to figure out what happened and why the airplane crashed as we did. As I was continuing to persevere and get well and set goals for myself, the first goal was to become an Advanced Ground Instructor. I had done some checking around with an examiner I knew out of the Flight Standards District Office in Charlotte, North Carolina, and he said, he recommended me getting the Advanced Ground Instructor license. I said, well okay, what do you suggest and how do you want to test me, so, in doing so, when I am ready? He said, I do not know, I will have to call Washington D.C. and see what they suggest. Therefore, he got to checking into what the expectations were of the FAA, and they said, we do not know, we have

never had a blind man take a test. So, they said, we have to call Oklahoma. So, they contacted Oklahoma and Oklahoma said, we don't know, we have to contact Washington back.

Jerry stated they contacted the Civil Air Medical Institute. I continued,

They got to checking back and forth, they finally came up with the summary, that if Rich can test me orally, you know, on the written test, he can read the test to me, so let's do it that way. Rich Burns, the examiner gave me the test orally and he said, after the test was over, I made higher on it than he did.

We laughed, and Jerry stated, "Rich Burns, a good man. We'll tip the hat to him as well."

I continued,

It was really funny because after I did that he said, the FAA brought him to Washington and gave him a Certificate of Achievement and of course, all they gave me was my license. I am like, hey, I want one of those certificates to hang on my wall.

Jerry said, "We have to make that right."

I laughed! Jerry stated, "That is great, so a certified ground instructor. And what did that enable you to do?"

"Well, that allows me to teach private pilots, commercial pilots, you know recreational pilots, sports pilots, flight instructors, airline transport pilots, and so forth."

"The whole shebang, and where did you do that?"

"I did not teach in the pilots program until I started working on my master's degree at Embry-Riddle."

"So did you move to Florida to Embry-Riddle?"

"Not immediately, no, sir. I had to attain the bachelor's degree before I could begin the master's degree."

"You got that at the University of North Carolina at Charlotte."

"My first guide dog and I walked 1,800 steps one way to class every day for three and a half years."

Jerry said, "Did you really? Wow."

"Yes, sir."

"We have been remiss in not introducing your partner, Jet. Jet is out of range here, but he is right there on the floor, loving this cold floor."

"He is relaxed, I believe."

"That is awesome"

"Yes, sir."

"So you graduated from North Carolina. That is not an easy school to get through. That is highly respected. Then, you move to Embry-Riddle and you got a master's degree at Embry-Riddle."

"Yes, sir."

"The first blind person in their 83-year history, right?"

"Yes, sir, correct."

"In addition, you graduated, and what was your master's degree in, Barry?"

"A master's of science in aeronautics with specializations in aviation safety and aviation operations."

"Wow!"

I included, "I did so with distinction."

Jerry stated, "Again I go back. I do not know why I am interviewing you here. You are not disabled, okay, Barry? Now, you are finishing a PhD, what do you want to do when you finish with that? I mean you want to stay in aviation?"

I replied,

> I want to be able to go to an Association, preferably, the Federal Aviation Administration to write policies and procedures and be a part of General Aviation to pass along to pilots the

aspect of Safety. Teach to pilots what I encountered and if they ever encounter what I did that day, how to handle the situation, and what to do if they encounter that situation.

Jerry stated, "Let us talk about and get away from aviation. How did it change your life in other ways? I mean, have you looked at life differently as if 'Whoa, I dodged a bullet'? 'I am here to do something special,' or has it just given you more desire to do something with this second chance, basically?"

I explained,

> Yes sir, it has touched my life in several ways or possibly, in many ways. One, I do believe God kept me around for a reason and he has a purpose for me. Certain things that continue to happen in my life, I feel that the purpose is slowly rising to the top. In addition, I do not take things for granite like the one I did as a sighted person. I feel it when I am around my family and friends, when I am around people that are helping me, also my Guide dog and my previous Guide dog, Lincoln, and my fiancée, Nance.

Jerry stated, "Who is sitting here off camera. It is nice to have you here with us. Now life just has a special focus for you now, Barry."

I continued,

> Yes, sir, certainly, now more so than ever. I mean, I would not be where I am at today, if it were not for help of the community as well as the help of the compassion of individuals, the people who are reaching forward and helping me. It is an amazing story, I must say, but I am just very blessed to be alive and doing as well as I am.

Jerry asked, "So how did CFC-related agencies help you? In what sense did they do that?"

I answered,

> First off sir, Lincoln, my first Guide dog, he came from Southeastern Guide Dog Incorporated in Palmetto, Florida. The Guide dog school functions off the contributions of organizations like the CFC. As well as Jet, he came from Guide Dog Foundation in Smithtown, New York. Most of their contributions are from the CFC, the Combined Federal Campaign. That is very, very huge for me, because people need to be aware of how quickly life can change, which is in the snap of a finger, about that fast or faster. They may be in need of a particular sponsorship or organization like the CFC because all of us in life need help in certain aspects of life and some of us encounter obstacles that are smaller or bigger than others are. Lincoln as well as Jet has helped me face those problems or those obstacles.

Jerry said, "That is wonderful, Barry. Well, listen, Barry, I would love to sit here and talk to you all afternoon, but I am sure you have other things to do. I cannot tell you what a pleasure it is to meet you and have an opportunity to talk with you. I look forward to your talk tomorrow. Thanks so much for coming down and talking with me."

I said, "Yes, sir, you are more than welcome, and thanks for having me."

Jerry Lavey's Remarks

> Combined Federal Campaign off to a strong start: I have been going to CFC Campaign openings for literally decades, and I cannot remember

any one of them rising to the level of the one we had here at FAA Headquarters on Thursday. If you missed it, do yourself a favor and watch it when the archive webcast is available early next week. Those ceremonies can be deadly, and the speakers less than inspirational, but this one was a grabber from start to finish, from DOT Assistant Secretary Linda Washington's opening remarks and FAA Administrator Randy Babbitt's brief, effective statement, to the two inspirational speakers, Barry Hulon Hyde and Steven Fitzhugh.

Jerry Lavey's Last Word

The last word:

> I had the honor of interviewing Barry Hulon Hyde, one of the CFC speakers. Barry is an Aviation professional who, 11 years ago as an avid 26 year old pilot, was badly injured in an Aviation accident while riding in the right seat as a passenger. Among other things, he lost his vision, as well as the senses of smell and taste. His nose and one of his eyes was literally knocked off his face. Multiple bones in his face were shattered. It took him a long time to recover, but when he did, he was determined to continue in Aviation, no matter what. I sat there across from him and his Guide dog, Jet mesmerized by his story of courage and determination and gratitude. Yes, gratitude. He is very grateful to be alive and to have a chance to continue the pursuit of his passion, Aviation. Listening to him, I couldn't help, but ask myself: who's disable and who's not?

He is not clearly not, he is differently abled, as he likes to put it. He may be blind, but he has given so many of us this week the vision to see things differently. As I listen to him, all my trouble's vanished in a heartbeat. Enjoy the weekend. As Barry said, you never know how and when your life will change and it can happen in an instant.

Freshman Class Presentations at ERAU

On October 13 at 9:45 a.m., Nance, Jet, and I gave a presentation on the accident I lived through and on safety. This class was a university 101 class with twenty-five students. Rick Stickney was the instructor, and he participated and explained certain aspects to the class. On October 14 at 11:45 a.m., this presentation took place in the Student Village, in the Tallman Commons room, number 203. This class included thirty students, and it had more females in it. Both classes asked questions and participated in the presentation.

CFC Thank you letter

U.S. Department of Transportation
Federal Aviation Administration

October 21, 2009

Daytona Beach, FL 32119

Dear Mr. Hyde:

We would like to thank you for participating in this year's FAA Combined Federal Campaign (CFC) kick-off event as a guest speaker. Your motivating story, in addition to your remarkable personal and professional achievements, couldn't have been more suitable for what the CFC campaign is all about: helping those in need.

Employees are continuously speaking about your presentation and, because we captured it on video, they are able to show it to their peers and family members. Gerald Lavey, Deputy Assistant Administrator for Corporate Communications and longtime FAA employee, stated that he has been attending these events for decades and this was by far the best. This was possible because of your contribution and for being living proof that contributing to CFC charities can make a difference in our own aviation community.

Should you wish to review or share the video, it may be found at the following website for the duration of the campaign which runs through December 15:

We are certain that your story of success will lead others to participate in this life-changing campaign and become more compassionate individuals. It was an honor meeting one of our own aviation lovers, and we hope you have remarkable success in your future endeavors. Many thanks to your lovely fiancée, Nancy, for attending and supporting this initiative as well.

We hope you had a safe return home and that Jet enjoyed his time in Washington, DC.

Sincerely,

James H. Washington
FAA CFC Deputy Vice Chair

Seeing New Horizons

Janet Barns, a wonderful lady that graduated high school with my brother, came back into my life during November 2009. We connected through Facebook and have reunited. As she has learned more about me since she was unaware of the accident and my recovery, she is now interested in writing a song about my circumstance. The following is a rough draft of what is put together by Janet and her friend Kirsti Manna.

Seeing New HORIZONS

-

-G D
-Niner four Yankee is going in-
G C
--prayed To God forgive my sins
C d
-And that's the last thing I remember
C G
-of niner four Yankee going in--

(maybe second verse stuff)???
When I woke up I said turn on the lights
-my mom said son they're shining bright
-NEED MORE SECOND
VERSE LYRIC HERE

-

CHORUS:--
C
-I'm seeing new horizons
D
-I'm living and I'm surviving
-EM D C
-that day that I fell from the sky

-G
-never thought I'd climb out
-D
there were tears and there were doubts
EM
--but the angels held my hand
C
--and made me see
-D C
-I'm still here, I'm alive and
G
--I'm seeing new horizons
-

-

-Of course another verse or a bridge here: -
I think this has to be about the degrees on your
wall, moving on, new life, something like
-

- -now I got my seeing eye dog, Lincoln at my knee
- -hanging' on the wall, a doctorate degree-

--THEN THE ENDING BRIDGE OF ALTRO
COULD BE SOMETHING LIKE THIS...

- -one day I'm gonna fly again
- -my friend
- -one day I'll have my angel wings
- And I'm gonna fly, fly high.
- -thru the clouds, above the sky

Janet said, "These are all temporary lyrics. You have to tell me
what you don't like. I can change anything. If I am saying too much
about one thing or not emphasizing enough on another thought, you

just need to direct me as to what you want it to sound like. We can make this a specific song about your story with selective details, or we can write it more generically for the common folk with struggles. It's your song, so you tell me what you would like it to be."

Experimental Aircraft Association

November 14, 2009, I received a letter from Jan Peterson. Jan wrote a nice letter thanking me for the thank-you letter that I sent her and EAA for the Bud Milligan Scholarship I was awarded.

Dear Barry and Jet;

Thank you so much for your lovely thank you letter for the H.P. Bud Milligan Scholarship you received from EAA. There is no doubt in my mind that there could not have been a more deserving recipient.

Your love of aviation and your story will be such a gift to so many others. I believe there is usually good that comes from adversity and you have taken that concept to a new level!

I have to tell you that your letter arrived to me on the third anniversary of my husband's passing from a traumatic brain injury sustained in a fall after passing out from a heart problem. He was 55 years old, just like your father. My husband Tim, spent his life in aviation working as a corporate pilot, a mechanic, and most of all his favorite love, a CFII.

My father, Bud Milligan, also lived his life filled with a passion for aviation. He flew Spitfires for the RAF in WWII and was shot down on the island of Malta. He recovered from his injuries and went to work for Bell Aircraft test flying

P38s, and flying the first jet, the P59. His closest friend throughout his life was Slick Goodlin who flew the first 26 flights on the X-1. Following Bell Aircraft, Bud went to South America and flew DC 2's and 3's over the Andes. He later came back to the states and flew for the non-scheduled airlines until 1967 when he went to work for the Douglas Aircraft Company as a production test pilot. He retired from flying in 1978 and passed away in 2001.

I learned to fly in 1982 and earned a CFI although I only did some teaching for a short period of time. Tim was such a good instructor I usually referred people to him.

I have been a puppy raiser for Canine Companions for Independence for the past 5 years and have raised 4 puppies for them. CCI trains wheelchair service dogs and hearing dogs. Of course I was thrilled to learn that you have a Guide Dog as I understand the special bonds that are created with service and guide dogs.

Your story of triumph over adversity touched me so much and I wanted to let you know that. I feel that great things are just beginning for you! I want to wish you the very best in everything you do.

If you ever come to Idaho I would love to meet you and jet. Wishing you and your family all the very best.

Sincerely,

Jan Peterson

University Aviation Association

Saturday morning, November 20, 2009, I received the twenty-fifth scholarship from the University Aviation Association in the mail. The scholarship was valued at $2,000 and was in memory of Dr. Paul A. Whelan.

Federal Aviation Administration Job Proposal

Thursday morning, December 3, 2009, James Davis in human resources contacted me with the Federal Aviation Administration. He emailed me the job proposal and pay band for an aviation safety analyst position. My prayers had been answered!

On December 3, 2009, Lincoln turned eleven. I found it rather ironic that my first guide dog's eleventh birthday occurred on the same day the FAA contacted me. They offered me a G pay band position. I considered the offer, and I thought about it and discussed the proposal with Nance and Rich Burns. I contacted Mr. Davis that afternoon, and I explained to him that the pay band was not what I interviewed for. In addition, I explained that I did not think that pay was enough for me to live on in that area. He and I talked about it, and he said he would present my concern to his upper management and try to adjust the pay band closer to the higher part of G.

Thursday morning, December 10, 2009, Davis contacted me and offered me the original pay band. He told me I had forty-eight hours to consider it. James stated for me to call him back with an answer by Monday, December 14. I contacted Mr. James Davis on Monday, December 14, and accepted the proposal. In addition, Nance faxed him the documents he needed to start the security clearance as well as for the credit check and the six papers signed that he needed.

Salisbury Post Update

Clear skies ahead: Job with FAA latest comeback step since losing sight in plane crash

Friday, December 25, 2009

Barry Hulon Hyde lost his sight in 1998, while barely surviving the crash of a 1965 model Piper Twin Comanche. Today, after going back to school and becoming a Doctoral Candidate and receiving his Master's degree with a 4.0 GPA from Embry-Riddle Aeronautical University has landed himself a job.

By Kathy Chaffinkchaffin@salisburypost.com

KANNAPOLIS—It has been almost nine years since the Post ran a story about Barry Hulon Hyde's brush with death in a plane crash.

It was a story of miraculous survival, the unwavering love of a family and tremendous faith.

Hyde, who lost his eyesight in the crash, was quoted in the Nov. 12, 2000, story as saying, "The good Lord's got a purpose for me..."

He was right.

To recap what happened: June 1, 1998: Twenty-six-year-old Barry Hulon Hyde was flying high—literally.

A 1990 graduate of South Rowan High School, he had completed flight school at American Flyers in Addison, Texas, in January 1996 and was enjoying his job as an instructor for Lancaster Aviation at Concord Regional Airport.

Hyde had completed a morning flight and was flying to Roanoke, Va., in a Piper Twin

Comanche as safety pilot for another pilot who was working on getting his instrument rating current. Thirty minutes into the flight, the right engine failed, then the left.

Hyde's left eye was ripped out on impact, and the damage to his right eye was severe. Doctors said the bones in his face were crushed, describing it as an "eggshell crushed in 10 million pieces," according to his mother, Brenda.

Surgeons grafted tissue and bone and used 15 steel plates to rebuild his face.

February 1999: For the first time, Hyde was alert enough to become fully aware of what had happened. He wanted to die and talked openly about suicide.

His steady girlfriend, having stuck by him while he was in the hospital and rehabilitation center, had broken up with him months before, saying "she couldn't handle it anymore."

July 1999: Hyde underwent another surgery at Carolinas Medical Center in Charlotte, during which a plate was put in to lift his nose from his face and several screws from the previous surgery were removed.

August 1999: He enrolled at the Rehabilitation Center for the Blind in Raleigh, living on campus while learning to get around, learning to read Braille and working on the computer using software designed for the blind.

Dec. 30, 1999: Hyde's father, Barry Edward Hyde, died suddenly at age 55 after four surgeries following a massive heart attack.

April 2000: Hyde interviewed as a candidate for the Southeastern Guide Dog School program in Palmetto, Fla.

June 6, 2000: He took an aviation test and became the first and only blind advanced ground instructor.

June 12, 2000: Hyde was matched with a 19-month-old, black Labrador retriever named Lincoln.

The dog became his constant companion, helping to heal him emotionally and regaining his freedom.

October 2000: He earned his aviation license to become an instrument ground instructor.

About a month after the story ran, Hyde met Kendra, a blind woman who was taking classes at the University of North Carolina at Charlotte, and they began dating.

In May of 2001, Hyde was accepted at UNC-Charlotte, and he and Lincoln moved to a nearby apartment. "We walked back and forth to class," he says, "1,800 steps one way."

Life as a blind student was challenging, but Hyde recorded the lectures on a tape recorder and played them back at home, using another tape recorder to make verbal notes.

He took his tests at the university's Disability Services Office on a computer with JAWS (Job Application With Speech) software, allowing him to take them verbally.

The N.C. Division of Blind Services paid Hyde's tuition and assisted with his expenses and rent.

He graduated in December of 2004 with a 3.45 grade-point average.

Lincoln led him across the stage to accept his diploma at commencement services, and the audience honored them with a standing ovation.

"It was really awesome to be recognized like that," Hyde says.

The following May, he underwent another surgery on his face, during which surgeons removed several metal plates and screws and took bone from his cranium to rebuild his face and nose.

In July 2005, Hyde moved to Daytona Beach, Fla., and began working on his master's degree in aeronautics at Embry-Riddle Aeronautical University, the world's largest flight school.

He received financial assistance from the Florida Services for the Blind, a $12,000 scholarship from the university and several other scholarships, including two from the Greater Miami Aviation Association's Batchelor Aviation Scholarship Fund and two from the Air Traffic Control Association.

He had only been there four months when Kendra died suddenly from complications of diabetes. "It was a heartbreaker," he says. "Lincoln and I came home for her funeral service."

When Hyde returned home to Kannapolis a month later for the holidays, he and his cousin took Kendra's ashes up in an airplane, releasing them over both their homes.

The following year, Hyde's friendship with Nancy Riedel developed into a romance. They had gotten to know each other when he spoke at fundraisers for the Carolina Outreach Program of Southeastern Guide Dog Inc., of which she was director.

When the Concord outreach program closed a few months later, she and her Labrador retriever, Jackson, a retired guide dog, moved to Daytona Beach to be with Hyde and Lincoln. Soon afterward, Riedel, who Hyde calls "Nance," got a job with Embry-Riddle.

Hyde remained dedicated to his studies, graduating on May 7, 2007 with a 4.0 grade-point average with distinction.

"I had lots of family and friends there for the commencement," he says.

"Lincoln was hooded when I was hooded."

And when Hyde and Lincoln walked across the stage at commencement services, they received another standing ovation. "I was the first blind graduate in Embry-Riddle's 81-year history," he says.

On June 1 of that year, Hyde began working on his doctorate online from Northcentral University in Prescott, Ariz. "It was almost like it was God's plan that I started on the nine-year anniversary of the plane crash," he says. "That was the driving force for me to prove that I could continue on."

Hyde received two more scholarships from the Greater Miami Aviation Association and Air Traffic Control Association. He has received 25 scholarships in all while continuing to work on his doctorate with a 2011 completion date for his dissertation.

Last Dec. 3, Hyde's faithful guide dog, Lincoln, was retired to the status of beloved pet. On Jan. 20 of this year, Jet, another black Lab, took over as his guide dog.

"Jet is a city dog," he says. "He grew up in Albany, N.Y."

Hyde says there's never a dull moment for him and Riedel with their three dogs, each one valued at $60,000.

While continuing to work on his doctorate this spring, Hyde taught an online aviation class for Daniel Webster College in New Hampshire.

The topic of his dissertation: "The Proper Execution of the Preflight Checklist to Ensure Flight Safety."

Hyde says the pilot's failure to properly execute the preflight checklist was the cause of his June 1, 1998, crash. He is working on a book about the crash and his struggle to remain in aviation as a blind man. It will be titled, "Seeing New Horizons: How Blind Aviator Barry Hulon Hyde Views Aviation Safety."

In early October, Hyde flew with Riedel, Lincoln and Jet to Washington, D.C., where he received his fourth scholarship from the Air Traffic Control Association on Oct. 7. The next day, Hyde interviewed for an aviation safety analyst position with the Federal Aviation Administration (FAA).

The interview was held on the eighth floor of the FAA's Flight Standards District Office in downtown Washington, he says, and lasted two hours. Later that afternoon, the deputy director of communications for the FAA did a live interview with Hyde and Jet for its Web site.

The next day, Hyde met FAA Administrator Randy Babbitt at a Combined Federal Campaign Kickoff that encouraged employees to donate money to nonprofits. Speaking in front of an audience of more than 150, Hyde told them about his plane crash and how he had benefited from various nonprofit organizations for the blind.

As part of the event, Hyde presented Babbitt with an alumni pin from Embry-Riddle, his alma mater, and Babbitt returned the favor with a limited edition book on the history of the FAA.

Hyde, who contacted the Post when he arrived in Kannapolis last week to spend Christmas with his mother, says he was offered the job on Dec. 3—Lincoln's 11th birthday. "Once again, I think that's God's way of showing how He's continuing to make things very memorable for me," he says.

Part of his duties when he begins work on March 1 will be developing policies and procedures for general aviation and flight schools.

"This is just a huge honor," Hyde says. "This is what I've worked so hard for to accomplish over the past 10 years. It's like a dream come true.

"It shows me that God has a purpose for me and that He's making it known with each door that opens up."

E-Pilot

December 28, 2009 the Aircraft Owners and Pilots Association electronic version over email included the following link in the third headline of the email:

Former flight instructor to develop GA safety procedures

A flight instructor who lost his eyesight in a plane crash 11 years ago has landed a job with the

Federal Aviation Administration. Barry Hulon Hyde received a job offer on Dec. 3 for an aviation safety analyst position with the FAA. Hyde, who is also writing a book about his experience, will develop safety procedures for general aviation and flight schools.

Tommy Hyde's Passing

December 29, 2009, around 10:30 p.m., my cousin Tommy Hyde passed after many health issues. He had organs removed that were causing problems and he had pancreatic cancer. Tommy and I spoke weekly, and I miss him dearly. He missed my dad's anniversary by one day or a couple of hours.

Daytona Beach News Journal

January 11, 2010
FAA job marks latest comeback for blind man
By MARK HARPER
Education writer

DAYTONA BEACH—Twelve years have passed since Barry Hulon Hyde's career ambitions crashed and burned in the Virginia woods.

On June 1, 1998, Hyde—an aspiring pilot—survived a plane crash. His sight, though, did not. His dream of becoming a private pilot for a NASCAR team was gone.

But his passion for aviation—and aviation safety, in particular—still burned.

Now a 37-year-old doctoral student with a master's degree from Embry-Riddle Aeronautical University, Hyde has landed a new career. In March, he starts as an aviation safety analyst with the Federal Aviation Administration in Washington.

"I'll be writing policies and procedures for general aviation and flight schools," Hyde said in an interview recently. "Embry-Riddle will be using some of the policies and procedures I'll be writing."

Hyde is six courses and a dissertation short of a Ph.D. in business administration specializing in aeronautical safety. He plans to finish the degree by taking the courses online through Northcentral University of Prescott, Ariz.

An FAA spokesman said he couldn't yet comment on Hyde. But the Embry-Riddle professor who coordinated his master's program in aeronautics said the FAA made a good choice.

"He's all grit and go," said Marvin Smith, a professor of aviation sciences at ERAU. "He's got a way of capturing people's affection."

Hyde actually interviewed for the job at the same time he was a guest speaker for an agency event.

Next month he will move with his fiancee Nancy Riedel and his guide dogs Jet and Lincoln to the Washington area so he can start learning his way around.

"I never dreamed I would live through a plane crash, attend the world's largest aeronautical university, then from there go to the FAA," he said. "I never dreamed of attaining these goals."

Blessed

I could not get this far if I did not have certain individuals like my family, Nance, and my guide dogs Lincoln and Jet to help me around the obstacles in my life.

The thirty-seven years I have lived has taught me that we can succeed no matter how many obstacles we experience along our path in life. The loss of my sense of smell, taste, and sight happened eleven years, six months, and six days ago. The incidents in my life have taught me no matter how bad of shape we are in, life goes on and so do we.

Monday, March1 2010, I began work at the FAA Headquarters in Washington, DC. The name of the building is the Orville Wright, and it is ten floors high and is located on Independence Avenue. My title is an aviation safety analyst, and my cubicle area, Flight Standards 820, is on the eighth floor.

Wednesday, March 3, Nance, Jet, and I went to the cafeteria to have lunch. Upon entering, we were stopped by the FAA administrator Randy Babbitt. He stopped me and shook my hand and welcomed me as his newest employee. We spoke for about five minutes, and he asked if I needed anything and if things were going okay. In addition, he asked where I was located and he said he would come visit me after coming back from a trip. He said, "I have to go, I have to go catch a flight."

The first project assigned to me was the hot topics for general aviation. This project was questions and answers submitted to Lynn McCloud, who wrote the memo to submit to Babbitt. This memo prepared him for a forum at Sun N' Fun in Lakeland, Florida.

Tuesday, March 22, 2010, Nance, Jet, and I were standing outside the cafeteria speaking with Nancy Kalinowski. Administrator Babbitt approached us, and he shook my hand and said, "Barry, Randy Babbitt. How are you doing?" He then said, "Secretary. Secretary, I want you to meet my newest employee. This is Barry Hulon Hyde, and Barry, this is the secretary of transportation, Ray LaHood." I shook his hand, and Babbitt introduced Nancy and Jet. We spoke briefly to them, and they went into the cafeteria. We turned around and walked off as well. I was overwhelmed with excitement! We walked by the elevators, and there stood one of the secretary's guards.

Barry & Jet at FAA

INVITATION: Come Meet Mr. Barry Hulon Hyde & his Guide Dog Jet

Melvin Cintron, Manager, General Aviation and Commercial Division, AFS-800, would like to introduce you to our new employee in AFS-820, Mr. Barry Hulon Hyde and his guide dog, Jet. When: 10:00 a.m., Thursday, March 4, 2010 Where: Bessie Coleman Room, 10A, 2nd floor.

Barry is a person with a blindness. He and Jet, his trusty sidekick (guide dog), joined AFS-820 on Monday as an Aviation Safety Analyst. Since many of you may not be familiar with guide dog etiquette and related safety issues,

Barry's going to address his new colleagues here at 10A and give us some tips and pointers.

Barry comes to us from Embry-Riddle where he's been a ground instructor and earned a Master of Science degree in Aeronautics. He's currently working toward his Ph.D. in Business Administration with an Aeronautical Safety Specialization.

You'll be seeing Barry's fiancée, Nancy, here too, for a while as she assists him in getting acclimated to his new digs. Nancy is a guide dog trainer (guess how they met?) so she's helping both of the guys get used to the new surroundings.

Please share this invite with other co-workers in the FOB-10-A Building.

Lincoln's and Nance's Departure

In early May of 2010, I ended the relationship with Nance. I wanted to see if I could make it on my own. In preparation of Nance's decision on leaving, I thought about Lincoln being there alone without Jackson while I would have to go to work with Jet. The final decision was to send Lincoln with them. I now feel it was the wrong decision, and it really bothers me. However, I know he was taken care of and with two really close companions.

Nance took care of all my financial living issues, so they would be paid automatically, such as the power and water bills, credit card, and added important information onto the computer, so I could have a list of them. She was always a phone call away, and she helped me significantly. Nancy was a great addition to our life and she did so much for the boys and me. It was really difficult to let her go after all she had done for us.

Member Spotlight

Aircraft Owners and Pilots Association May 2010 Issue

PILOT BRIEFING
Starting over

A new life after an accident

It was 13 years ago when Barry Hulon Hyde lost his eyesight in an airplane crash that almost ended his life. Since then, Hyde has made aviation history by becoming the first FAA advanced ground and instrument ground instructor who is blind. He is the first blind student to earn a master's of science in aeronautics from Embry-Riddle Aeronautical University—with a perfect 4.0 GPA. In December 2009, Hyde landed an aviation safety analyst position with the FAA.

"I want to prevent fellow pilots from encountering what I did and teach them how to handle the situation if they do," said Hyde, who had to abandon his dream—with 1,600 flight hours—of becoming an airline pilot after the crash. Barry Hulon Hyde and his guide dog are now full-time employees of the FAA. "With this job, I will have the opportunity to contribute my knowledge, research, skills, abilities, and flight experience by writing aviation safety policies and procedures for GA and flight schools."

Hyde was riding right seat as a safety pilot in a 1965 Piper Twin Comanche for a pilot who wanted to practice his instrument skills. The airplane took off from Concord, North Carolina, bound for Lewisburg, West Virginia. About 22 minutes after takeoff, the engines started spitting. A few minutes later, the right engine stopped. About 10 minutes after that, the left engine quit. An emergency landing site, a baseball field, was selected but the airplane didn't make it. The Comanche crashed into a patch of trees between two houses, approximately 100 feet short of the intended field and 30 miles from Roanoke, Virginia. The right seat broke on impact, both wing tips with the auxiliary fuel tanks outside were sheared off, and the tail section completely separated from the fuselage.

Doctors saved Hyde's life and he spent almost three months in the hospital as machines kept him alive. After returning home, Hyde struggled with memory loss and had to learn to walk again, but would do it blind. From this experience, Hyde said he has learned several things.

"First, anytime something occurs, I teach students to immediately land the airplane, then diagnose the problem. Second, always do a proper preflight and this action will help eliminate some questions to the pilots in the cockpit. Third, do not trust anyone but your mother—and keep an eye on her," he said.

With a sense of humor and humility, Hyde is also writing a book about his experience, which will highlight questions about the accident that, according to him, should never have happened. Whatever the cause of the accident—improper preflight planning, lack of fuel—Hyde feels better knowing that his experience may help prevent unnecessary accidents.

"I feel what I learned can help other pilots because I have encountered a situation that pilots, hopefully, will never encounter," he said.

"Accidents are caused by negligence, error, or a combination of both," he said. "I want to help prevent those costly mistakes."

Administrator Randy Babbitt's response on the AOPA article:

Good morning Barry,

Thanks for forwarding the great article. You continue to be just great to work with both as a fellow aviation professional and as a colleague, not to mention as an inspiration to so many folks! I will look forward to dropping by soon and catching up with you and getting feedback from you on how things are going.

With kind regards, (and say
"hi" to Jet too) Randy

Tuesday, May 18, 2010, Jet and I attended a training class for the FAA in the FAA Headquarters. There were twenty-three of us in attendance, and there were four presenters to the class. We all had to stand up and give a brief description about ourselves, and at the break, Dwayne Hunter, out of the Richmond Flight Standards District Office, approached me and shared with me that he investigated the plane crash that I was involved in on June 1, 1998.

Robin and Rascal Meet Hyde and Jet

On August 1, 2010, Jet and I met Robin and Rascal. We were standing out in the front of the house located on Ridge View in Alexandria, VA. Robin and Rascal came walking up, and Robin asked if she could pet my dog. We made our introductions, and I invited them inside. I asked her if she could take Jet and me to the vet on Friday, and she did. I brailed her, and we have been together ever since.

Interviewing for FAASTeam

Thursday, September 2, 2010, I met with Mel Cintron, Florence, and Don Wood, the fill-in manager of 810, and we talked about me joining the Federal Aviation Administration Safety Team (FAASTeam). I spoke on how I did not feel I was contributing to safety and the agency in the Airman Certification branch of 800 Flight Standards. I told them I wanted to utilize and share my experience, knowledge, and education with fellow pilots and help with safety. I wanted to use my story and share other important aspects of safety by giving presentations.

High School Reunion

Friday, September 10, Jet and I flew on US Airways to Charlotte, North Carolina, to attend my graduation anniversary. Robin Watson (future wife) took us to Ronald Reagan National airport that morning, and Mom met us at the gate at Charlotte Douglas Airport. She drove us home, and we visited with Aunt Margie and Grandma Absher as well as my brother.

On Saturday, I visited with Uncle Rudy and Uncle Randy along with my grandma Hyde. During the visit, we attended my twenty-year class reunion. Deric Harrington drove us to Salisbury, North Carolina, to the Holiday Inn where it was held. We visited with some people we had not seen in twenty years and others that we saw in the past ten years. There was a big turnout, and we had a whole lot of fun. Sunday morning, we returned to Mom's. We visited with family and friends. Sunday, Tony Therrill fried catfish for the family and me. We had a really nice visit and enjoyed that great catfish.

On Monday the thirteenth, Mom took us to the airport, and we flew back into Reagan National, where Robin met us at the gate.

On Wednesday, September 15, Robin, Jet, and I attended a symposium for Embry-Riddle Aeronautical University at the Russell Senate building, downtown DC. We entered the building and went to check in, and Maury Johnson, the wife of the president of the university, greeted us. We spoke briefly, and she offered to pay our way in. I thought this was a very nice gesture, and this reminded me once again how nice of a woman she was. We walked into the room and was greeted by a woman who was on the Embry-Riddle Senate. As I was speaking with her, Dr. John Johnson came up and greeted us. We spoke briefly, and shortly thereafter, the FAA administrator Randy Babbitt greeted us as well. I shared being transferred to the FAASTeam with him, and he was happy to hear this news. Dr. Johnson, the administrator, and a US representative spoke to the group, and it was a very good presentation by the gentlemen.

On Tuesday through Thursday, 21–23, I met with the FAASTeam in the Wilbur Wright building. I met with the managers who made up the eight districts throughout the country. For lunch on Thursday, I met with the head manager, Kevin Clover, who was out of Long Beach, California, and the assistant manager Phil Randal, who was out of Greensboro, North Carolina. I also met a coworker who is now a long time friend, Felice Bruenner.

Sabrina Jones with the communications department in the FAA, interviewed me on Monday, September 27, and took pictures of Jet and me. She wrote the following article, and it was published on the 29.

Seeing New Horizons

September 29, 2010 –

Barry Hulon Hyde's dreams of piloting a corporate jet for a NASCAR team or a commercial jet abruptly ended one day 12 years ago.

He was a 26-year-old flight instructor in North Carolina who had logged more than

1,600 hours in the air. Then, on June 1, 1998, he boarded a 1965 Piper Twin Comanche as a passenger with a pilot who wanted to practice his instrument skills. About a half hour after take-off, the plane's engines stopped, and the aircraft crashed into a patch of trees near Roanoke, Va.

He was initially pronounced dead on arrival at a hospital, but a medical team revived him. He was left with no sight and no ability to taste or smell. He was no longer able to fly a plane, drive a car, or engage in everyday activities, such as cooking.

But, eventually, Hyde was able to create a new life from the devastating wreckage of that day. Over the years, he earned college degrees, including becoming the first student who is visually impaired to earn a master's of science degree in aeronautics from Embry-Riddle Aeronautical University. He then became the first blind advanced ground and instrument ground instructor certified by the FAA, and joined the agency earlier this year as an aviation safety analyst based at Headquarters. A few weeks ago, he became a member of the FAA Safety Team (FAASTeam).

"I did not think I would be working here," he said one morning, while sitting at his desk with his three-and-a-half-year old Black Labrador guide dog, Jet, resting nearby. "This is a dream I never thought of achieving."

He hopes his new position will enable him to achieve another goal—protecting pilots from accidents like the one that left him severely injured. He aims to use his story to emphasize the importance of conducting thorough preflight tests and other safety procedures.

"That's how I'll be able to contribute to safety," Hyde said. "I want to be an example. Wherever I go, people are going to listen to me because of what happened to me and what I lived through."

His mornings now consist of waking up with Jet around 4 a.m., waiting for a van service that caters to people with disabilities to pick him up and take him to his downtown Washington, D.C. office. At work, a screen reader—a software application that translates text on Hyde's computer screen into a speech form that he listens to through earphones—allows him to check his e-mail, work on reports, and perform other functions.

Hyde is focused on safety in other areas of his life, as well. He is four classes and three assignments away from completing his doctorate in business administration with a specialization in aeronautical safety. The 27 scholarships and grants he has received total nearly $90,000. He has also written 220 pages of a book on his life, tentatively titled, "Seeing New Horizons: How Blind Aviator Barry Hulon Hyde Views Aviation Safety."

The years have not been without obstacles. The accident left him with multiple injuries, including the detachment of his nose, the loss of his left eye, a broken vertebra, and missing teeth. Once, he suffered a seizure that lasted 45 minutes—a condition that is believed to be a symptom of his severe head injury. Before the FAA hired him, Hyde had lived on $599 a month in Social Security disability income and depended on food stamps and other assistance.

Hyde's compelling experiences could lend themselves well to instructing pilots on what could happen if they fail to properly pre-flight airplanes or perform other safety functions, said his supervisor, Phil Randall, assistant national FAASTeam manager. He recalled Hyde's visit to Headquarters last year as a speaker for the agency's kick-off of the Combined Federal Campaign, a charitable-giving drive.

"He's got his own story," Randall said. "I think he touched everybody enough that everybody wanted to hear more."

Hyde hopes that what some individuals hear could potentially prevent them from suffering the same hardships that altered his life.

"This is a big picture for me," he said. "Now I see God's plan hard at work."

On October 6, the following responses were included in the Focus FAA, Your Two Cents link.

Chris Harnish
Manager, Pacific Operational Support Facility, ATO
Western-Pacific Region

Most Inspiring

The story "Seeing New Horizons" is one of the most inspiring accounts of human triumph I have ever read. Barry's story of faith and determination transcends being the success story it is by teaching us an important lesson about life in that we can reach our goals, and our dreams can come true, despite the toughest odds, if we are willing to work hard enough to achieve them. Thank you, Barry, and welcome to the FAA. You are an inspiration to us all; your story makes me proud to work here.

Ron Johnson
Great Lakes Region

The Right Man

It sounds like FAA hired just the right man for the job with Barry Hulon Hyde. I've always believed that your attitude defines your altitude, and it's obvious that the sky's the limit with this inspiring individual. All the story needs is a cute dog. Wait! It's got that, too!

Peggy Wade
Airports Environmental Specialist
Southwest Region

So Passionate

Barry Hulon Hyde is an inspiration for all of us and the reason why we in the FAA are so passionate about our jobs.

Jean Hardy
Safety Inspector, AVS
Headquarters

Wonderful

Thank you very much for publishing this inspirational story concerning Barry Hulon

Hyde. What a wonderful person. Kudos to Barry Hulon Hyde.

American Council of the Blind Convention

October 08, 2010, Jet, Robin, and I flew from Reagan National Airport to Memphis International Airport on Delta Airlines in an Airbus A-319. This airplane had three seats on each side of the aisle. The flight was full, and we had a lady that sat beside us on the same row where we sat on the seventh row behind bulkhead. It was a two-hour flight, and then we had a layover in Memphis, Tennessee, for one and a half hours. We then boarded an Atlantic Southeast Airline on a Canadair Regional Jet 700 that carried us on a flight for fifty-seven minutes to Montgomery, Alabama.

Saturday morning, the ACB convention continued from Friday. A doctor took the podium at 9:00 a.m., and he talked about macular degeneration. I took the podium at 10:00 a.m. and spoke about my life history, the accident, the rehabilitation, the education, and the scholarships. ACB paid me a stipend of $500, our airline ticket, hotel reservations, and meals. It was a very nice convention.

Official Blog of Ray LaHood

October 14, 2010

FAA's Barry Hulon Hyde: blind safety analyst achieves aviation dream

October is National Disability Employment Awareness Month, and this year's theme is "Talent Has No Boundaries: Workforce Diversity Includes People with Disabilities." It's an opportunity for all of us to appreciate the contributions people with disabilities have made in the workplace.

I'm proud of the diverse group of employees we've brought together here at DOT. One of them is Barry Hulon Hyde--a man whose story exemplifies how much we benefit from having people with disabilities in the workforce.

Then, on June 1, 1998, he boarded a 1965 Piper Twin Comanche with a pilot who wanted to practice his instrument skills. A half hour after takeoff, the plane's engines stalled and the aircraft crashed into a patch of trees near Roanoke, Virginia.

At the hospital, Barry was pronounced dead on arrival, but a dedicated team of medical professionals continued working and saved his life. The accident's effects, however, were devastating. He was blinded in the crash and left without the ability to taste or smell.

Eventually, he was able to piece together a new life from the wreckage of that day. And while his career in the air may have been over, his career in aviation wasn't.

Through hard work and dedication, he became the first blind student to earn a master's degree in aeronautics from Embry-Riddle Aeronautical University. He also became the first blind advanced ground and instrument ground instructor certified by the Federal Aviation Administration. Barry now works as an aviation safety analyst at the FAA and is a member of the FAA Safety Team (FAASTeam).

Barry's work at DOT is aided by his guide dog, a three year old Labrador named Jet.

Stories like Barry's are evidence of the tremendous value we stand to gain by employing people with disabilities.

Here at DOT, we're committed to ensuring all people have access to jobs so they can live independently and realize their dreams. And we're also intent on building the strongest team possible. Recruiting and retaining skilled professionals like Barry Hulon Hyde achieves both of those important goals.

Brother's Loss of Life on December 20, 2010

The weekend before taking vacation to go home for Christmas, I spoke with Todd on Saturday, and he was looking forward to Jet and me coming home and he was excited to meet Robin and Rascal. Mom shared with me that she learned that he received a DUI on Saturday night. Judy Therrell and mom went to pick him up Monday morning. He drove his truck to mom's, and then, he disappeared. Mom and Judy started looking for him, and mom found him in front of a neighbor's house hanging in the woods. He was pronounced dead, and ¾ of a bottle of Rebel Yell was found under the table that he put it under before doing the deed. He was so upset because he was sure he was going to lose his license and his job due to the DUI. If that happened he would not be able to have his family back since he and his wife were separated. A big part of their problems was his alcoholism. He had chosen a long-term solution for a temporary problem. I am sure on the day of his funeral, he was the happiest ever, since everyone's focus was on him.

Loss of Grandma Hyde

On March 16, 2011, my grandma Hyde took her last breath at home with Rudy and Randy. She lived a long and productive life. It was a great loss and she is dearly missed, but we know she has gone to be with our loved ones. Grandma's service was held at Hope Lutheran Church, in Kannapolis, NC. Uncle Charles was not doing well, therefore, he sent his oldest son, Mark, in his absence. One evening over the next couple of days, we had fried catfish that Tony Therrell cooked for us, and we were joined by Mark, Randy, Stewart, Rudy, mom, Judy, Robin, and myself. Tony was giving Stewart a hard time, since he was a sand-lapper! I will never forget that after Grandpa Hyde's passing, she bought a brand new Cutlass Supreme, and received her license at age 68. Whether she was cooking or watching TV, she would say, you boys get out of here, and go play!

Purchased house in Alexandria, Virginia

On January 17, 2012, the closing on 8214 Ackley Street in Alexandria, Virginia, took place. We did not need to put a dollar down on a thirty-year loan with 4.5 percent. This mortgage payment lowered my rent payment from $2,000 to $1,650 per month. The move took place February 9, 2012. The house includes four bed-rooms and two baths with a fenced-in backyard.

Loss of Lincoln

Another memorable aspect of the month of June was losing Lincoln at 9:15 in the morning of June 5. Unfortunately, I did not learn of his passing until Friday afternoon at 12:54 p.m. I cried like a baby, and I am still upset for losing him. His death is so permanent, and because of this, it makes it so hard dealing with his loss. A couple weeks later, I did receive a thank-you card for Nance donating money in his memory to Guide Dog Foundation. Those people who learned of his passing have been real supportive, and it reminds me how many lives he touched.

Vacation to North Carolina

On Thursday, July 19, 2012, Robin, Rascal, Jet, and I went to Mom's in North Carolina. We went by Randy's to visit him and Stewart, his roommate, and then we went to Mom's and arrived around eleven o'clock at night. We visited Grandma, Mom, Randy, Rudy, Lauren, and Austin. Tony Therrill cooked fish for us as well. We attended a concert at the Verizon Amphitheatre in Charlotte with Deric Harrington and Scottie Stewart. The concert featured Motley Crue, who opened for KISS on Wednesday, July 25, 2012. Motley Crue rocked the house and sang all their hits plus a few new songs. KISS opened with Detroit Rock City. They were really good as well.

Dukes of Hazard Reunion

Saturday, August 11, 2012, Robin, Jet, and I went to Amissville, Virginia, to the Dukes of Hazard Homecoming. This homecoming was advertised to take place at Cooter's place. Daisy, Enos, and Rosco were present signing autographs. Music was playing, and Robin made our picture standing in front of 75 General Lees and one of the Plymouth Police Cars with Bo and Luke dummies in the rear seat. Attending the event was memorable and an experience.

Proposal to Robin

My birthday occurred on February 3, 2013, and I proposed to Robin Darlene Watson. We looked at rings in Concord while we were home for Christmas. We needed financing, and I applied for a loan from Fifth Third bank, and they sent a letter to me the following week. The letter stated that I was out of their loaning area. I received a letter in the mail from Falls Jewelers. They offered the sale for five hours on Sunday, February 3, since the special included the Super Bowl. They sold wedding rings to us for half price, and Fall's Jewelers made the sale to us the Thursday before my birthday. We have spoken about being married at Graceland in Memphis, at Elvis's place.

New Heat and Air System

The last week of March, the gas furnace went out. I had to borrow $9,000 from the Federal Credit Union to pay for a new heat and air conditioner. A business named Select installed the new system and began new duct work on Monday, April 8, 2013. This project took them three days, and next, the Sheetrock had to be fixed and painted.

Grandma Absher Passing

On Friday, December 20, 2013, Grandma Absher went to become an angel in heaven. She left us on the same day my brother did, and it was three years later to the exact day. My mom was visiting her, and Pastor Bost came in and prayed with them both. Shortly thereafter, Grandma took her last breath. It was like she needed permission to go. Jet, Robin, and I came down on Sunday. Mom, Margie, and Wayne put together all the funeral details. The viewing was on Monday, December 23, at Whitley's funeral home in Kannapolis. Pastor Bost did the service, and the viewing was real nice. All but a few of the family attended. We attended the graveside service, and it was raining. One detail I can remember Grandma saying was if it is raining when someone is being buried, that meant they were going to heaven. We definitely think she went to heaven. Once the graveside service was over, it stopped raining, and the weather started clearing up.

Graceland Wedding

Robin and I decided to marry in Graceland at the Chapel in the Woods with just a few family members in attendance. We also decided to have a reception in North Carolina, so all of our family and friends could celebrate with us. Robin handled all the trip arrangements as well as wedding details and she set up the reception also. It all came together except mom was suffering from a pinched nerve in her back and she could not make the trip. On Wednesday morning, July 30, 2014, Robin, Jet, and I drove to Mom's and arrived around 3:15 p.m. We had to do some last-minute shopping at Sam's Club, and then Randy, Rudy, and Lisa shared a nice visit and barbecue from the Varsity restaurant. On Thursday morning, Randy, Robin, Jet, and I left Moms to go to the airport. At the airport, lots of construction was occurring, but we parked and rode a shuttle bus to the terminal. We flew out of Charlotte/Douglas airport around 9:30 a.m. on a Canadair Regional Jet.

We arrived at Memphis around 11:00 a.m. and rented a Dodge Charger. We drove it to downtown Memphis to get our marriage license at the courthouse. Then, we left there and eventually found Elvis Presley Boulevard that took us to find Lonely Street and followed it to the Heartbreak Hotel.

We toured Graceland that afternoon—the layout of the Graceland mansion, how the house was set up, and the memorial garden in the back. That night, we watched an Elvis impersonator at the Rock 'n' Roll Cafe. Friday morning, August 1, we had breakfast at the Heartbreak hotel. Then, we went through the gift shops and museums. His airplane was a Convair 880 named the Lisa Marie. In addition, we had our pictures taken with the Jetstar, the Hound Dog II. The museum was filled with cars, such as two Rolls Royce, a white and a black one; Ferrari; Cadillac; Harley Davidsons; a pink Jeep; and many more cars.

Around eleven on Friday morning, we took Robin to have her hair and makeup done. Randy and I had lunch and found a bar to hang out in until she was finished. Robin came to the bar, then we left there and went to the Heartbreak Hotel to dress for the wedding.

On August 1, 2014, Friday afternoon, around 3:30 p.m., Robin and I were married, and my uncle Randy Hyde was the best man. We chose this date, since it was the anniversary of when we met four years earlier. We arrived at Elvis's Chapel in the Woods. Robin's sister Anita and her husband, Doug, their son David and his wife, Ashley, met us outside the chapel. We also met the pastor, the photographer, and the coordinator. The ceremony was perfect, but the only thing missing was my mother being present. We left there and followed Robin's family to Beale Street.

Elvis's Chapel in the Woods at Graceland

Wedding picture on steps at the Graceland mansion

We had dinner at King's Palace on Beale Street. There was an acoustic guitar player and Robin's brother-in-law Doug requested "Can't Help Falling in Love" that Robin and I danced to for the first time as husband and wife. Robin's family, Randy and us shared a great dinner, and we went down the street and had our picture taken by David in front of the Elvis statue.

On Saturday morning, we checked out and had breakfast at IHOP. We were home just after 3:00 p.m. on another CRJ. We took Randy to my mom's for him to retrieve his car and to visit Mom briefly. We drove by and picked up cousin Ferrell, so he rode with Randy to the hotel in Mooresville for the reception. We had a terrific reception. Around eighty people attended, and we had a great time. We received nice gifts and lots of great company.

Early, Sunday morning, Robin told me my uncle Wayne, Mom's brother, had a stroke. That issue was the reason he and his girl-friend did not show up at the reception. In addition, Aunt Margie, Mom's only sister, was unable to attend the reception as well due to her having a heart attack.

Sunday afternoon, Dale Earnhardt Jr. won the race at Pocono. This helped complete a really nice weekend, although we missed Mom's presence in Memphis, and learning of my uncle's stroke made us sad.

The loss of Uncle Wayne & Aunt Margie

Wayne, Mom's only brother, died on August 13, 2014. He had a very nice service, and it was like a family reunion. We saw lots of family members at the funeral.

On August 28, Margie, Mom's only sister, had a massive heart attack and died that night. Her funeral was on Sunday, and it was like attending another family reunion.

Mom's surgery

Mom had surgery on her back to lift the bone off the pinched nerve on September 15, 2014. Her surgery was on Monday, and we drove to visit her after she came home on Thursday. We were there with her from Friday, September 19, through Tuesday, September 23. She was doing amazingly well and walking more during each day. While we were visiting, it was nice to visit Garvey, Pat, Pod, and Sharon as they came by on Sunday afternoon. It was super to visit Pat and Garvey one last time. In addition, on Monday evening, we visited Carrie Reavis and talked about her eleven horses.

Passing of Aunt Leisa Caldwell

My dad's only sister died from liver cancer on July 2, 2015. She was survived by her son, Jason, daughter, Shayla and brothers Charles, Rudy, and Randy. We were very blessed to have her for 54 years. Her service was held at Hope Lutheran Church, as well.

Accident remnants seventeen years in the making

Saturday, September 19, 2015, Robin took me to the Quickcare to have my knee examined. The PA had it x-rayed, and everything looked normal to him. He told me to start a double antibiotic and come back in a week to see how it was healing. I was still in tremendous pain, and I was walking with my support cane to help offset the pain. On September 22, 2015, in the shower, I washed my knee real lightly because of the pain I was encountering from three weeks ago where I hit my knee on a washer door in the kitchen. I heard something ding, and it was a piece of plexi-glass that fell out onto the floor of the tub as I was standing taking a shower. Robin identified it, and we were just dumbfounded. It was a piece of glass from the windshield of the airplane that I had crashed in over seventeen years ago! The piece of glass left a hole in my knee, and the plexi-glass was an inch long, a half inch wide, and three-sixteenths thick. Historically, this day was important because this afternoon the pope arrived in town for the week from Cuba. The next day, Robin took me to the orthopedic doctor. The doctor claimed he had never seen anything like this, glass being rejected by the body after seventeen years, three months, and twenty-one days after the accident.

POC for the FAASTeam

On May 22, 2017, an article from the Flight School Association of North America was written by Bob Rockmaker, the president of the school. The article described that I would be the POC for the FAASTeam in my new undertaking.

Completion of the Doctorate

On June 1, 2017, the nineteen-year anniversary of the plane crash, I received approval on the final chapter of my dissertation. On June 11, I submitted the final dissertation manuscript. On Wednesday, July 5, 2017, the oral defense took place with the mentor and the subject matter expert, and it lasted only forty minutes. I officially became Dr. Hyde on this date.

Several important people assisted me in accomplishing this unbelievable goal and I would like to say thanks to them. I would like to begin with saying thanks to Nance for all of her graciousness and for all of the scholarships I received, and for many other great things she did for the boys and me. Next, I would like to say thanks to uncle Rudy. All of his proofreading and helping me to do research paid off. Thanks much uncle Rudy. One more person that helped me tremendously was Dr. Shirley Phillips. I would have never made it this far without her helping me writing that dissertation. Thanks always Shirley. Lastly, my lovely wife, Robin Darlene! Robin and I worked almost every day for almost seven years writing and rewriting that dissertation, and we continued to call on Shirley to help us with our mentor's recommended changes. You are the greatest, so patient with me, and you continue to help Bravo and me with each passing day. I thank God for you and I sure do appreciate you!

Celebration of the Doctorate

On August 13, 2017, Uncle Rudy gave me a reception to celebrate the achievement of the doctoral degree at New Hope Lutheran Church, Sunday, 2:30 p.m. to 4:30 p.m. It was similar to a family reunion. We celebrated with around seventy people—everyone from Rudy, Randy, Mom, Robin, Jet, Eloise McClean, Dayton, Regis, Frank, Donna, Eric, Ferrell James II, Kit Caldwell, Jan, Jason, his daughter, his wife, and Shayla. Also, Ray and Diane Johnson, Larry Morris, Sharon Harrington, Tom Grady, Chad and Kelly Hyde,

Brandon, Linda, and Blake went. Freddie and Elaine Query, Gene and Lynn Goines, JoAnn and Albert Wingler, Pastor Larry Bost, and many more enjoyed the great party.

Passing of Uncle Charles

On January 3, 2018, Charles Wrenn Hyde passed at 3 am, age 80. He is survived by his wife, Annaleisia, and sons, Mark and Christian and his two brothers, Randy and Rudy. I am told that he had a 6-gun salute, and a very memorable funeral. He and Annaleisia were together for about 60 years. Rudy went out to be with them during this great loss. I felt very honored when he and Annaleisia sent me a name plate for my desk.

Bravo

My third guide dog arrived in my life on Monday, July 30, 2018 from Southeastern Guide Dogs of Palmetto Florida. He is a one-year-and-six-month-old yellow Labrador retriever. We flew home for his first flight on August 11 in an Embraer on Jet Blue. We were in class for two weeks with nine total participants present, but one lady had to drop out for medical reasons, and this class of eight was number 269 for the organization. Bravo was named by the calendar girls, and he was the third dog they had named regarding military relations. His birthday is January 18, 2017. He and Jet played together and one could tell the age difference. Bravo likes to retrieve whatever you throw and Jet would just lay there and watch.

Barry & Bravo at the FAA office

University Aviation Association

After some time passed and upon completing the degree, the subject matter expert Dr. David Cross participated in the oral for the doctoral degree, and he summarized the information from the dissertation down to eighteen pages, and it was accepted by the University Aviation Association as a scholarly journal. He and I are the authors listed on their website. Here is a link that will take you to this area to read it:

http://ojs.library.okstate.edu/osu/index.php/CARI/index

Dr. David Cross presented this scholarly journal over five minutes in Dallas, Texas, on September 27. I declined to attend, since it was due to me not being home long enough to feel comfortable with my new guide dog Bravo. Also, it was going to cost me to attend—hotel stay, meals, and transportation.

Beginning work at AFS-630

I reconnected with my friend and fellow aviator Margaret Morrison when I went to work for the FAA in 2010 and I am so happy I did. During October of 2018, Margaret recommended me to her manager, Kieran O'Farrell, to give me an opportunity to contribute my knowledge, experience, and my education to AFS-630. It is very rewarding being a part of such a great group of people! The manager, Larry West is keeping me busy and I am very glad to be enjoying my work and playing a part in safety. All the people are a joy to work with. I am blessed once again.

The loss of Jet

We lost Jet on September 24, 2019 at 3:00 p.m. that afternoon. It was so hard letting go of him after we had been together for 10 and a half years. He and I did everything together and he was so dedicated and had a lot of unconditional love to give. The vet said Jet's abdomen was full of blood that either came from a spleen or tumor rupturing. She gave him a relaxing shot, and Robin and I sat on the deck with him as the vet gave him his shot that led him to taking his last breath. What a great Guide dog he was and I miss him dearly. Bravo is great and I am glad that he and I have already bonded.

Conclusion

Aviation is what I do for work and fun. I am fortunate enough to still do it for fun. I feel like I am a walking miracle!

I am passionate about aviation safety, and I want to prevent an accident like I was involved in from ever happening again to another pilot. My dream was to become an airline pilot and enjoy the lifestyle that comes with that privilege. Now I have the opportunity to contribute my knowledge, education, and experience with others who share my enthusiasm for aviation and safety.

Today, I unquestionably possess a unique and special perspective on aeronautical safety. My life goals include sharing this profound insight with as many developing aviators as possible.

About the Author

"My work to enhance aviation safety is not just a job…it is my life!"

The author is a North Carolina native, and from an early age, absolutely aspired to be an aviator. A year and a half ago, he met Bravo at Southeastern Guide Dog Incorporated in Palmetto, Florida, and believes he was sent to him from God. Dr. Hyde is an aviator, and now, a perfect fit with a dog that is named after a letter in the phonetic alphabet for the military and aviation.

In May 2019, Dr. Hyde began an exciting new chapter for the FAA as a member of the Airman Testing Standards Branch AFS-630. It is their goal to prevent an accident, like the one in which Dr. Hyde was involved, from ever happening to another pilot. He truly desires to use his passion, education, and experience to further safety and help pilots and the blind to attain their goals.

Dr. Hyde currently resides in Fredericksburg, Virginia with his wife Robin and his current guide dog Bravo. He currently teleworks from home on a full-time basis. In his free time he enjoys visiting local airports and spending time with fellow aviators. He also enjoys one of his favorite pastimes, listening to NASCAR races on satellite radio as well as the Dallas Cowboys.

CPSIA information can be obtained
at www.ICGtesting.com
Printed in the USA
LVHW070749050321
679525LV00015B/31

9 781684 567591